THE NEW NATURALIST
A SURVEY OF BRITISH NATURAL HISTORY

A NATURAL HISTORY OF MAN
IN BRITAIN

THE NEW NATURALIST

A NATURAL HISTORY OF
MAN IN BRITAIN

Conceived as a study of changing relations
between Men and Environments

H. J. FLEURE F.R.S.

and

M. DAVIES Ph.D.

COLLINS
ST JAMES'S PLACE, LONDON

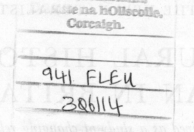

ISBN 0 00 213153 6

First published 1951
Revised edition 1970

© in the Revised Edition, H. J. Fleure
and Margaret Davies 1970

Printed in Great Britain
Collins Clear-Type Press,
London and Glasgow

"BRITAIN, best of islands, lieth in the Western Ocean betwixt Gaul and Ireland, and containeth 800 miles in length and 200 in breadth. Whatsoever is fitting for the use of mortal men the island doth afford in unfailing plenty. For she aboundeth in metals of every kind; fields hath she, stretching far and wide, and hillsides meet for tillage of the best, whereon, by reason of the fruitfulness of the soil, the divers crops in their seasons do yield their harvests. Forests also hath she filled with every manner of wild deer, in the glades whereof groweth grass that the cattle may find therein meet change of pasture, and flowers of many colours that do proffer their honey unto the bees that flit ever busily about them. Meadows hath she, set in pleasant places, green at the foot of misty mountains, wherein be sparkling well-springs clear and bright, flowing forth with a gentle whispering ripple in shining streams that sing sweet lullaby unto them that lie upon their banks. Watered is she, moreover, by lakes and rivers wherein is much fish, and, besides the narrow sea of the Southern coast whereby men make voyage unto Gaul, by three noble rivers, Thames, to wit, Severn and Humber, the which she stretcheth forth as it were three arms whereby she taketh in the traffic from oversea brought hither from every land in her fleets . . ."

extract from HISTORIES OF THE KINGS OF BRITAIN *by Geoffrey of Monmouth (died c. 1152), translated by Dr. Sebastian Evans*

". . . This fortress built by Nature for herself
Against infection and the hand of war,
This happy breed of men, this little world,
This precious stone set in the silver sea . . ."

from Shakespeare, RICHARD II, Act II, Scene I

But now the gentle dew-fall sends abroad
The fruit-like perfume of the golden furze:
The light has left the summit of the hill,
Though still a sunny gleam lies beautiful,
Aslant the ivied beacon. Now farewell,
Farewell, awhile, O soft and silent spot!
On the green sheep-track, up the heathy hill,
Homeward I wend my way; and lo! recalled
From bodings that have well-nigh wearied me,
I find myself upon the brow, and pause
Startled! And after lonely sojourning
In such a quiet and surrounded nook,
This burst of prospect, here the shadowy main,
Dim-tinted, there the mighty majesty
Of that huge amphitheatre of rich
And elmy fields, seems like society——
Conversing with the mind, and giving it
A livelier impulse and a dance of thought!
And now, beloved Stowey! I behold
Thy church-tower, and, methinks, the four huge elms
Clustering, which mark the mansion of my friend;
And close behind them, hidden from my view,
Is my own lowly cottage . . .

FEARS IN SOLITUDE, *by S. T. Coleridge; written
in April 1798 during the alarm of an Invasion*

CONTENTS

CONTENTS

COLOUR PLATES

*Throughout this book Plate numbers in arabic figures
refer to Colour Plates, while roman numerals are
used for Black and White Plates*

PLATES IN BLACK AND WHITE

TEXT FIGURES

ACKNOWLEDGMENTS

FOR PERMISSION to reproduce text figures acknowledgment is made
to:—
University of Bristol Speleological Society (Fig. 6); Society of
Antiquaries of London (Fig. 14); Prehistoric Society (Fig. 13); Royal
Archaeological Institute of Great Britain and Ireland (Figs. 16, 25, 26,
30 and 31); Eric S. Wood, *Collins Field Guide to Archaeology in Britain*
(Figs. 9 and 17); *Acta Archaeologica* (Fig. 20); the Trustees of the British
Museum (Figs. 21, 22 and 46); the Royal Commission on the Ancient
Monuments of Scotland (Fig. 23); the Ministry of Public Building and
Works (Fig. 27); R. G. Collingwood and J. L. N. Myres, *Roman Britain
and the English Settlements* (Fig. 29); R. H. Hodgkin, *A History of the
Anglo-Saxons* (Fig. 34); Cambrian Archaeological Association (Fig.
36); National Museum of Wales (Figs. 28, 35 and 37); B. T. Batsford
Ltd. (Figs. 38, 39, 62, 70 and 73); Royal Anthropological Institute
(Figs. 56 and 57); Honourable Society of Cymmrodorion (Figs. 58,
59 and 60).

AUTHOR'S PREFACE

THE IDEA of a book with this title came from the Editors of the *New Naturalist* series of books, and the writer is very grateful to the Editors for their active and sustained interest in the book as it grew. The author has tried to trace main lines of evolution in matters in which deliberate choice between alternatives has been somewhat less important than response to environment. No hard and fast line can be drawn so what is included or excluded is the result of decisions that are submitted to the tolerant judgment of the reader.

Dr. Julian Huxley has made very many valuable suggestions, Dr. Dudley Stamp, Mr. James Fisher and Mr. J. Gilmour have also helped the writer considerably, and he would wish further to express his special gratitude to Miss Joan Ivimy, as well as to the artist, Miss Alison Birch, who has drawn the text figures. His friends, Doctors Elwyn and Margaret Davies, have kindly contributed to overcome some difficulties and Mr. F. Smith of Messrs. Collins has given valuable help.

Mr. Robert Atkinson and Mr. John Markham added greatly to such interest as the book may have by their initiative and enthusiasm in taking nearly all the photographs. Others who kindly contributed towards the colour illustrations are Mr. P. L. Emery, Mr. Eric Hosking, Mr. Cyril Newberry and Mr. S. C. Porter. Sir Charles and Lady Darwin most kindly allowed reproduction of the photograph of Charles Darwin (Plate X).

Two special notes need to be added here. The inferences published here for the first time in Chapter 9 are results of work in progress since 1905. Some fourteen years ago the Leverhulme Trust, through Lord Haden Guest, made a generous grant to aid this work. It is hoped that a fuller and more closely argued account of these researches will appear independently before long; the delays of publication have been due largely to an effort to avoid certain grave errors into which statisticians dealing with these matters have been led.

The aim of this book, a picturing of British life, is to stimulate interest in our evolution and in its portrayal in our museums. The museums of local culture as well as the Folk Culture department of the National Museum of Wales at Cardiff and at St. Fagans Castle point to the need for a great effort to collect and preserve vanishing types of objects, especially in rural life. The strengthening of our museums of local culture, the collecting and storing of material in danger of being lost, and perhaps the making of an ENGLISH MUSEUM and a MUSEUM OF SCOTTISH LIFE are aims to be cherished.

H. J. FLEURE

London,
January, 1950

AUTHOR'S PREFACE
TO THE REVISED EDITION

THE senior partner in preparing this edition wishes gratefully to acknowledge the very large share which his age and infirmities have made him leave to Dr. Margaret Davies. Her archaeological knowledge and wide experience as a member of the Countryside Commission have much enriched the book. In the preface to the first edition reference was made to an anthropological survey of Wales. The results of this research were published by the Royal Anthropological Institute in 1958.

Since 1950 several centres for the study of folk culture have been established. Among them are the Museum of English Rural Life at Reading and many regional and local folk museums. The University of Edinburgh now has a School of Scottish Studies and there is a lectureship in Folk Life Studies in the University of Leeds. Ulster has its Folk Museum in Belfast, the Welsh Folk Museum at St. Fagans, in a fine setting near Cardiff, is expanding, but we still need English and Scottish national folk museums.

Cheam   H. J. FLEURE
January, 1969

CHAPTER I

A GENERAL INTRODUCTION

THE INTRODUCTORY quotation from the translation of Geoffrey of Monmouth's work is eloquent of the characteristics of the various parts of Britain but it does not go so far as to picture for us the differences between the various parts of our island. That island is almost unique in its possession of a very rich series of geological records from the pre-Cambrian to the post-Pleistocene, from mountains, admittedly not very high, to lands below sea-level, from acid-soiled moorlands to rich loams of lasting value once they were cleared for cultivation. The broad general gradation from older, harder, less fertile, to younger, softer, easier lands is from north-west to south-east, and we shall introduce our discussion by trying to follow this gradation in giving brief sketches of our chief regions as homes of men.

An outstanding feature of the story of man in Britain is that, in the course of the historic centuries, a considerable measure of unity has been achieved without a great deal of forcible repression of diversity. Unity in diversity, both in considerable measure, is a feature of Britain. How that diversity should be described in a brief sketch is a question to which many diverse answers could be given. Politically and in a sense historically we might speak of Scotland, England, Wales. Archæologically Fox has emphasised "Lowland" and "Highland" Britain, a division which has much value. But it is too broad, in that Highland Britain includes both the Atlantic coastlands and the great moorland areas of the north and west, while Lowland Britain includes the south-east of England and also the Midlands north-west and west of the Jurassic scarp. Belloc with some justification argued that the Jurassic scarp is the most important dividing line in England; it includes the Cotswolds, Edgehill, the Northampton heights and Lincoln Edge, south of the Humber. The line Mersey, South-Pennines, Humber is another dividing mark with strong claims on various grounds. Climatically the division into Atlantic coasts, Southern and Northern Moorlands (the latter north of the Highland line in Scotland), South-eastern and North-eastern lowlands has some value and some limitations.

Relief and structure mark as units the Scottish Highlands and Hebrides, Midland Scotland, the Southern Scottish Uplands and the Cheviots, Northern England, Wales, the Midlands, South-east England with a special sub-division for East Anglia and one for Kent and, finally, the South-west. Islands, notably Shetland and Orkney and Man, need to be added as distinct elements.

As this book attempts to look at the Natural History of Man in Britain it must concern itself with folk-life. One acknowledges freely that many features have been introduced, even imposed, by conquerors and infiltrating leaders of various kinds, and, where the will-power of a leader or leader-group is heavily involved, we may allow the conventional acceptance of the connotation of "natural" to exclude such matters as being more appropriate to political retrospect. Where they have left a permanent regional impress on the life of the people, i.e., when the people have assimilated a good deal of what was introduced or imposed by leaders, the present review must obviously take these things into account. There will be, as usual in human considerations, a marginal zone in which the writers' limitations, aptitudes and experience will inevitably affect treatment. That this may perhaps give added vitality must be pleaded in defence of human fallibility which should also ask for leniency when, inevitably, treating subjects within the fields of other specialists.

Atlantic Britain includes the lands which look towards the western seas (Fig. 1). They may front on the open Atlantic, as do the Scillies and Cornwall, western Scotland and the Western and Northern Isles, or on to the Irish Sea as do Wales, Lancashire, the Lake District, the Isle of Man and Galloway. All these lands have physical and climatic features in common, and for nine millennia seafarers who have used the seaways along the Atlantic route have imprinted their occupation patterns on the landscape. The rocks of Atlantic Britain are our oldest and hardest rocks and disintegrate into thin soils. Good freely-drained soils are found only in limited patches where limestone outcrops occur, or where sands and gravels are spread over valley bottoms or behind beaches. Much of the upland is covered by heavy glacial clays, sometimes capped by peat. Such land was extensively tilled only in the Bronze Age, before much of the peat was formed, and when the climate was warmer and drier than it now is.

For much of its prehistory and history, settlers have been attracted to the narrow coast fringes of Atlantic Britain, to beaches, estuaries and to the lower coast plateaux. Here the sea routes have linked com-

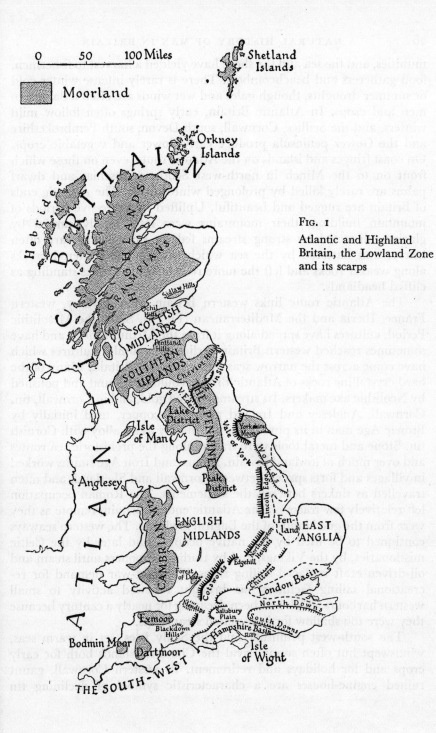

0 50 100 Miles

Moorland

Shetland Islands

Orkney Islands

Hebrides

BRITAIN

HIGHLANDS

GRAMPIANS

Sidlaw Hills

Ochil Hills

SCOTTISH MIDLANDS

Pentland Hills

SOUTHERN UPLANDS

Cheviot Hills

ATLANTIC

N. Tyne

S. Tyne

Lake District

V. Eden

PENNINES

Isle of Man

Yorkshire Moors

Vale of York

Wolds

Peak District

Anglesey

CAMBRIAN MTS

Lincoln Edge

Northampton Heights

ENGLISH MIDLANDS

Fenland

EAST ANGLIA

Forest of Dean

Cotswolds

Edgehill

Chilterns

London Basin

North Downs

Mendips

Salisbury Plain

South Downs

Exmoor

Blackdown Hills

Hampshire Basin

Isle of Wight

Bodmin Moor

Dartmoor

THE SOUTH-WEST

ATLANTIC

FIG. 1

Atlantic and Highland Britain, the Lowland Zone and its scarps

munities, and the sea and the shore have yielded a harvest to fishermen, food gatherers and beachcombers. There is rarely intense winter cold or summer droughts, though gales and wet winds are often a danger to men and crops. In Atlantic Britain, early springs often follow mild winters, and the Scillies, Cornwall, south Devon, south Pembrokeshire and the Gower peninsula produce early flower and vegetable crops. On coast fringes and islands on the Atlantic route, even on those which front on to the Minch in north-west Scotland, fuschias and dwarf palms are rarely killed by prolonged winter frosts. The Atlantic ends of Britain are rugged and beautiful. Uplifted by successive periods of mountain building, their mountains were later boldly carved by glaciers, dissected by strong streams fed by rains, which are often heavy, and battered by the sea which probed out sheltered creeks along weaker rocks and left the more resistant rock masses standing as cliffed headlands.

The Atlantic route links western Britain with Brittany, western France, Iberia and the Mediterranean (Fig. 2). Since the Mesolithic Period, cultures have spread along it from the Mediterranean and have sometimes reached western Britain earlier than similar cultures which have come across the narrow seas into south-east Britain. Many of the hard crystalline rocks of Atlantic Britain could be ground and polished by Neolithic axe makers. Its streams yielded gold, and in Cornwall, tin. Cornwall, Anglesey and Ireland produced copper, used initially by Bronze Age man in its pure form, but mainly as an alloy with Cornish tin. Stone and metal tools were traded along the prehistoric sea routes and over much of lowland Britain. Bronze and Iron Age smiths worked in villages and forts spaced between Cornwall and Shetland, and often travelled as tinkers between the settlements. The Roman occupation left relatively few traces on the Atlantic ends of Britain, remote as they were from the good lands of the English lowlands. The western seaways continued to be used by the native peoples, and later by the Celtic missionaries, by the Vikings, and by trading schooners until steam and oil-driven craft replaced sailing ships. The post-war demand for re-creational sailing facilities has brought renewed activity to small western harbours which had been decaying for nearly a century because they were too shallow for iron-plated steamships.

The south-west peninsula and the Scilly Isles, set in warm seas, windswept but often sunny, rival the Channel Islands both for early crops and for holidays and retirement. In western Cornwall, gaunt ruined engine-houses are a characteristic symbol of declining tin

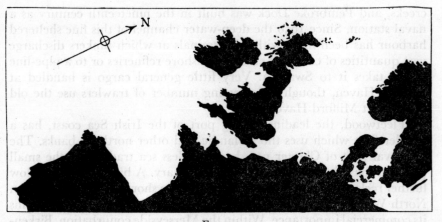

FIG. 2

Diagram showing the intermediate position of the British Isles between North-west and South-west Europe

mining. New bungalows for retired folk, chalets and caravan sites for tourists, usually placed on the fringes of holiday resorts and of the ports which handled tin and china clay, now contribute substantially to the economy of Cornwall and south Devon.

The sheltered inlets of western Britain were and are nurseries for the sailors who man naval, trading and fishing vessels. At Plymouth old-established links with the navy have produced the communities of Devonport and Stonehouse, at the head of the splendid anchorage of Plymouth Sound. Bristol-Avonmouth, the leading port of the Severn estuary, handles substantial general cargoes in addition to older trades in sugar, flour and tobacco. The ports of south-east Wales developed, and since 1913 gradually declined, as exporters of coal. They are not deep natural harbours; their docks were excavated largely on reclaimed mudflats. Their coal exports have been replaced by oil imports at Swansea, tropical fruit imports at Barry, and Port Talbot, Cardiff and Newport handle iron ore for nearby coastal steelworks. On the west Welsh coast, shallow harbours to which schooners brought in lime and took out slates, copper or lead, are full of pleasure craft in summer.

Neolithic seamen rafted bluestones from the Presely Mountains down Milford Haven, and in Tudor times vessels of sixty tons left it for Newfoundland, and brought back dried cod. Coal from Pembrokeshire's coalfield, unworked since 1945, was exported from its tidal creeks, and Pembroke Dock was built in the nineteenth century as a naval station. Since 1950 the deep-water channel of this fine sheltered harbour has been lined with oil terminals at which tankers discharge vast quantities of crude oil either to onshore refineries or to a pipe-line which takes it to Swansea. Very little general cargo is handled at Milford Haven, though a decreasing number of trawlers use the old harbour at Milford Haven town.

Fleetwood, the leading fishing port of the Irish Sea coast, has a trawler fleet which uses the Icelandic and other northern banks. The medieval port of Chester now has even less sea trade than the small ports on the Flintshire side of the Dee estuary. A barrage would allow further reclamation of this silted estuary and a shorter road link between North Wales and Liverpool. On the Mersey estuary, Liverpool retains its commercial importance. Within the Merseyside conurbation, Birkenhead's shipbuilding, and the developing oil and petro-chemical industries south of the estuary, are also based on the Mersey waterway. Liverpool's growth was based on the grain, fibre, sugar and tobacco trades and it remains a leading British port for general cargoes. Like Cardiff, it has accepted at least three generations of West African and Arab sailors who have usually married local girls. Both cities have also attracted a continuous stream of Irish immigrants for more than a century. Glasgow too, has taken in many Irish families who have come across the North Channel. Clydeside is a conurbation with a population of one-and-a-half million which still looks to the river to provide employment in shipbuilding and in cargo and naval traffic. Tanker traffic uses Gareloch, a deep fjord north of the mouth of the Clyde. Glasgow, with its old cathedral, university, and leadership in engineering, dominates most of the Scottish Midlands, and its interest in modern technology is reflected in the foundation of the new university of Strathclyde. The fine anchorages of north-west Scotland are backed by poor hinterlands and carry on only local trade. They provide shelter for crofters' vessels and training for seamen, a notable feature of the Northern Isles and particularly of Shetland. This lean land has made the Shetlander a fisherman with a croft; the men of Orkney are, rather, crofters with boats. Viking settlers have contributed more than place-names to both groups of islands and one of our great naval anchorages was Scapa Flow in Orkney.

The Isle of Man was also settled by the Vikings, but few onshore fishermen now practise their craft there. Island life is geared to farming and to tourism. Lancashire folk who prefer a fine natural coast to the concrete promenades of their own popular resorts have taken holidays in the Isle of Man for many years. Lancashire resorts like Morecambe, Blackpool and Southport increasingly house retired people and residents who commute daily to the industrial towns.

Farming of coastal lowlands in Atlantic Britain varies from highly specialised cultivation of flowers, early potatoes and broccoli, in the south-west, to crofting in the Northern Isles. Dairying is widespread on the lush pastures of the broader valleys which break up the hilly sea frontage. The coastlands provide winter tack for breeding stock and young animals from the hills. On the lower hillsides and lower plateau-tops near the coast the arable land produces cattle fodder, notably roots and oats. These lands are not the granaries of Britain.

The Highland Zone of western Britain is a region beset with difficulties. It is thinly peopled and its hills have been depopulated in the past century. Mining enterprises once flourished here and quite large groups of miners have lived for short or longer periods in its mountain valleys. The lead miners of the Lake District, the Pennine Dales, and of Cardiganshire are among them. In Cumberland, North Wales and north Pembrokeshire, slate quarrying was at one time important and there are still large active quarries and slate mines in Snowdonia. In South Wales, coal is mined in mountain valleys. This is the only major upland coal basin in Britain, and although much coal is now won from opencast workings in the highest parts of the coalfield, many pits on or near its high northern border have closed down.

In Scotland and Mid-Wales hydro-electric schemes produce power for the grid system rather than for many local industries. As the Forestry Commission's plantations mature in both areas wood processing could become more widely established, but depopulation is often so far advanced that little surplus labour is available. Generally speaking, integration of stock-rearing, forestry, water conservation, recreation and local industry seems to be the pattern best suited to highland Britain. The Forestry Commission has set up several National Forest Parks in Scotland, England and Wales, which are increasingly used by tourists. After the 1949 act enabled National Parks to be set up, ten were established in England and Wales. They include, in highland Britain, the Northumberland, Lake District, Yorkshire Dales, Peak District, Snowdonia, Brecon Beacons, Exmoor and Dartmoor National Parks. The others are the Pembrokeshire Coast National Park, which extends into the Presely Mountains, and the North York Moors National Park, which covers the highest coastal hills of eastern England.

The Highlands of Scotland (Plate 2, p. 33), are comparable in natural beauty with English and Welsh National Parks and cover a much larger area than any of them. Fig. 1 shows the north-west Highlands and the Grampians, separated by the Great Glen. Along it the hard granites, gneisses and quartzites have been deeply cleft along fault-lines. As a result there is a lowland route along a chain of lochs which has been used since prehistoric times. Deep glens parallel to, or at right angles to, the Great Glen cut the Highlands into steep-sided mountain blocks topped by vast wet moors. Valley communities have been isolated from each other, and, until the mid-eighteenth century, mutually hostile clans were a feature. Farming centred on cattle, and cattle-droving and cattle-raiding were common. The sparse population lived in scattered farms, hamlets and valley villages which were sometimes under the shadow of the chief's castle. The late eighteenth century, however, saw some opening up of the Highlands. The chiefs no longer needed fighting men and themselves became landlords of sheepwalks and, later, of deer forests. Depopulation of the Highland glens followed, at first outwards to the coasts and to the developing industrial centres, and in the nineteenth century to North America and to the Commonwealth countries. The tourist industry is now bringing work to highland communities, notably to those of Speyside, where settlements like Aviemore have both winter and summer holiday seasons. This and other valleys have notable whisky exports, and multiple use of land and the establishment of suitable industries is being encouraged by the Highlands and Islands Development Board.

In north-east Scotland more open country with better soils derived from Old Red Sandstone is found in Orkney, Caithness, and Ross and Cromarty. These windswept lands were relatively densely settled by Neolithic families who came in from the south, and also attracted Viking settlers from across the North Sea. The south shore of the Moray Firth and east Aberdeenshire are also long-settled areas; in the latter the rearing of beef cattle, especially shorthorns and Aberdeen Angus, brings prosperity to farmers. Aberdeen, the granite city between the mouths of the Dee and Don, has a historic university and flourishes on North Sea trade, on fishing, as a holiday resort, and on the products of a well-farmed hinterland. Deep-sea fishing and fish-processing is a feature of other Aberdeenshire ports such as Peterhead. Many ports of north-east Scotland have long been linked with countries around the Baltic and with Norway, the Faroes and Iceland.

The Scottish Midlands are bordered by two great fault-lines which run from the north-east to south-west. The strip of land which has been lowered below these fault-walls forms a valley, forty miles wide, floored with Old Red Sandstone and with Carboniferous rocks. Faulting has preserved here the raw materials of good farming and industry which have been eroded off the surfaces of mountains beyond both faults. The northern fault runs from Stonehaven in the north-east to Helensburgh on the Clyde, while the faulted front of the Southern Uplands, which extends from Dunbar to Girvan in Ayrshire, is generally less abrupt, and less deeply dissected, than that on the north side of the Scottish Midlands. Nor is there on the south side a broad outcrop of red sandstone comparable to that which runs along the north side of the Scottish Midlands from Stonehaven and the Tay estuary south-westwards to a narrow terminus on the Clyde estuary. The broad eastern end of this belt of warm red soils is Strathmore, a desirable and highly coveted valley at the foot of the difficult Highlands. Strathmore is best known for its soft fruit crops, especially raspberries. It is a well-tended land with a line of towns which have, or had, both defensive and market functions. Among them are Brechin, Forfar, Coupar and, the best known, Perth, at the southern entrance to Strathmore. Stirling and its finely poised castle command many routes, and control the way provided by the Forth valley between the Scottish Midlands and the Highlands. High masses of igneous rock, such as the Campsie Fells and Ochil Hills, separate Strathmore and its western continuation from the industrial Midlands of Scotland.

The Scottish coalfields, on both sides of the Forth estuary and in Lanarkshire and Ayrshire, are surrounded by larger areas of Carboniferous Limestone. These support, in east Fife and on the big mixed farms of the lowlands, a relatively dense rural population. Men have farmed both areas since prehistoric times. St. Andrews, on Fife's peninsula, was an important medieval ecclesiastical centre and retains its old university, its great dignity and its golf links. The main industrial areas of Scotland, which support four-fifths of its people, lie in the isthmus between the Forth and Clyde estuaries. They centre on the coal, iron, and oil shale deposits, and on the great cities of Glasgow and Edinburgh. Both firths carried early seamen into the Scottish lowlands and prehistoric settlers farmed on the sites of both cities. They grew at control points of seaways and of routeways across narrow coastal plains and along valleys which led into the hills. Glasgow, like St. Andrews, was a medieval ecclesiastical centre. As the religious focus of the west coast, it honoured a Celtic saint rather than a missionary apostle. Edinburgh was linked historically with France and the Low Countries, Glasgow, later, with the American trade. Hills within the capital city have provided sites for dignified public buildings and Craig's New Town of Edinburgh, finely planned in the late eighteenth century, is unmatched in Glasgow. Edinburgh also has areas which are as squalid as those of Glasgow and London but, like them, are gradually being rehabilitated. The greater amount of rehousing necessary in Glasgow is responsible for new towns, such as that at East Kilbride, where open country is readily accessible and Cumbernauld, Glasgow's most outstanding new town scheme.

The most important single contribution to the Industrial Revolution was James Watt's steam engine, and since then engineering has dominated industrial development in the Scottish Midlands. Applied particularly to shipbuilding on the Clyde, Scottish skills have also extended to structural engineering and have been much sought after abroad. The manufacture of plant for the sugar, textile, paper and printing industries, iron-founding at Falkirk, and many related industries based on iron and steel are also found in the Scottish Midlands. Old established textile industries include Dunfermline's linen, Kirkcaldy's linoleum and Dundee's jute industry, but Lanarkshire's former cotton industry is now represented chiefly by specialised branches such as Paisley's thread-making and the man-made fibre industry.

Beyond the southern boundary fault lie the Southern Uplands, high rolling moorlands of old sedimentary rocks with, in the west, protruding igneous intrusions like Merrick (2,765 feet). The upper valleys of major rivers dissect these moorlands and allow penetration by road and rail. Annandale and Nithsdale link the Solway and Clyde estuaries. This is cattle- and sheep-rearing country, with the higher hills given over to the native black face or to the big Cheviot, a breed which came originally from Northumberland. Their wool, together with that of cross-bred sheep, supports the hosiery and tweed industry of the Tweed and its tributaries. Centred on Hawick and Galashiels, this industry is having to adapt itself to competition from synthetic fibres. Along the lower Tweed valley the hummocky boulder clay is tilled on good mixed farms.

From the Bronze Age onwards, North British peoples on both sides of Cheviot have been culturally linked. These pastoral hills of the border culminate in the igneous mass of "The Cheviot" (2,676 feet), while from their southern slopes headstreams run down to the Northumbrian lowlands, to river mouths flanked by fine beaches and backed by good

PLATE I SHAKESPEARE CLIFF and Down, Dover. The chalk cliff named from the scene in "King Lear".

PLATE 2 BRAERIACH and Carn Eilrig, Cairngorms.

farmland or, farther south, to the coalfields and Tyneside. Here memories of the folly of over-dependence on mining and shipbuilding spur on attempts to broaden the industrial pattern and to improve the environment.

At the western end of Cheviot the sheepwalks have been replaced by Kielder Forest; beyond it lies the Solway Firth and its mosslands. The proposed barrage across Solway Firth offers possibilities for water storage, power schemes, road-building and industrial development on both sides of the border. Carlisle and Newcastle are linked by one of the few direct west-east routes through the highlands of northern England. The Romans built a line of forts along this valley and, north of them, Hadrian's Wall. Sections of the wall, its ditches and its milecastles, are still very impressive, especially where the wall is poised on the cliff formed by the igneous intrusion known as the Whin Sill.

South of the Roman Wall lie the Pennines and the Lake District, separated by the Eden valley but linked by the high limestone country of Shap Fell. Fairly low passes lead from Shap Fell over limestone grazing land into Wensleydale and Swaledale. Since the Bronze Age men have passed this way between Yorkshire and the Eden valley. The Lake District is a dome of rocks which centres on jagged volcanic peaks like those around Borrowdale. Scafell Pike (3,210 feet), the highest English mountain, is one of them. By Alpine standards, the glaciated Lakeland mountains and lakes are small, but their perfect proportions give them grandeur and beauty. Their tourist season has lengthened since Wordsworth's day, and they are also popular for retirement. From Lakeland, water supplies go to much of Lancashire, and to coastal towns like Whitehaven and Barrow where industries based on iron and steel are being partly replaced by chemical and light industries.

The Pennines are a deeply-cut faulted arch whose steeper flanks are on their western side. Barriers like Cross Fell (2,930 feet), which overlooks the Eden valley, and the Edges, which rise out of the Cheshire Plain, are typical. The northern half of the Pennines, and their southern end which forms the White Peak, are underlain by Carboniferous Limestone. Formerly a source of lead, it is now worked for cement and fluorspar, and its caves and sink-holes provide sport for potholers. High up the Yorkshire Dales, colourful meadows dotted with stone hayhouses, in the limestone country, recall similar scenes in mountain Europe. Elsewhere the Pennines are capped with Millstone Grit, often blanketed by peat, and the soft water which drains downslope is stored in numerous reservoirs. Coalfields, and industrial communities based on them, flank both sides of the Pennines. The Yorkshire Dales and the Peak District, both National Parks, have fine walking and touring country which is being conserved for the thousands of day visitors who come from the surrounding towns.

Around Manchester, the Forest of Rossendale and the Pennine Edges form a funnel for wet south-westerlies. In settlements at the foot of the hills, the spinning of cotton came to displace that of wool, which became concentrated east of the Pennines. Plentiful soft water, a humid atmosphere, and cotton supplied through Liverpool were responsible for this change-over. Cotton-weaving and processing occur on both sides of Rossendale Forest. Engineering and chemical industries are dispersed throughout south Lancashire. Its flat western lands, which have patches of fertile drained peat mosses, are given over to mining, glass-making at St. Helens, vehicle-building at Leyland, and specialised farming which supplies milk, eggs, poultry, potatoes and vegetables. Popular coastal resorts supply fresh air at all seasons, a necessity in spite of reduced atmospheric pollution in conurbations like Manchester-Salford in which over three million people live.

The Ribble valley and the Fylde have retained since the sixteenth century many families who adhered to the Roman Church. This was also a feature of isolated valleys on the Yorkshire side of the Pennines, as it was of those on the southern borderland of Wales. The Yorkshire aristocracy, however, often enriched by the dissolution of Cistercian monasteries, went over to the Anglican Church much more readily than the squires of the Fylde. Yorkshire's landowners were more closely linked with the court and with York Minster. York, which could be reached by small ships sailing up the Ouse, was the second city in the kingdom until medieval Bristol outstripped it. The restored guildhall of York's Merchant Venturers recalls this leadership.

It is interesting that the dukedoms of Lancaster, York, Chester and Gloucester should have been held by the Royal Family. These were areas immediately below or behind the Scottish and Welsh borders and in non-royal hands these titles, and that of the Duchy of Cornwall, might have led to rivalries like those between France and Burgundy. The medieval Bishop of Durham was another frontier lord, suzerain of a splendid fortress and cathedral, whose writ reached over all the area north of the Wear and Ribble; but he threatened the king less than a military leader who might found a family.

Yorkshire's broad acres are far more productive than those of

Lancashire, both in their surface tillage and in their underground coal-seams. Many of the large pits of the Yorkshire-Derbyshire coalfield, and those south of it, feed coal to a line of power stations along the Trent. The Cistercians reared sheep in the Yorkshire valleys and a woollen industry developed there. Concentration on industries such as worsteds, in which the wool is combed flat so as to make a finer cloth than tweed, hosiery, skilled steel manufacture at Sheffield and Rother-ham, and brewing at Burton-on-Trent, are still features of towns on the flanks of the Pennines. But from Darlington southwards through Sheffield and Derby to the Black Country, technological advances are integrating complex engineering and light industries into the older industrial patterns. On both sides of the Pennines and in the Midlands, the current technological revolution, calling for a greater variety of skills, has produced changes as radical as those of the first Industrial Revolution and has made for a more soundly based industrial structure. Many local authorities are planning better housing and social facilities to match modern industrial plants and are gradually clearing the appalling legacy of the past century.

Wales is a largely upland country, and from Snowdonia south-wards along the Cambrian Mountains to the Brecon Beacons, the land-scape is rugged and beautiful, but often masked by cloud. Though deeply cut by the upper valleys of rivers like the Dee, Severn and Wye, high moorlands dominate the core of Wales. Its industrial areas lie behind the north-east and south-east coasts, and, unlike the Scottish Midlands, its interior industrial valleys are neither wide nor low-lying; they are gouged out of a high plateau with a mountain rim. Regional groupings which originated in the Iron Age have made for differences of outlook in communities separated by the mountains. North and South Welsh people differ markedly, and look increasingly to differing areas of England. Valleys and coastal plains have allowed English armies, settlers and language to penetrate westwards at vary-ing rates. The peoples of West Wales, Snowdonia and Anglesey, and many who have moved from these areas to Swansea and Cardiff, have retained Welsh speech and use a living literature. Welsh speakers are more numerous in rural Wales than Gaelic speakers in Scotland, and there are more of them in Swansea or Cardiff than there are Gaelic speakers in Glasgow. But Cardiff is a post-war capital, a much younger administrative centre than Edinburgh, and its choice was disputed by Caernarvon and other towns. Nonconformity dominates the religious life of Wales and its disestablished church lacks the prestige of the

Church of Scotland. Unlike Wales, Scotland retains its own legal system.

As in Scotland, the oldest Welsh rocks are those of the north-west. They lie under the planed-down farmlands of Anglesey. Across Menai Strait, Snowdonia rears up to culminate in pointed peaks like Snowdon (3,561 feet), in the summits of the Carneddau range, and, farther south, in the jagged silhouettes of the Rhinog group, behind Harlech, and in Cader Idris. Ancient volcanoes injected lavas into all these mountains and glaciers have ground out high cwms and valley lakes. On the east side of Snowdonia, slopes plunge steeply into faulted valleys like those of the Conway and Dee. Around Bethesda and Blaenau Ffestiniog quarries or slate mines yield purple slates. The quarrymen also work small-holdings which have left a distinctive field pattern on the western hillsides of Snowdonia. They have also contributed considerably to the intellectual life of Wales. The hillsides supported both sheep and cattle until Tudor times but are now sheep country only (Plate 3, p. 48). Here and elsewhere in Wales the flocks were taken up to the sweet mountain pastures from May to October and *hafod* and *lluest* (found farther south), which both mean summer dwelling, are common constituents of farm names.

Tourism supplements the income of many farms and is important along the north coast, in Anglesey, the Llŷn peninsula and along Cardigan Bay. Snowdonia, the core of Gwynedd, was the main Welsh medieval stronghold and to counteract its influence, Edward I built imposing castles in walled towns. These castles and walled boroughs stand by the sea which kept them provisioned, and survive, flanked by less imposing modern accretions, at Conway, Beaumaris, Caernarvon and Harlech.

The central uplands of Wales are very thinly peopled. The lean land makes farming difficult and over the past century they have become the empty heartland of Wales. Migration is often only to valley farms, or to market towns like those which lie by the Severn and its tributaries, or to westward-facing valleys. But depopulation has also taken Mid-Wales folk to the Welsh coalfields and their ports, to the Midlands and to the south-east of England. Birmingham has a large Welsh community, as has Slough, to which South Welsh miners and steelworkers made the largest contribution in the 1930s. Quarrymen have also gone from Snowdonia to the building and contracting industries of Liverpool. For over a century the lean farmlands of Wales, like those of Scotland, have seen an exodus. Farmers' sons from the hills of Cardiganshire and Carmarthenshire have become dairymen in London; milk trains still run from Carmarthen to London. Drapers have gone to London from the valleys of south Cardiganshire and north Pembrokeshire, where small woollen mills make colourful tweeds, blankets and rugs. Many Welsh doctors and teachers have also worked in England.

In the country which they left, hill farms have often become sheep ranches, and much afforestation has taken place. A hydro-electric scheme has been completed on the west side of Plynlimon and a pumped storage and a nuclear power scheme in Snowdonia also contribute to the grid system. Conventional and regulating reservoirs have been built in the narrow wet valleys of Mid-Wales. The tourist industry, with walkers and pony-trekkers especially in mind, could be fostered there, for Mid-Wales has some of the most beautiful and remote valleys in Britain and a good series of west-east green roads which were once used by drovers taking cattle to the Midland plains for fattening.

The Highland Zone of Wales passes southwards into the fine red scarps of the Brecon Beacons. Flanked by Black Mountains on both sides, and bordered by the pastoral Usk valley, they form a National Park which is often visited by people from the adjoining coalfield of Carmarthenshire, Glamorgan and Monmouthshire. The greater warmth of the Bronze Age allowed settlement to expand on to hills in Mid-Wales, and the round barrows which covered Bronze Age burials can be seen on many hilltops. They are found in the Black Mountain of Carmarthenshire, high above a lovely mountain lake called Llyn y Fan Fach. The best-known Welsh folktale, which centres on this lake, reflects the clash of cultures between the peaceful Bronze Age hillfolk and the boisterous Iron Age intruders who came up the valleys which penetrate the hills. The features common to many versions of the legend of Llyn y Fan Fach are a tall, fair farmer from the valley who marries a slight, dark, fairy bride who rises from the lake. If he strikes her with iron she will disappear into the lake, and, after many happy years, a carelessly thrown bridle brings this about. Hill people are skilled in country lore and the Lady of Llyn y Fan Fach taught her sons the use of herbs. They became the physicians of Myddfai, and many have claimed to have used their remedies. Maenor Myddfai extends upslope from the Vale of Towy into the Black Mountain, and in the Middle Ages its free tenants had the unusual feudal duty of providing their lord of the manor with a physician whenever he was travelling in Wales.

Early nineteenth-century topographers described the beauty of the Rhondda valleys, and the "Alps of Glamorgan" at their heads, in lyrical terms. The mining valleys of South Wales are now ribboned with houses, chapels, roads and railways, and slag-heaps extend from the pit-heads up the steep hillsides. Living conditions are difficult in the narrow and often sunless valleys. Numbers of pits and miners have been considerably reduced, but the attachment of valley communities to villages which cluster around the pit-head and chapel persists. There is still an outward flow of population, especially of younger families to the new industrial centres on both sides of the Severn estuary. Labour forces in the valleys are much more mobile, and daily travel to industrial estates at their mouths is now commonplace. Local authorities strive to improve unsatisfactory living conditions and social services, and the Civic Trust has outlined a scheme to rehabilitate the Rhondda valleys. Dangers and disasters are met with courage, and many older Welsh miners live with their scars and with the dust disease, pneumoconiosis. But industrial scars on the landscape, here and elsewhere, are wounds which could be more rapidly healed if larger grants were available. Experiments on slag-heaps in the devastated lower Swansea Valley, and by the Forestry Commission on several coal-tips, have shown what could and should be done.

The Highland Zone of Wales presents a broken wall of hills to the English Midlands. Relatively easy communication from Montgomeryshire and other eastern Welsh counties has made Shrewsbury almost an auxiliary capital of Wales. Border counties like Shropshire, Herefordshire, and Gloucestershire, still well-wooded, are regions of half-timbered farms and villages set in fine farmlands. Beyond them lie the industrial Midlands of England, whose former forests have been largely cleared. Bordered on the east by the Jurassic scarp, which runs from Lyme Bay to the North York Moors, the grasslands of the Midlands are underlain by New Red Sandstones, Triassic rocks which are new compared with the Old Red Sandstones of Herefordshire. Clay and gravel spreads are common, and the Severn and Trent and their tributaries take a rather sluggish run-off from these lowlands. North-westwards the Cheshire Plain provides a lowland link with Merseyside. Where coal-bearing rocks are exposed, in east Shropshire, west and east of Birmingham, and around Stoke-on-Trent, industry is old-established, and many outlying towns such as Redditch and Stafford are important engineering centres.

This heartland of England, because of its dense forests, was unattractive to prehistoric man except on its hill borders. It was opened up by the Romans who drove roads through it which are still major highways between southern and northern England. Watling Street, now the A5, is one of them. The Midlands subsequently became the kingdom of Mercia, with Offa's Dyke as a western boundary against the Welsh. In Mercia the forests gave place to common fields surrounding nucleated villages and, after enclosure, to a mixed farming system. Dairying increased with industrialisation, to meet the demand for milk, as did cheese-making, notably of Stilton and Cheshire cheeses, and fattening of cattle reared on poorer pastures has long been a feature of farming in the east Midlands. Drovers who brought in cattle from Wales avoided the turnpikes and sought ridgeways which are still called "Welsh Ways" in the Cotswolds and elsewhere. Cattle hides formed the basis of the boot and shoe industry of Northampton.

Large medieval manors and rich pastures gave wealth to a squirearchy which was largely Royalist in the Civil War. Boroughs set at bridgepoints in the rich valleys gradually grew as market and service centres. But industry grew most rapidly outside the incorporated towns and, especially in the eighteenth century, in towns such as Birmingham and Stoke-on-Trent. These towns, and northern cities like Manchester, Leeds and Sheffield, became centres of religious dissent after the enactment of oppressive laws such as the Act of Uniformity, the Conventicle Act and the Five Mile Act. The generations of thoughtful and enterprising men who guided their development were often Presbyterians, Unitarians, Quakers or Jews. Civic pride expressed itself in substantial public buildings and this tradition continues in the redesigning of civic centres at Coventry, Birmingham, Stoke and elsewhere.

Coalbrookdale, on the western fringe of the Midlands, was a birthplace of metallurgical techniques. Craftsmen in metals multiplied in Birmingham, around James Watt, and in nearby towns. Modern skills go into a very wide range of metallurgical and engineering industries and into the manufacture of vehicles and their components. Raw materials like sheet steel are brought in from many plants beyond the Midlands, and finished products supply British and overseas markets.

Fig. 1 shows the Jurassic scarp, a major cultural divide, and southeast of it a series of chalk scarps like the Chilterns and the North and South Downs. The long Jurassic and Chiltern escarpments have steeper northward-facing scarps and fall only gently southwards. Their porous tops were less densely forested than the plains and, from the Neolithic Period, men have travelled along both the Jurassic Way, and along ridgeways like that along the Berkshire Downs which continue north-eastwards as the Icknield Way. Parts of the Chilterns are clay-capped and have extensive beechwoods which have been cropped by the furniture-makers of towns like High Wycombe. Now conifer plantations are replacing the deciduous woods.

The nodal point of the chalk scarps and their routeways is Salisbury Plain. It could also be approached by early settlers up rivers, and along gravel terraces, from landings in the Christchurch and Bristol areas, and up the Thames valley. Salisbury Plain, in the heart of Bronze Age Wessex, was the home of the aristocratic trading community which built Stonehenge and other ceremonial henge monuments. Dorchester-on-Thames, one of their religious centres, was the seat of an early diocese which extended to Lincoln. The South Downs and their southern lowland fringe shared in some of the prehistoric achievements which centred on Salisbury Plain. The juxtaposition of good grazing land, and, after clearance, rich valley arable, gave wealth to scarp-foot villages situated on spring-lines, and to market towns built by rivers which cut through the scarps.

The sheep of the Jurassic scarp provided wool for cloth-making and for export, and wool merchants built fine churches, cathedrals and houses from the Cotswolds northwards to Lincoln. Oolitic limestone has been used for a greater number of satisfying buildings of all kinds than any other of our building stones.

Sited near points where rivers break through the scarps, Oxford and Cambridge are of special interest. Their strategic importance was recognised by the building of motte-and-bailey castles in each city. Hill, vale and waterway provided produce for their fairs, St. Giles at Oxford and Stourbridge at Cambridge. It is characteristic of British tradition that the older English universities developed at these two centres and not, as in the case of the Sorbonne in Paris, in the immediate vicinity of the royal court.

The northern end of the Jurassic scarp reaches the sea in high cliffs around Whitby. In the Cleveland Hills the escarpment rises above Tees-side. Its iron and steel industries were founded on Cleveland ore and the North York Moors provided alum and jet for many centuries before Tees-side grew. Parts of the Moors and their coast now contribute to the chemical industries of Middlesbrough-Billingham, yielding potash and natural gas. The lowlands of Yorkshire and Lincolnshire, focusing on the ecclesiastical centres of York and Lincoln, formerly traded along rivers like the Ouse, Trent and Witham. Kingston-upon-Hull is the leading modern port. Across the Humber lie the expanding port of Immingham, and Grimsby, a large trawling and fish-processing centre. Oil, North Sea gas and a new Humber bridge could considerably enhance the industrial possibilities of Humberside.

Numerous fine sandy beaches between Scarborough and the Thames estuary have attracted holidaymakers from much of England for half a century. Caravan and chalet sites are now numerous around the holiday resorts. However, coasts fronted by salt marshes, around the Wash, in north Norfolk, and in Essex, are less crowded at the height of summer. All these coasts were badly flooded in 1953 and their sea walls have since been rebuilt and strengthened against the winter wildness of the North Sea.

Since farming communities first entered Britain, the rich lands of East Anglia have invited settlement by peoples coming in from the North Sea up navigable estuaries, or along the chalk scarp into Breckland. Neolithic men sought the river gravels and the lightly forested heaths which were underlain with chalk layered by bands of flint. Their Bronze Age successors also frequented the chalklands, but Iron Age farmers cut into the woodlands around the river mouths and founded tribal capitals like Colchester which were taken over by the Romans.

Before the Romans left Britain, peoples from the Frisian coast began to come across the North Sea to settle in East Anglia. They initiated the English settlement of Suffolk and Norfolk, clearing and tilling and imposing a pattern of communal cultivation on the landscape. Their medieval descendants made East Anglia both a grain land and a grazing land, with a wool surplus which was exported from many estuarine ports to the Low Countries. In Suffolk, towns like Lavenham and Long Melford worked up the wool and their wealth was used for the building of churches which rival those of the Cotswolds. Norwich was the main port, market and guild centre of medieval East Anglia, and its splendid cathedral dates from the Norman foundation of the bishopric. When the woollen industry moved to Yorkshire, other craft-based industries replaced it in Norwich. Among them were boot and shoe industries and the processing of locally grown mustard. Here, as in textile regions in northern England, dissenters have been made welcome and manufacturers have contributed greatly to civic development. Medieval Flemish weavers, Huguenot refugees and Dutch drainage engineers have all practised in East Anglia and the Fenland. Constant interchange of goods and ideas between East Anglia and the Low Countries brought in during the seventeenth century the use of clovers and root-crops. Turnip Townshend and Coke of Holkham were Norfolk landowners who advocated and successfully practised root-crop cultivation to augment cereal cropping and replace fallowing. Their Norfolk four-course rotations completely altered arable farming in Britain and led to widespread enclosure of common fields. In both East Anglia and the drained Fenland west of it, farming today is of a very high standard. It produces not only cereals and roots as advocated by the improvers, but large sugar-beet, vegetable and soft fruit crops which are processed at local factories. The sandy heaths of Breckland, where the improvers experimented, are now partly covered by Thetford Forest, but some intensive vegetable cropping is practised there.

Medieval peat extraction, followed by flooding, produced the Broads between the Yare and Waveney rivers. The sheltered waters of Broadland now form the most intensively used sailing and cruising area in Britain, and old trading centres like Yarmouth have fishing harbours, and fine merchants' houses, on their sheltered estuarine sides, and promenades and holiday facilities on their bracing North Sea frontages. Productive wells of the North Sea gas-field lie offshore and pipe-lines from them could lead to petro-chemical industries at several points on the East Anglian coast.

Fig. 2 shows the British Isles in relation to the European mainland. The seas which have often been regarded in modern times as a barrier, or as a defensive moat, have functioned as linking highways during much of our history and prehistory. Along the Atlantic route both settlers and ideas have come from the Mediterranean and Western Europe. South-east England has been more closely linked across the narrow seas with north France, the Low Countries and north-west Germany. Trade links with the Paris Basin, and the conurbations round the mouths of the Rhine and Elbe, give south-east England commercial advantages which are obvious from the map.

The peopling of south-east England began before the Dover Strait existed, and hunting groups used both the Thames river gravels and the downs and heathlands as they foraged for food. Neolithic, Bronze and Iron Age farmers sought the same areas and carved out farmlands and hamlets. The Romans moved into Britain from landings in the southeast, and, secure in military bases like London and Verulamium, extended their power over most of Britain. South-east England was their granary, and large estates were carved out of it around their villas.

English settlers, Norman warriors, and a succession of refugee groups came first into south-east England, and trading enterprises were then sent out from it. Pilgrims used the old North Downs Way to Becket's tomb at Canterbury; the metropolitan church, like the older universities, was established outside London. Crusaders and generations of travellers went farther along the ridgeway and left England from Dover. This harbour below the chalk cliffs was and is the leading Cinque port and has played a glorious role in British naval history, not least as the base of the Dover Patrol (Plate 1, p. 32). The building of a Channel Tunnel and of hovercraft bases will alter the pattern of communications across the Dover Strait, but will also add development pressures to those which already exist in south-east England.

But communications will centre on London, as they have done since the Roman Period, and its immense wealth and growth will increase. London is unique among great cities for a succession of notable buildings which have been erected between the Norman and the modern periods. Its explosive modern growth, heralded by stately squares too often accompanied by miserable tenements, its royal parks, its commercial heart, its peripheral light industries, its octopus-like tentacles which have engulfed old villages and market towns, its impersonality that is yet of the very essence of its collective being, all give it a character which no other city is likely to develop. The orbit of London has now reached the Channel on the south and is spilling over the Chilterns on the north. Commuters travel to London from all these areas, and attempts to stem this movement have established new towns like Bracknell, Crawley and Stevenage, beyond the outer fringe of London's green belt. Modern industries have multiplied in and around these towns. More recent overspill schemes seek to distribute people farther afield, beyond the Chilterns around Bletchley, in Hampshire and in several East Anglian towns.

A complex rail network has spread residential development over the lower downlands around London and into heathlands south-west of the city. Sandy soils in the Weald are still well cropped and well wooded, and though small towns here and in the marginal valleys have slightly expanded, the countryside between the North and South Downs is still predominantly rural. Due south of London, its most accessible coastal belt, around Brighton, supports a conurbation of half a million people. Many work in the holiday industry and many are retired folk. The developed coastland continues beyond Selsey Bill to Portsmouth and Southampton, engulfing old cities like Chichester, in which a fine cathedral, consecrated in 1108, is surrounded by increasingly heavy traffic.

Southampton benefits from tides coming up both the Solent and Spithead and most of our great passenger liners are based on its riverside docks. On the west side of Southampton Water, around Fawley, a complex of refinery and petro-chemical plants matches those of the Medway and lower Thames estuaries. Behind Fawley, the New Forest, formerly a royal hunting preserve, provides grazing for ponies and recreation for the people of Southampton and towns farther afield. Spithead has the great naval base of Portsmouth on its shores, but from the harbours of Chichester, Ryde, Cowes and Lymington, pleasure craft seek the waters round the Isle of Wight and are far more numerous than naval vessels there. The harbours of Christchurch, Poole and Weymouth are also full of sailing craft. These are the waters used by Neolithic men who came up the Atlantic route in skin-covered boats and dugout canoes, and ventured inland into Wessex. For much of prehistory the focus was Salisbury Plain and, later, a royal Saxon seat and a medieval bishopric was centred on Winchester. Southampton, itself an old city, is now dominant, based on an Atlantic route of wider significance.

This brief review of the major regions of Britain has attempted to show some of the opportunities and problems which they have presented to successive settlers over the past 5,500 years. Our natural regions grade into one another and none has been sufficiently isolated to persist in working out its fate separately. Intermingling has given us a tendency to objectivity and compromise among ourselves, and an appreciation of adventure and innovation, all characteristic features of British thought.

CHAPTER 2

IN THE BEGINNING

As MAN did not originate in Britain, a study of his natural history there should describe how he reached our island and when.

The discoveries of Boucher de Perthes in the Somme valley, verified by Sir John Evans in 1859, the year of *The Origin of Species*, finally established the existence of Palæolithic man as the contemporary of extinct animals and led to modern chronologies. The age of man on earth has been extended from Archbishop Usher's 6,000 years to a period of at least 100 times that length. Africa has yielded many forms that in one way or another approach mankind, so the old search for the "missing link" is superseded. Darwin suggested that man originated in Africa and it now appears that some of the most significant stages in the evolution of modern mankind occurred there and in the Middle East. South-east Asia has also been claimed as an alternative birthplace of our species. We need no longer be haunted by the myth of a single couple of parents for mankind. We are dealing with a being that early acquired unique powers of adapting his mode of life to widely varying surroundings and who wandered far and wide. Consequent divergences of evolution resulted both from the effects of diverse environmental influences on growth and on natural selection, and from the accumulation of differing variations in more or less isolated groups. A variety of hominid forms need not be considered as biologically distinct, mutually infertile species.

Some widespread human characteristics, which are old-established, may be mentioned. Most human beings prefer a temperature of 62°-75° Fahrenheit, but many enjoy colder intervals, finding them bracing, especially to the nervous system. This suggests that a region which had temperatures of this kind had a good deal to do with the evolution of man. In the Pleistocene Ice Ages, when apparently man was evolving towards his present physical condition, such temperatures were probably characteristic of parts of East and North Africa. The East African Rift valley and the wadis of the Western Sahara have yielded many implements of early man.

As a species we are remarkably poor in body-hair and must have lost it very early in the special evolution of mankind. Our animal relatives have hairy bodies; and, among mankind, some Europeans, the Ainu of North Japan, a few groups in the Philippines, and the Australian aborigines have most body-hair. The majority of Africans and many Asiatics have lost almost all save the head hair.

Humanity typically has brown pigment granules in hair, eye and skin; though, in fair-haired blue-eyed north-west Europeans, the melanin, as this pigment is called, is very much reduced. It is possible, even probable, that early man had a good deal of this pigment. It is a product of metabolism which, so far as the skin is concerned, is shed as the skin wears away, but it is of great value for stopping excess of ultra-violet rays, whether direct from the sun, or pouring through a blue sky, or reflected to some extent from a snow surface.

The erect posture, with the head balanced on the vertebral column and the hands free from the duty to help support the body, is another universal feature, probably not quite fully attained in some hominids (Near-Men) of the Pleistocene Age. This posture and balancing of the head still has to be learnt in the first two years of life, and the reduction of the relative size of the jaws has been an essential accompaniment of the change of posture and balance. Our animal relatives have relatively heavier jaws, and jaws and head there are held in place by strong neck-muscles. Their reduction in mankind has given the larynx and mouth a new freedom which may well have promoted the ability, so characteristic of man, of producing varied sounds. Language is a universal feature of mankind, going beyond expression of feelings and having sounds denoting things and ideas.

Some of the hominids nearest to man were still very heavy-boned in head, face and jaws, and it is probable that vestiges of this boniness remain here and there among us; and this characteristic reappears in some cases of abnormality of a part of the pituitary endocrine gland at the base of the skull. The reduction of this boniness has been a marked feature of the early story of man. It is justifiable to connect the changes just mentioned with man's spread, after he abandoned a tree-life, from woodland or bush margins out on to open grasslands. On these sparse grasslands the long-inherited forward look, the increasingly free hands, the quick run might all help success in the food quest very effectively.

The human hand is another of our general characteristics, and its working is closely linked with the eye and with the large brain. All men use implements, at least of wood and stone; and this is to be correlated with the character of the hand.

All men use fire or flame, and this is no doubt a very ancient acquisition; it has often been suggested that at first men could maintain a fire but could not light one, i.e. they were dependent on prior fires, ultimately on natural fire. There is the famed story of Prometheus, stealing fire from heaven and bringing it to earth in a hollow reed. Some rituals suggest that firemaking was a process of skill in ancient times and that the maintenance of fire, by women in many cases (note the Vestal Virgins), was a ceremonial affair. The use of fire not only to scare wild beasts, but also to give warmth and to make food easier to eat for people with jaws reduced from animal strength, suggests the immensely important part fire has played in the growth of civilisation, and especially in helping man to spread northwards to Britain and colder lands.

Human babies are more tender than those of apes for lack of hair on the body, have heads too heavy to hold up at first and need months to learn to walk, so maternal devotion has found enlarged scope, and tempers power over the infant with love's restraints. In such ways maternal devotion has become one of the most important factors of progress. Durable social life has made communication by sound a means of categorical statement as well as of communication of the emotions, and thus has contributed enormously to the growth of reasoning. Much of this can be looked upon as an outcome of a process of foetalisation, involving the maintenance throughout life of characteristics which, in animal ancestors, were transient phases of pre-natal or early post-natal growth. This foetalisation is associated with the enlargement of the brain and the advantage accruing from longer training.

Use of tools appears to have preceded major growth of the brain in mankind and is associated with fossil men of the *Australopithecus* type. In 1959, Leakey found a skull of what he called "nutcracker man"— *Australopithecus (Zinjanthropus) boisei*—at Olduvai in Kenya in association with Pre-Chellean tools. Nutcracker men, carnivorous hominids who made pebbles into tools by chipping cutting edges on them, lived early in the Pleistocene Period, perhaps 600,000 years ago. The making of Pre-Chellean pebble tools gradually spread throughout South and North Africa and the Chellean tools which succeeded them were used in Europe where they are found, for example, in the Somme valley.

Hominids of *Pithecanthropus* stock, men with receding chins and other ape-like characteristics, were the first inhabitants of Eurasia. These Lower Palæolithic hunters lived in Europe during or between the second and third Pleistocene Ice Ages. Penck and Brückner identified four Ice Ages: Gunz, Mindel, Riss and Würm, occupying, very roughly, 800,000-10,000 B.C. and separated by long warm interglacial periods. The jaw found in interglacial sands at Mauer near Heidelberg may be that of a hunter from the great interglacial period before the Riss glaciation. It belongs to the Middle Pleistocene and may be c. 400,000 years old.

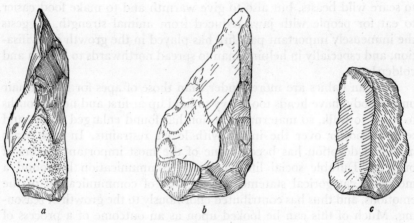

a   b   c

FIG. 3

Lower Palæolithic implements: *a.* and *b.* core implements. *c.* rough flake. (x 1/3)

The Mindel-Riss interglacial period covered thousands of years, during which small nomadic groups of lower Palæolithic hunters followed far more numerous herds of game northwards across Europe. A few of them may have reached Britain about 200,000 years ago. They were the makers of Clactonian and Acheulian tools, hand-axes, often with points, which could be rapidly fashioned by a practised hunter (Fig. 4). These flint cores were not hafted but were used as hand-tools for scraping and cutting skins and flesh. Small animals could have been stunned with hand-axes but larger ones were probably caught in pit traps and speared. Clactonian hunters also fashioned flakes whose edges were trimmed and sharpened to make scrapers and knives. Wooden spears could have been shaped with the scrapers and a spear of yew was found at Clacton in Essex.

PLATE 3 HOUSE OF MAN WHO MARRIED A FAIRY, a mountain farmhouse near Snowdon.

PLATE 4 MODERN WELSH CORACLES, River Towy. Wickerwork (well developed in the Early Iron Age) forms a frame for stretched oxhide.

Large numbers of hand-axes were struck where the families halted in their hunting forays. Where flint was plentiful, on the gravel terraces of large river valleys, and on downlands south and east of the Cotswolds, thousands of hand-axes have been found, but they could have been made over the centuries by only a few nomad groups. Higher land in western Britain did not attract these first visitors from Europe. The Trent and Severn basins have produced less than a hundred of their axes and beyond the Severn only one surface find has been found in Wales, at Penylan on the east side of Cardiff. None has been found in north-west England.

In one of the gravel terraces of the Thames valley at Swanscombe Clactonian axes in the lower levels are succeeded by Acheulian axes in the upper gravels. The Acheulian axes were found with a skull not unlike that of *Homo Sapiens*, except for its exceptional thickness. But this is an incomplete skull and lacks the forehead bones: it is roughly 200,000 years old.

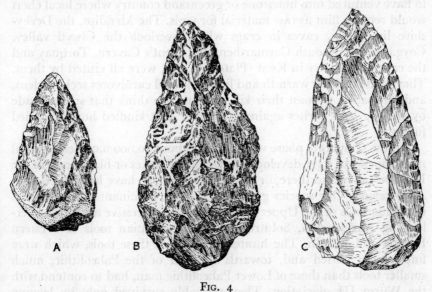

FIG. 4
Acheulian axes with characteristic shallow flaking

The Riss glaciation would have forced Lower Palæolithic hunters to retreat southwards out of Britain. Men reappeared there during the last interglacial period (Riss-Würm) and in the first phase of the Würm glaciation. These were Neanderthal men, makers of Mousterian tools, and they appear to have been more numerous than the Acheulian hominids and to have ranged more widely over the tundra during their hunting expeditions. One of their sites near Hamburg has been dated to c. 55,000 B.C. Though some phases of the Würm glaciation were less intense than much of previous Ice Ages, Neanderthal man and his successor *Homo sapiens* were often forced to become cave-dwellers in winter half-years. It has been suggested that their spread was facilitated by a temperate phase which ended about 30,000 B.C. between Würm I and II and a second temperate phase which followed Würm II and ended before 25,000 B.C. Würm III appears to have been at its maximum between 25,000 and 12,000 B.C. but after about 10,000 B.C. the climate became progressively warmer.

The cave-dwellers of Würm I hunted the mammoth, bison and woolly rhinoceros across the tundra of Europe and southern Britain. Ebbsfleet by the Thames was one of their camps and others were scattered over England south of the Trent valley. Hunting bands seem to have ventured into limestone or greensand country where local chert would replace flint as raw material for tools. The Mendips, the Derbyshire limestones, caves in crags which overlook the Clwyd valley, Coygan Cave in south Carmarthenshire, Kent's Cavern, Torquay and the cave at Oldbury in Kent (Plate 6, p. 85), were all visited by them. They made fires for warmth and light, to repel carnivores seeking dens, and, probably, to roast their kill on spits. We think that sparks made by striking iron pyrites against quartz or flint kindled heaps of dried fungus.

In the temperate phase which ended about 30,000 B.C. Neanderthal man appears to have developed long narrow flakes or blade tools in the Danube valley and there, or in the Near East, to have hybridised with *Homo sapiens*. Our species gradually became dominant and produced the blade tools of the Upper Palæolithic, the successive and often overlapping Aurignacian, Solutrean and Magdalenian tools of Western Europe and Britain. The hunters who made these tools, which were finer, more varied and, towards the end of the Palæolithic, much smaller tools than those of Lower Palæolithic man, had to contend with the Würm III glaciation. They probably survived only by leaving Britain during its most severe millennia around 20,000 B.C. The caves already mentioned again provided shelter. In Kent's Cavern an Aurignacian woman left the scrapers with which she cleaned skins and a pin with which she pierced them. Caves overlooking the Clwyd valley, such as Cae Gwyn and Ffynnon Beuno, near St. Asaph, sheltered

Aurignacian hunters as did Paviland Cave in Gower which then looked down over the wide valley which subsequently became the Bristol Channel. The so-called Red Lady buried at Paviland was a young huntsman whose body had been plentifully covered with red ochre. This may represent life-blood or may reflect painting of bodies for the chase or ceremonies.

Several caves under Creswell Crags near Worksop were occupied during Magdalenian times and gave their names to the Creswellian industry of the millennia around 12,000 B.C. Creswellian hunters occupied Kent's Cavern, Torquay, Aveline's Hole at the north-west end of the Mendips, King Arthur's Cave in the Wye valley limestone, Cathole Cave near Paviland and Nana's Cave on Caldy Island off Tenby. Like the Eskimo the Creswellians hunted reindeer but also, as the climate improved, stag, pig and *Bos primigenius*. This was the aurochs which was the predecessor of domesticated cattle. He may then have stood six feet high, though some aurochs drawn by the Upper Palæolithic hunters of the Dordogne valley resemble modern cattle.

Wandering hunters whose lives are controlled by the movements of the herds on which they prey can visit their cave shelters only sporadically. But memories of these refuges would linger and several show intermittent use over the centuries. King Arthur's Cave was occupied at intervals from 25,000 to 1,500 B.C. by nomad groups, that is from the Aurignacian to the Bronze Age.

Upper Palæolithic men were close observers of the animals on which they depended, and skilful flint-workers and artists. They made gravers or burins for engraving bone, antler, wood and soft stone, and they were interested in the fertility of animals and women. Though Britain has nothing to equal the brilliant assemblage of cave art of France or Iberia, nor their "Palæolithic Venuses", statuettes of pregnant women, there is some good Magdalenian work on bone at Kent's Cavern, and an engraving on bone of a human figure and another of a horse's head from two of the Creswell caves. Bone, frequently broken to extract marrow, and breaking naturally with a fine point, was increasingly used in the Upper Palæolithic. Fine bone sewing needles were made for sewing skins to make clothing or to provide roofs for tents. Harpoons were made to spear fish, and the bone, ivory and antler tools of the Magdalenians, the last Ice Age hunters, like their way of life, are reminiscent of that of the Eskimo. In France and Spain their cave paintings recall his artistry, notably, for instance, the Magdalenian reindeer of Font de Gaume or the bisons on the roof of Altamira cave.

Britain in the long Palæolithic ages was the outer fringe of a thinly peopled continent. Over the rolling plains which linked Britain and northern Europe herds of game and hunting bands ranged widely. It has been suggested that not more than 250 hunters would have been present in Britain at any one season during the Palæolithic. On the European steppes more numerous hunters may have reduced the herds considerably. In Britain most of the animals and nearly all of the edible roots, nuts and fruit would have been unaffected by the very small population.

About 10,000 B.C. the Würm glaciation ended and vast masses of meltwater flowed into the seas and valleys round a Britain which was still a peninsula of Europe. The sea-level rose and the land surface also rose as it was released from the weight of the ice caps. Willow and birch spread over the land and later, as it warmed up, pine forests developed. The reindeer moved out over Northsealand into Scandinavia, or died out and were replaced by red deer. This was the Pre-Boreal Period of c. 10,000 to 6,800 B.C., and towards its end the Straits of Dover and the Bristol Channel probably came into being. Rises in sea-level had exceeded rises in the level of the land. In the succeeding Boreal Periods (c. 6,800-5,000 B.C.), hazel, oak, elm and lime replaced pine as the climate became warmer and drier. During the warm damp Atlantic Period (c. 5,000-2,500 B.C.), mixed deciduous woods dominated by oak covered much of Britain. Alder would be dominant in wet valleys and mixed scrub on valley gravels, chalk and limestones, or on coastlands exposed to high winds and salt spray.

In the Pre-Boreal, Boreal and first fifteen centuries of the Atlantic Period, Mesolithic hunters and collectors ranged over Britain. The great herds of game disappeared after the ice retreated. As Mesolithic man hunted over the coastal fringes, the sea gradually rose, eventually to cover many of his shelters and hearths. Women gathered much of the food supply, hammering shellfish such as limpets off the rocks. Offshore fishing from dug-out canoes and, probably, skin-covered boats, and even fishing in deeper waters, are suggested by fish bones in middens. Men hunted with the bow and arrow, using dogs to help them and hunting equipment that was more varied than that of the Palæolithic. Man worked in stone, bone and red deer antler, and in wood, and his axes had cutting edges which could slice through small timber. But he was still a nomad living at subsistence level on the fringe of temperate Europe. Mesolithic men were hunting along the broadening Straits of Dover when, in the Fertile Crescent, farmers had already settled down

PLATE I.   AVEBURY, Wiltshire. Aerial view of the bank, ditch and
surviving stones of the circles

PLATE II.   STONEHENGE, Wiltshire. Aerial view

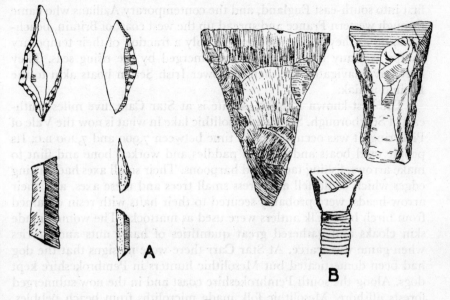

FIG. 5

Mesolithic implements: *a*. Microliths or pigmy flints. *b*. Tranchets or flake axes

and built large villages like Jericho because they were not wholly obsessed by the search for food.

Before 7,000 B.C. Mesolithic families moved to and fro across Northsealand. These Maglemose folk take their name from a type-site called Magle Mose, or great bog, in Denmark. Northsealand must then have been a great fen which would attract fowlers and fishers. A Maglemose harpoon was brought up by a trawler from the Leman and Ower Banks, off East Anglia, in a mass of submerged peat or moorlog. Camps of Maglemose hunters have been found at many lowland sites in eastern England, notably in the Thames valley. As the climate became warmer and drier the population increased and there was a good deal of intermingling with other Mesolithic peoples and an exchange of skills in fashioning tools.

On the windswept coasts of western Britain, on sandy inland heaths and on high hilltops above the forest margins, Mesolithic people who used small flints or microliths (Fig. 5), often mounted in rows, made temporary camps. They were food collectors and left large shell middens on or near the seashore. These were Tardenoisians, who probably came first into south-east England, and the contemporary Azilians who came through western France and spread up the west coast of Britain, beach-combing as they went. We know of only a fraction of their temporary camps as many must have been submerged by the rising seas. They may have navigated the then narrower Irish Sea in boats akin to the Eskimo umiak.

The best-known Maglemose site is at Star Carr, five miles south-east of Scarborough. Set by a Mesolithic lake in what is now the Vale of Pickering, it was occupied some time between 7,900 and 7,200 B.C. Its people used boats and wooden paddles and worked bone and flint to make arrows, fishing tackle and harpoons. Their small axes had cutting edges which could fell and dress small trees and these axes, and their arrow-heads, were probably secured to their hafts with resin obtained from birch bark. Elk antlers were used as mattocks. The women made skin cloaks and gathered great quantities of hazel nuts and berries when game was scarce. At Star Carr there were no signs that the dog had been domesticated but Mesolithic hunters in Pembrokeshire kept dogs. Along the south Pembrokeshire coast and in the now submerged forests offshore, Mesolithic folk made microliths from beach pebbles. Maglemose tools found there suggest a penetration from eastern Britain in the Atlantic Period. The Mesolithic people of south-east England have left many traces in the Weald and adjoining sandy areas. Occasionally, as at Abinger and Farnham, shallow wind-shelters were hollowed out near springs, the pits being covered with a rough roof of skin or saplings supported on stakes.

In western Britain Mesolithic fishers used bone fishing hooks, harpoons, stones to hammer shellfish off rocks, and when they were lucky enough to find stranded whales, mattocks to remove blubber. Their camps are widely scattered along the coasts of Cornwall, South Wales, the south-west tips of the Llŷn peninsula and Anglesey, the Flintshire coast, and in Galloway, Arran and Bute and up to and beyond Oban. Caves were occupied but many of the finds come from open-air workshops partly covered by later sand-dunes, or from cliff-tops. Here they squatted and chipped flint and worked bone. Mesolithic hunters sought the grit hilltops of the Pennines, possibly during summer hunting forays, and here, above 1,500 feet, many microliths have been found. More recently, trench ploughing which precedes afforestation has cut into the thick peat mantle of similar hilltops in South Wales to reveal microliths scattered on the grit surface below the peat. On Dartmoor and on Bodmin Moor small groups seem to have

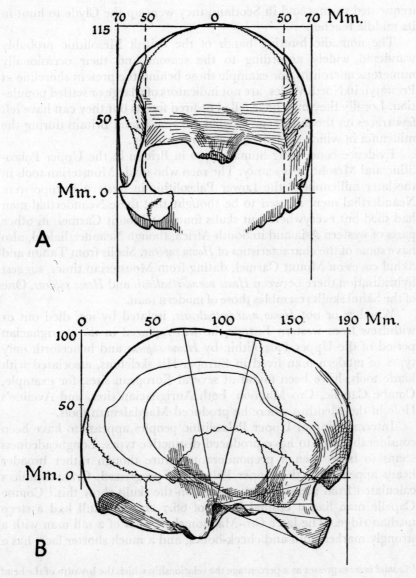

FIG. 6
The Aveline's Hole skull: a) front and b) side views

frequented springs and in Scotland they went up the Clyde to hunt in its middle reaches.

The nomadic hunting bands of the British Mesolithic probably wandered widely according to the seasons and their occasionally numerous microliths, for example those behind the present shoreline at Prestatyn in North Wales, are not indicators of a large or settled population. Locally they may have felled or fired forests but they can have left few traces on the landscape of what became Island Britain during the millennia in which they lived there precariously.

Evidence concerning human types in Britain in the Upper Palæolithic and Mesolithic is scanty. The men who made Mousterian tools in the later millennia of the Lower Palæolithic in western Europe were Neanderthal men. It used to be thought that these Neanderthal men had died out everywhere but skulls found at Mount Carmel, in other parts of western Asia and in South Africa, though Neanderthaloid, also have some of the characteristics of *Homo sapiens*. Skulls from Tabun and Skhul caves on Mount Carmel, dating from Mousterian times, suggest hybridisation there between *Homo neanderthalensis* and *Homo sapiens*. One of the Skhul skulls resembles those of modern man.

Whether or not *Homo neanderthalensis*, isolated by ice, died out or withdrew from western Europe, he was replaced in the Aurignacian period of the Upper Palæolithic by *Homo sapiens* and henceforth only types of modern man lived in Europe. His skeletons, associated with blade tools, have been found at several European sites, for example, Combe Capelle, Cro Magnon, both Aurignacian sites, and Aveline's Hole in the Mendips where he produced Magdalenian tools.

Intermingling of Upper Palæolithic peoples appears to have been considerable and to have produced distinctive types. Longheadedness seems to have been a preponderant feature though rather broader heads appeared as the Upper Palæolithic progressed. Cranial indices calculated from measurements taken on the skulls show this.[1] Combe Capelle man had a cranial index of 66.7 and his skull had a steep median ridge. The later Cro-Magnon skull, that of a tall man with a strongly marked chin and cheek-bones, and a much shorter face, has a

---

[1] *Cranial index* expresses as a percentage the relationship which the breadth of the head bears to its length, calculated on the skull. *Cephalic index* expresses the corresponding relationship measured on the living head. Extreme longheads are those with an index of less than 72.5 on the skull and 73.5 on the living head. Longheads are those between 72.5 and 77.5 on the skull and 73.5 and 78.5 on the living head, while broadheads have indices of over 81.5 on the skull and 82.5 on the living head.

cranial index within the range 73.7-74.8. The Aveline's Hole skull, shown on Fig. 6, has a cranial index of 70.8, but two others from this cave, with cranial indices of 80, show the trend towards broadheadedness which occurred in the Magdalenian period and is also found in some of the skulls from the Creswell caves.

In Mesolithic times both long and broadheaded types were found in Europe and Britain. In Central Europe, as at Ofnet in Bavaria, and in Portugal, broadheaded skulls characterise Mesolithic finds. Mesolithic hunters and fishers spread to Britain from both central and western Europe, contributing differing elements to its sparse population. Longheaded types with cephalic indices of 70 and 75, as represented by the skulls from the Mesolithic habitation site in MacArthur Cave at Oban, probably preponderated. But we must assume some Upper Palæolithic survivals of extreme longheads, some racial intermixture and some differentiation into the distinctive types which characterise the population of modern Britain. In it, in areas of difficulty and isolation, are people who show the marked longheadedness and strong brow ridges which are found on late Palæolithic skulls (Plate VIII, p. 141 and Chapter 9). Other modern peoples show the same analogies.

CHAPTER 3

EARLY IMMIGRATIONS AND HUSBANDRY

WHILE Britain was still peopled by Mesolithic hunters and collectors, groups of families had settled down to till the fertile ground along great rivers like the Euphrates, Tigris and Nile. They also grouped themselves around perennial springs like those which watered the oasis of Jericho. This relatively low land, curving from the Tigris-Euphrates delta round to the lower Nile valley, is often called the Fertile Crescent. In it, and in the mountains which surround it, wild forms of wheat and barley, and the wild ancestors of cattle, sheep, goats, dogs and pigs, could all have been found when Mesolithic families hunted and gathered their food there. What probably happened is that dogs in search of carrion attached themselves to these groups, lambs, kids and calves were captured and reared, and women discarded wild grass seeds and watched them germinate. At more fertile camp-sites the young plants would have thrived and increased, and a more settled life with an assured food supply would gradually have replaced nomadism.

The wild grasses of the genus *Triticum*, from which our wheats evolved, gave rise to einkorn (*T. monococcum*), widely cultivated in Neolithic times, and to the more productive emmer (*T. dicoccoides*). By the Iron Age bread wheat (*T. aestivum*), a cross between emmer and the wild grass *Aegilops*, was sustaining increasing populations in much of Europe and Western Asia. Its relative club wheat (*T. compactum*) was grown by Neolithic farmers, notably those of the Swiss lake-side villages. Spelt (*T. spelta*), still a bread wheat in remote parts of the Balkans, was probably first sown and harvested in the Bronze Age.

Both two- and six-rowed barley grew wild in Palestine and were cultivated throughout Neolithic Eurasia. They were evolved by Neolithic farmers into *Hordeum tetrastichum*, the ancestor of modern varieties of barley. Oats and rye may have grown as weeds in the corn patches of many Neolithic cultivators. They appear as food grains in late Bronze Age and Iron Age deposits in parts of Central Europe where, during the cool wet summers which characterised the Iron Age, it may have been realised that they were a more profitable crop than wheat or barley.

By 7,800 B.C. a Mesolithic settlement, centred on a platform which was probably a shrine, existed at Jericho. The Neolithic people of Jericho developed corn plots in their oasis and by 7,000 had built on the Mesolithic site a considerable village sustained by the waters of springs. At Jericho and at Jarmo in Iraq, in the hills east of Kirkuk, wheat and barley were grown. This wheat was emmer and at first both it and the varieties of barley grown were very like the wild forms. Seed was stored in stone bowls and leather bags. There was no pottery in these Fertile Crescent villages of the 7th millennium B.C. In Egyptian villages like those of the Fayum, dated at 4,500 B.C., seed corn was stored in pits carefully lined with basketry.

The leather containers were not necessarily made from animals which had been hunted down. The Mesolithic Natufians of Jericho had tamed the dog and their Neolithic successors kept goats. At Jarmo both sheep and goats were kept, the sheep being the Asiatic mouflon. Elsewhere, at Anau in Turkestan, for example, the urial was the local wild sheep and this too was tamed. Pigs appear in Neolithic Iraq and Iran, and, later, at the Fayum and in Neolithic Switzerland. Cattle, then much larger beasts than our domesticated breeds, would be more difficult to domesticate and more demanding in their pastures. *Bos primigenius*, the aurochs of Pleistocene Eurasia and North Africa, or smaller breeds which developed from it, may have been domesticated in the Fertile Crescent about 5,000 B.C. These long-horned breeds were taken throughout the Near East and Europe by Neolithic herdsmen. In the late Bronze Age they were largely replaced in western Europe by *Bos longifrons*, the short-horned ancestor of our modern cattle.

Animals attached to settlements, perhaps tethered in the fields or grazing on stubbles, would provide manure in return for more nutritious pastures than those which they usually found in the wild state. Relatively safe from carnivores, their young would more readily survive. Thus both human and animal populations increased more rapidly as the Neolithic progressed.

Mixed farming, combining tillage with the rearing of animals, thus developed as early as the 7th millennium B.C. in the Fertile Crescent and spread westwards through the Mediterranean lands and northwestwards along the European steppes. There wind-blown loess, fertile, porous and less densely wooded than heavier soils, was farmed as

Neolithic man spread. The loess lands were beginning to be settled around 4,000 B.C. The oldest Neolithic houses so far located in Bulgaria date from 3,600 B.C. although the Danube basin in north-east Bosnia has Neolithic settlements which are said to date back to about 4,400 B.C.

Over the centuries families spread more widely, the men and their flocks sought land for grazing and the women needed new ground to sow seed. Woodland would be fired, and the ashes made the ground temporarily easier to work. Shifting cultivation by slashing and burning began to leave its mark. On the forest margins the flocks would eat or uproot saplings and slow down regeneration. In Mediterranean lands the goat began what J. L. Myres called its age-long nibble up the mountainsides. The early Neolithic in Italy dates from the fifth millennium B.C. Deforestation has a very long history in Mediterranean lands.

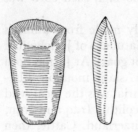

FIG. 7
Neolithic hoe blade: front and side views (× 1/3)

There would still be much hunting and gathering to supplement food supplies, especially in autumn and winter. Large crab apples were gathered and dried by the women of the Swiss lake-side villages, and wild animals would provide furs for the cloaks which they made. Neolithic women grew flax; linen cloth occurs in early levels (c. 6,500 B.C.) at Jarmo, at the Fayum in 4,500 B.C. and in the Swiss lake-side villages. Flax is not common farther north in Neolithic Europe though it may have been grown there for both fibres and seed.

Tillage demands a settled life and the building of homes. Small, usually rectilinear, houses spread throughout Europe. Though they often had stone foundations, timber was frequently used in building them and trees had to be felled and dressed for this purpose.

Maglemose men of the Mesolithic had already fashioned tree-felling axes with transverse cutting edges from chipped flint. This raw material was obtained from beach deposits, or, on land, from glacial gravels. Neolithic men used more efficient axes of polished stone and were able to rely not only on flint but also on a variety of fine-grained rocks of greater geological age and wider distribution. Experiments with polished stone axes have shown that 600 square yards of birch forest can be felled by three men in four hours. An axe-head is effective on about one hundred trees and then needs to be replaced or sharpened. Tools

PLATE III. a. SILBURY HILL, Wiltshire. A prehistoric mound near
Avebury

b. CEFN AMWLCH, Llŷn peninsula, Caernarvonshire. A single-
chambered tomb overlooking the sea

PLATE IV.   CAPEL GARMON, Denbighshire. A transepted gallery grave

made by grinding and polishing included the axes with which men attacked the forests and the hoes with which women cultivated (Figs. 7 and 8). Digging sticks with their points hardened by fire and weighted with stones were probably also used by women and children. When they reaped their corn, cutting off the ears with a flint sickle, Neolithic women dried it in clay ovens to harden the grain and ground it in saddle querns, rubbing it with a rounded stone against a larger grit slab.

Many Mesolithic men had lived by seas or rivers which provided much of their food, and had made boats and wooden paddles. Neolithic man in the Fertile Crescent would be a fisher and fowler in the rivers, lakes and deltas. He would use boats on the rivers and on the Mediterranean and in them he and his successors slowly spread coastwise or between islands which were often intervisible. Some craft must have been driven from the tideless Mediterranean through the Straits of Gibraltar into the wilder Atlantic. Out there he would try to keep to the coast. Voyagers gradually spread around the Iberian coast, or they went overland, using one of the great trans-peninsular routes, that from Languedoc to

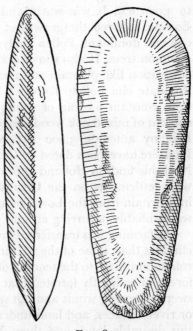

FIG. 8
Neolithic polished axe: front and side views (× 1/3)

the Gironde estuary. They went northwards to Brittany and Normandy. From northern France Neolithic families came to south-west Britain about 3,500 B.C. and, lured on by lands projecting into the Irish Sea, and seldom out of sight of land in good weather, they moved up the west coast of Britain to the Shetland Isles. This was the Atlantic route which, with varying significance, influenced the settlement pattern of Britain throughout prehistory (Fig. 2). On present evidence it appears to have brought in Neolithic settlers more speedily than the Central European overland route between the Fertile Crescent and south-east England. But early Neolithic families with their beasts and seed corn came not much later across the English Channel from the chalklands of northern France to augment the farming groups of Britain.

The diffusion through Europe of Neolithic seafolk and farmers occurred during the Atlantic Period which is roughly dated from 5,000 to 3,000 B.C. It was warm and damp, a climate which, in Western Europe, fostered the growth of mixed deciduous woodland in which oak was dominant. Pollen analysis shows that elm and alder were also common trees. It also shows that, in Brittany and elsewhere, weeds of cultivation like plantain and mugwort increased after 3,500 B.C. From this date elm pollen decreases, and this decline is thought to result from constant feeding of young elm shoots, the most palatable constituent of mixed oak woods, to tethered cattle. Neolithic settlements in Brittany antedate 3,000 B.C., while cultivation levels examined in Finistére have been dated by C 14 analysis to at least 3,200 B.C. Early Neolithic finds in Holland appear to be contemporary and to be linked with settlements on the Central European loess lands. Immigration into Britain from the Low Countries and the north French chalklands was probably occurring around 3,000 B.C.

As farming was transferred northwards in Europe to more boisterous climates than those of the Mediterranean, tillage may have assumed a role subordinate to the tending of flocks. Both demanded land free from forest, or so lightly forested that it was easy to clear. In Britain, shores swept by strong winds and salt spray, gravel deposits on raised beaches or river terraces, and land underlain by chalk and limestone provided this desirable land, and there Neolithic families settled. They found Mesolithic families already roaming over the coastlands and river gravels and, eventually, native British Neolithic cultures arose from their fusion with these groups. This merging, and the expansion of the Neolithic population, occurred between 3,000 and 2,000 B.C., in the Sub-Boreal Period. It too was a time of warmth, but it was drier than the Atlantic Period.

The equipment of the western Neolithic settlers included, in addition to their polished axes and hoes, round-based pottery based on leather bags, and leaf-shaped arrowheads which they used when hunting (Fig. 9). Broken yew bows dating from c. 2,600 B.C. have been found preserved by peat in Somerset.

Bag-shaped round-based pottery has been found at Windmill Hill

near Avebury and at other causewayed camps of the southern chalklands (Fig. 11). The first of these causewayed camps to be built appears
to have been the most westerly one so far discovered, that at Hembury
in Devon, dated by C 14 analysis to *c.* 3,200 B.C. The building of Windmill Hill itself is dated to *c.* 2,900 B.C. Other C 14 dates for the early
Neolithic suggest that south-west Britain and
Ireland, in the mainstream of the Atlantic
route, were settled earliest and that, on
present evidence, Neolithic farmers then
spread eastwards in Britain. They also
suggest that the spread of settlement up to
and past Northern Ireland, perhaps by
groups swept along by the Irish Sea tides,
was relatively rapid. Neolithic occupation
sites in Co. Antrim and in Cumberland are
dated before 3,000 B.C.

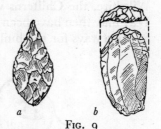

FIG. 9

Neolithic implements: *a.*
Leaf-shaped arrowhead. *b.*
Scraper, showing end view

   The causewayed camps of Neolithic farmers shown on Fig. 11 were
set within incomplete ditches and banks which were not built for
defence. If surmounted by brushwood palisades they could have
served as cattle corrals. The ditches were not continuous; causeways
crossed them between pits into which waste food and bones were
thrown. Causewayed camps may have been mainly used for autumn
feasts, when, for days or weeks, cattle were rounded up and, except
for the breeding stock which could be fed through the winter months,
were slaughtered by pole-axing. Autumn fruits and nuts accompanied
the feasts of meat. Cooking-pots used during the feasting were bag-
shaped. Many are plain, like similar pots from north-east France,
others have lugs by which they could be held and these suggest that
people from Brittany could have influenced their style. Windmill Hill
people were clothed in fur and in the hides of their cattle. The women
dressed the skins with flint scrapers and used bone awls and flint perforators before they sewed them with leather thongs. They were not
wholly dependent on their cattle for food but made gruel and bread
from wheat (emmer and einkorn), and barley, whose growth on porous
soils would be encouraged by the warmth and damp. Barley forms
only about a tenth of the food grains of these early British farmers.
Their cattle were small longhorns related to *Bos primigenius,* their sheep,
descended from the urial, were the turbary sheep of Swiss lake-side
villagers, and they also kept small pigs and dogs. Horses were lacking;
they did not spread through Europe until the Bronze Age.

The distribution of causewayed camps suggests that Neolithic farmers, landing in Devonshire, Dorset and Sussex, spread with their flocks along the chalklands and intermingled in Wiltshire. Salisbury Plain and the Marlborough Downs became a focus of prehistoric Britain and remained so for two thousand years. From the downs of Wiltshire, the Chilterns were settled and the Ridgeway and Icknield Way may then have been tramped out by men and herds as they served as droveways for the builders of the causewayed camps.

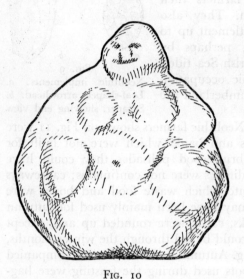

FIG. 10

Mother Goddess figurine from a flint miners' altar in Grimes' Graves, Norfolk (about half actual size)

Flimsy wooden Neolithic farmhouses have naturally not survived for five thousand years. Their postholes have occasionally been found under later tombs. In western Britain, where plentiful surface stones made it easier to build foundations or walls, a few Neolithic huts have been recovered. Such are the house at Haldon, in Devon, a timber-framed rectangular house with wattle-and-daub walls, at Mount Pleasant overlooking Porthcawl in Glamorgan, a smaller though similar structure, the houses at Rhos y Clegyrn, three miles south-west of Fishguard, and Clegyr Boia near St David's where a rectangular house twenty-four feet long and a smaller round structure were found. The Clegyr Boia pottery was of a basic round-bottomed type found in Ireland and at Carn Brea in Cornwall. At Carn Brea early farmers had rough shelters on a site which later became an Iron Age fort. Other Neolithic shelters have been found on Hazard Hill near Totnes, in Flintshire, at Storrs Moss near Lancaster (a lake dwelling), and near flint mines.

There are nine sites on the Sussex Downs where bands of flint were sought by miners, and others are known in Wiltshire and Hampshire. At Durrington near Stonehenge the workings seem to have been open-

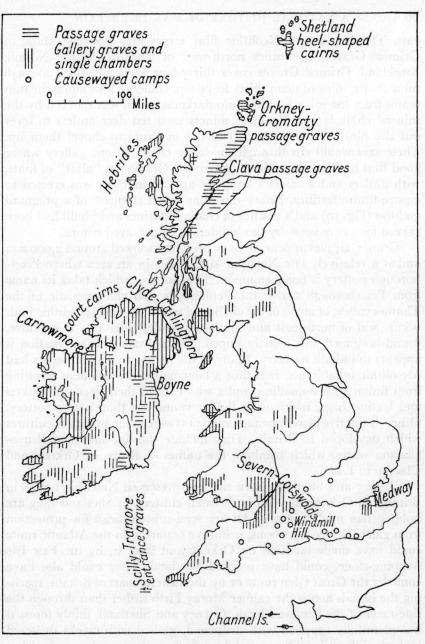

Key:
≡ Passage graves
⦀ Gallery graves and single chambers
○ Causewayed camps

0 ___ 100 Miles

Shetland heel-shaped cairns

Orkney-Cromarty passage graves

Clava passage graves

Hebrides

Clyde-Carlingford

Carrowmore court cairns

Boyne

Severn-Cotswold

Medway

Scilly-Tramore entrance graves

Windmill Hill

Channel Is.

FIG. 11

Distribution of causewayed camps and main types of megalithic monument

cast. The best-known Neolithic flint mines are, however, those of Grimes' Graves, five miles north-west of Thetford in the Norfolk Breckland. Grimes' Graves cover thirty-four acres and there are 346 mine shafts, some of them thirty feet deep. Galleries lead along the flint seams from the mine bottoms into darkness which was relieved by the miners' chalk lamps. Neolithic miners used red deer antlers to lever out the flints and the shoulder-blades of cattle to shovel them up. Their axes would cut through the softer chalk. In one gallery where good flint had not been found at Grimes' Graves, an "altar" of flints, with antlers and a miner's lamp set around its base, was erected to ensure future fertility. Before this altar was a statuette of a pregnant goddess (Fig. 10) and a phallus of chalk. Figurines and phalli had been carved for many years by the builders of causewayed camps.

Grimes' Graves appears to have been first worked around 2,000 B.C. and is a relatively late Neolithic site. It lies in an area where Peterborough pottery is fairly common. This pottery, which takes its name from Peterborough across the Fenland, is also characteristic of the Thames valley, of much of the chalkland where the early Neolithic finds occur, and of north-east and south-east Wales (Fig. 12). It is coarse, round-bottomed and heavily lipped. In its profuse ornamentation it appears to imitate basketry. Many of the areas in which it occurs had Mesolithic inhabitants. It is thus a later native development resulting from fusion with nomadic peoples who carried their goods in baskets and leather bags, which were lighter containers than heavy pottery. Other distinctive heavily ornamented pots were made by native cultures which developed in Britain. They include the flat-bottomed Rinyo-Clacton wares, which combine the names of Rinyo in Orkney and Clacton in Essex.

Orkney and Shetland have the best-preserved Neolithic houses in Britain. In Orkney they occur in small clusters, in Shetland they are isolated like modern crofts. All are semi-subterranean for protection from gales. Driven by storms, primitive seafarers on the Atlantic route could have made landfalls on Orkney and from it, by the Fair Isle stepping-stone, could have reached Shetland. They could also have come by the Great Glen route or up the eastern coast of Britain, reaching the islands across the calmer Moray Firth rather than through the tide-races of the Pentland Firth. Orkney and Shetland, thinly forested but plentifully supplied with driftwood, gashed with creeks sheltered by high cliffs and yielding a rich harvest from the sea, attracted settlers from the Neolithic to the Viking Period. Their Neolithic peoples were fisher-farmers, their economy based on sea and land like that of the Shetland crofter to-day.

The Orkney houses, at Rinyo on Rousay and at Skara Brae on Mainland, were built of the local flagstone. Its thin slabs needed little dressing and from them thick-walled square houses were built in groups around a central hearth. A larger house in each group suggests that they were the dwellings of a patriarch and his kin. The flagstones allowed box-beds, dressers and keeping-holes (small wall cupboards) to be built into the thick walls. Stone tanks stopped with clay which would have contained live fish and shellfish were let into the floor. The roof may have been of skins or reed thatch supported by whale-rib rafters. Around the semi-subterranean cluster, sheep, cattle and goats grazed, but no grain was grown. These were flesh-eaters akin to the Eskimo. In Neolithic Shetland the women grew barley and dried it over fires. The men tended flocks and fished. Small fields, some of which may be cattle pens, can still be seen scattered over the cultivable lowland fringes of the islands. Nearly sixty oval farmsteads have been found in the Shetland Isles: many were probably still used in the Bronze Age.

The Mesolithic element contributed nomadic strains to the native Neolithic cultures which developed in Britain. They were evident in groups of primarily travellers and traders, who carried the products of the Neolithic axe factories over long distances (Fig. 12). Polished axes, roughed out at factories in areas of old igneous rocks in western Britain, were traded widely, especially in areas where newer rocks like chalk supported many early farmers but could not provide them with durable raw materials other than flint. The axe factories often overlook the sea and that near Penzance, which has not been located, may even have been submerged by it. The trade in greenish polished axes was carried on by sea, down rivers and along ridge routes, notably the Ridgeway and the Icknield Way. The most vivid green mineral, jadeite, was brought in from Brittany for votive rather than everyday use. To the Wessex chalklands came axes from all the sites so far identified.

Christian forms of burial, with inhumation and often with memorial stones, date back nearly two thousand years. The tombs of Neolithic man were built over a similar period and some of the more important ones, such as West Kennet near Avebury, were in use for a thousand years. Like Christianity, Neolithic beliefs originated in the Fertile Crescent. They were centred on a goddess of the earth, a source of fertility for crops and animals. She appears in the finest tombs as a crude figure, or stylised as an eye goddess. She watched over the dead, from capstones or from the upright stones which supported them, as they lay with tools at their side and with their food in pots for use in the after-life. It may have been thought that only their souls would be released from the earth-covered tombs, and rounded holes or other openings were sometimes left for this.

On the chalklands of Britain the tombs were usually long earthen cairns and there is evidence from Dorset, Wiltshire and Lincolnshire that the bodies decayed first in mortuaries and that only the skeletons were buried. Earthen barrows were rectangular or wedge-shaped; extremely long ones occur in Dorset. Some, like Fussell's Lodge barrow, built near Salisbury about 3,200 B.C., covered long timber houses which enclosed the bones of the dead. White chalk would form barrows which could be kept outstandingly white by scouring. In western Britain white quartz pebbles were sometimes laid on the mound (as in passage-graves in the Bend of the Boyne in Co. Meath), or were heaped within it (as in the Isle of Man), recalling the giving of white stones in the Revelation of St. John, chapter 2, verse 17. Built of the great stones which give them their name, hundreds of megalithic monuments still bear witness in Ireland and western Britain to the importance of burial rites in the life of Neolithic man.

Fig. 11 shows the distribution of the two main types of megalithic monument in Britain and Ireland. It is a pattern related to the Atlantic route and to a seaborne dispersal of tomb styles which reached these islands from Spain and Brittany. The small group of late graves around the Medway are related to tombs found in Holland and north-west Germany and are the only ones which originated across narrower seas. Dutch megaliths date from about 2,600 to 2,000 B.C.

Up the Atlantic route, to land fronting on to the sea or linked with it by navigable rivers, seafarers brought two basic forms of tomb. One consisted of building galleried tombs set in long cairns (Fig. 14) and the other of having a passage leading to a burial chamber set in a round cairn (Fig. 13). Groups followed the tomb style of the homelands they had left. Where the farming population was relatively numerous, as it was on both sides of the Severn estuary, or in the northern half of Ireland, tombs multiplied over the centuries and the knowledge of how to erect them was not lost. There is considerable uniformity in tomb styles in these areas. Both were magnets which drew in many early settlers to the exclusion of peninsulas like Cornwall, Pembrokeshire and Llŷn. Although all these lie athwart the Atlantic route the megalith

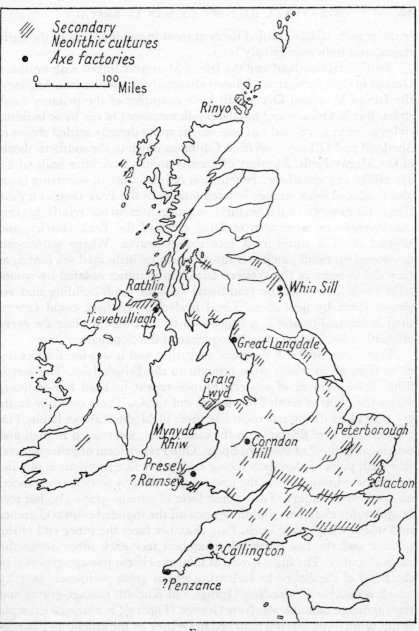

Secondary
Neolithic cultures
Axe factories

0 ——————— 100 Miles

Rinyo

Whin Sill

Rathlin

Tievebulliagh

Great Langdale

Graig
Lwyd

Mynydd
Rhiw

Corndon
Hill

Peterborough

Presely

?Ramsey

Clacton

?Callington

?Penzance

FIG. 12

Secondary Neolithic cultures and axe factories. The areas from which some axes
derive have been determined geologically but the factory sites have not yet been
located

builders seem to have settled them at most in small groups in the early stages, and only increasingly later.

South-west Scotland and the Isle of Man were linked with northern Ireland in their tomb styles. Islands attracted early settlement. Anglesey, the Isle of Man and Orkney all have examples of the primary tomb styles. But in Orkney and Shetland folk memories of the basic building styles seem to have died out and on the quite densely settled shores of Shetland and Orkney, and from Caithness down to the southern shores of the Moray Firth, a variety of massive tombs were later built which are unlike any elsewhere. Penetration of inland areas, occurring later, also produced some strange isolated tombs. In the Peak District it gave rise, so far as we can tell from surviving megaliths, to one relatively early gallery-grave on a western outlying ridge of the Peak District, and beyond it to a number of late gallery-graves. Where settlements developed on small patches of raised beach by little used sea routes, as they did in some of the Western Isles, communities isolated by mountains could have lost the traditional skills of tomb-building and replaced them by new ideas. Local leaders everywhere could express their individuality and it is fruitless to try to assign a place for every megalithic tomb in an orderly sequence of development.

France has over five thousand megaliths and it was tomb styles derived from them which were brought to the British Isles. The megalithic gallery-graves of western France repeat in hard free-standing stones the plans of south French rock-cut tombs. These could be easily cut only in relatively soft rocks like those of Mediterranean lands. The passage-graves of Brittany, on the other hand, are related in plan and ornament to those of southern Spain. One French form of gallery-grave, that with pairs of chambers facing each other like transepts across the gallery, was brought from the lower Loire basin by settlers who landed on the Severn estuary. The earliest form of passage-grave also has rectangular side chambers, but these open off the rounded central chamber into which the passage leads. One chamber faces the inner end of the passage and the two other side chambers face each other across the main chamber. The finest group of these cruciform passage-graves is in the Bend of the Boyne in Ireland, a site of great prehistoric sanctity which is notable for the New Grange and Knowth passage-graves and several henge monuments. New Grange (Fig. 13), is a superb example of this tomb form, but it is matched in Orkney by the cruciform passage-grave of Maes Howe, splendidly built of local flagstones. Both these tombs have corbelled roofs like Mediterranean tholoi and their

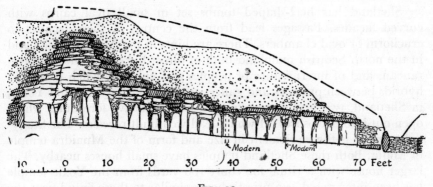

FIG. 13

Section through New Grange corbelled passage-grave and its cairn

consummate workmanship suggests that they are the tombs of revered leaders who may have pioneered migration over long distances. Maes Howe was pillaged by Viking raiders, later seafarers with long voyages to their credit who buried their leaders in great splendour.

Cruciform passage-graves are most numerous in Ireland, at the cemetery in the Bend of the Boyne, at Loughcrew west of it, and at Carrowmore and Carrowkeel in Co. Sligo (Fig. 11). Later small groups spread across the sea to Anglesey and built two passage-graves there. In Ireland they spread to the Wicklow Mountains, to the uplands of Northern Ireland and to hills in the north of Antrim which overlook the North Channel and the seaways along the west Scottish coast. From this coast passage-grave builders may have learnt that the Great Glen route would take them more safely north-eastwards than the seaway around Cape Wrath. They used it and settled and multiplied along the great valley. Passage-graves are relatively numerous at its northeast end. This Clava group has primary corbelled passage-graves in round cairns which recall Spanish passage-graves, though it also has locally developed variants including annular cairns which enclose a ceremonial area which may not have been roofed.

The passage-graves of Orkney and Cromarty are very varied. There are primary tombs like Maes Howe but, as at Clava, provincial styles of tomb developed under burial cairns which are either round or long. Some elongated mounds cover burial compartments in the form of stalls separated by large flagstones. The Camster cairn, which gives its name to a tomb group in Caithness, is a tholos with an antechamber which could have been built by settlers from Spain.

Shetland has heel-shaped tombs set in small oval cairns with curved façades. Passages lead from the centres of these façades to cruciform or oval chambers. There are hints in the Northern Isles and in the north Scottish mainland both of direct links with the Mediterranean, and of intermixture of peoples and cultures which produced hybrids between passage- and gallery-graves. At Stanydale and Yoxie, in Shetland, two heel-shaped temples have concave forecourts which open out into enclosures off which lead well-built recesses. The Stanydale temple is the equivalent in size and form of the Mnaidra temple in Malta. Both these Shetland temples have small houses nearby. The larger house with a ritual forecourt 100 yards from the Yoxie temple has been interpreted as a priest's house similar to those found near the Maltese temples like Mnaidra and Hal Tarxien; from the floor of a small Maltese temple comes material which by C 14 analysis is dated at 2,700 B.C.

The Northern Isles were obviously more attractive to megalith builders than the Western Isles of Scotland. On Skye and the Outer Hebrides, and in pockets of lowland on the western mainland, passage-graves were built with oval or polygonal chambers and several of them may be of late date. But a Neolithic settlement in Harris has produced an unusual C 14 date of 4,000 B.C. and hints at very early pioneering of a section of the Atlantic route which may not have been much used later.

Two main foci of gallery-grave builders are found along our western seaways. One imported the transeptal gallery-grave style of southern Brittany, while the other built the court cairns of the Clyde-Carlingford group and is found around landings of seafarers who were swept up the Irish coasts. Carlingford Lough was one of their entries. Both north-west and north-east Ireland have many court cairns and the coasts around the lower Clyde, those of south-west Scotland and the Isle of Man, intervisible in good weather, have smaller numbers of them. Court cairns (Fig. 14), in which the gallery leads into the long cairn from a crescent-shaped façade of tall stones, seem to have evolved in Northern Ireland. They are most numerous there and it has been suggested that they evolved around Carlingford Lough or in Mayo and Sligo. They then spread inland and are widely distributed in the northern half of Ireland. Related groups built similar cairns above landings in the east of the Isle of Man, in Galloway and in islands and peninsulas off the mouth of the Clyde.

These megalith builders were a restive and virile people. Dis-

satisfied with the limited patches
of good land which they found
around the Irish Sea, or perhaps, as the centuries went by,
driven from it by land hunger,
families with some of their
beasts took to the seas and rivers
and ventured coastwise and
inland. Their boats would provide quicker transport than
overland travel through the
forests. Such diffusion explains
a passage-grave at Calderstones
in Liverpool and the court
cairn called the Bridestones
on the western fringe of the
Peak District. This tomb may
be the burial place of families
which came up the Mersey and
its tributaries.

The builders of transeptal
gallery-graves settled around
the Bristol Channel, the Severn
Sea of older maps. Their landings were made in southern
Gower, along the Vale of Glamorgan coast and along the
east shores of the Severn
estuary below the steep scarp
of the Cotswolds. There, on
heights commanding the Severn Sea by which they had
come, they and their successors
built tombs like Hetty Pegler's
Tump. These large long bar-

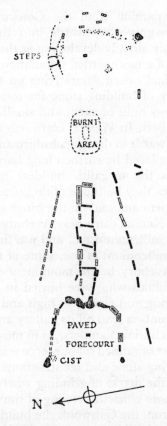

STEPS

BURNT AREA

PAVED

FORECOURT

CIST

N ←⊕

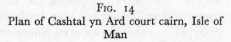

● Original stones unmoved
▦ New stones in identified holes
∴ White quartz pebbles

6 0   18   36 Feet

FIG. 14
Plan of Cashtal yn Ard court cairn, Isle of
Man

rows may contain as much as 5,000 tons of the local oolitic limestone. Both megaliths and small thin slabs of Cotswold stone were used
for the walling of façades, galleries and chambers. The skilled work of
Cotswold masons in this beautiful building stone has a very early
beginning.

Expansion from the Cotswolds took the builders of transeptal gallery-graves eastwards into the Marlborough Downs of Wessex, possibly already developing as the metropolis of prehistoric Britain, the land of a more settled population which had lost its urge for seafaring. Residual sarsen stones lying on the chalk surface provided a limited supply of building stone for tombs, and Wessex has about 160 long barrows built of earth and small stones. The majority have no burial chambers. In Wessex, eastwards along the chalk downs to Sussex and northwards to the Lincolnshire and Yorkshire Wolds, megalithic tombs are replaced by earthen long barrows.

As the megalith builders spread from the Cotswolds towards Wessex they built one of their transeptal gallery-graves at Lanhill near Chippenham, and on the fringe of the Marlborough Downs they built West Kennet cairn near Avebury. This was built in the first half of the third millennium B.C. and was finally blocked up in 1,600 B.C. During this millennium of use, some of the builders of the successive forms of the Avebury henge monument could have been among the forty-six individuals who were buried in it. The cairn at West Kennet is 350 feet long and eight feet high and it has a concave forecourt. Two pairs of chambers lead off its gallery and sarsen boulders were used in building its burial chambers. As in most sizeable gallery- and passage-graves a large organised labour force was needed for building the tomb and for carrying stone and constructional timber. Several West Kennet stones bear the marks of grinding where axes have been sharpened on them for more efficient dressing of timber.

From the Cotswolds the builders of transeptal gallery-graves spread across the Severn and up the Usk valley to the western slopes of the Black Mountains of Breconshire. Here, in forest clearings on patches of glacial gravel, which they could enlarge by slashing and burning, they settled and eventually built Cotswolds tombs. These people also spread to North Wales, possibly along river routes up the marches of Wales, and on the eastern slopes of the Conway valley a late version of a transeptal gallery-grave was built at Capel Garmon. Plate IV (see p. 61) shows that, in an area where rocks were much harder than those of the Cotswolds, they had not abandoned their traditions of using both upright stones and dry walling. It may have been the axe factory at Graig Lwyd which lured this group northwards.

In West Kennet and most of the early tombs of Neolithic settlers, round-based pots were placed with the dead for use after rebirth. These are pots of primary types, Windmill Hill near West Kennet providing a name for two of the main forms. The earlier Irish and Scottish passage-graves and gallery-graves have all produced round-based pottery. Some of it is ornamented, unlike the plain Windmill Hill ware. In the Alcala passage-graves of southern Spain and in early graves in Brittany, round-bottomed pots were buried with the dead. Leaf-shaped arrowheads were placed in the tombs, perhaps with men who had been good hunters. Axe-heads were sometimes placed with the dead, and at Cairn Holy in Kirkcudbright a jadeite axe from Brittany was included as an offering. Beads and pins adorned the corpses but metal is never found in primary deposits in passage-graves or gallery-graves in Britain. Nor is it found in Brittany, but copper occurs in Iberian passage-graves like those of the Los Millares group. It would seem either that some taboo had developed against this usage, or that copper, if the megalith builders had found it, had become something to be traded back along the Atlantic route rather than worked up in Britain.

Megaliths continued to be built throughout the third millennium in the British Isles and we have seen that, locally, distinctive forms developed from primary passage- and gallery-graves. Cruciform passage-graves lost their side chambers but the central round or oval chamber, off which they led, survived. This chamber is V-shaped in some Irish passage-graves and from it the so-called entrance-graves of Co. Waterford and the Scilly Islands may have developed. These are passage-graves in which the inner end of the passage forms a chamber only slightly wider than the passage. They lie under round cairns.

The latest forms of both passage- and gallery-graves are single chambers. They were still communal burial places, unlike later cists which covered burials of individuals. Great burial mounds and long galleries or passages ceased to be built and the curved façades of court cairns and transeptal gallery-graves were replaced by a pair of portal stones set across the entrance to a single chamber. Even these portals were discarded by some builders and late megaliths consist of a simple chamber under a massive capstone. The supports and capstone may be of considerable length and weight. These later megalith builders had not lost their skill in tomb-building and though the single chambers were usually covered by cairns, now that they are free-standing they are among the most impressive monuments of western headlands in Britain. Such are some of the Cornish and West Welsh single-chambered tombs and many Irish dolmens. Where the single chambers are polygonal in form, like that at Longhouse near the shores of north

Pembrokeshire, they are thought to be vestiges of passage-graves. Rectangular chambers, of which there are good examples on the Land's End peninsula, may have been built by the descendants of gallery-grave builders.

The last vestiges of megalith-building, the tombs of degenerate or poor groups, were the earthfast chambers in which an overhanging rock and one or two small uprights supported the capstone. The coasts of both North and South Wales provide examples of these makeshift megaliths. Both areas have fine tombs like the passage-graves of Anglesey, or Tinkinswood gallery-grave in Glamorgan, and also have many single chambers.

Tomb-building as practised by Neolithic peoples is reminiscent of the carving and erection of massive statues by another group of navigators, those of Easter Island. Thor Heyerdahl's experiments showed that considerable organisation was needed to erect one of the statues. Mrs. E. M. Clifford estimated that the transeptal gallery-grave at Rodmarton in Gloucestershire embodied 5,000 tons of stone which could have been provided in 250 days by 100 men. She calculated that the preparation of the site of the tomb and its erection would have occupied most of the following year. When prehistoric man transferred his loyalties from an earth goddess to a sun god and built the great henge monuments of the Bronze Age, we know that he brought similar skills and organisation to the building of his temples.

One may speculate on the forces which took megalith builders out of the Mediterranean and up the Atlantic route. They were not unique in this since Pacific and Viking peoples repeated their voyages and exploits. West European megaliths, set under great mounds, are very different from the early burial places of Mesopotamian and Egyptian peoples, but the impetus may have come from the Fertile Crescent. There, in the fifth and fourth millennia, great civilisations developed, elaborate tombs were built and burial rites centred on a belief in the afterlife. Good stone was not always available by the great rivers, and bricks were often used for tomb-building. Pottery, stone axes, copper daggers, figurines and beads were placed in tombs there and in Mediterranean islands like Crete. An ideology centred on committal to the earth and on rebirth may have spread westwards. Around the Ægean, settlement by builders of early tholoi and rectangular stone chambers may have been followed by expansion over the islands and coastlands. Tomb forms may have evolved there into more elaborate tholoi and rectilinear tombs. Far away in north-west Europe a different sequence developed from early tholos tombs but grave goods and forms of ornament such as spirals suggest that the builders of British passage-graves and the men who built the later tholoi of Greece had some beliefs in common.

Islands like Malta, at the crossways between the eastern and western basins of the Mediterranean, became centres of the megalithic religion. South Spain and south France were settled and, subsequently, the cult was carried across isthmuses and coastwise to the British Isles. Some have argued that priests like the later Celtic saints led these movements. There was an urge to voyage, settle and survive and a pre-occupation with elaborate burial rituals in graves built by and for the community which appears to have obviated warfare. Whether prospectors, pilgrims or priests, and perhaps all of these were found among them, they and the builders of the earthen barrows had peopled many British shores by 2,000 B.C., had settled a great deal of our downland and were spreading into such upland regions as could profitably be tilled by their primitive tools.

CHAPTER 4

CRAFTSMEN IN METAL

LATE IN THE Neolithic Period, about 2,000-1,800 B.C., considerable groups of pastoralists and prospectors began to immigrate into
southern Britain. They came from the Low Countries across the narrow
seas to the lands around the Thames and East Anglian estuaries. Soon
afterwards other waves of related immigrants came up the Atlantic
route to south-west England and South Wales. The distinguishing
feature of their equipment was the drinking vessel known as a beaker.
It was often of good red ware and more finely fashioned than earlier
Neolithic pottery. Bell-shaped beakers (Fig. 15) usually came in with
the early Beaker immigrants. Later waves of settlers brought in more
richly ornamented ones and over the next three hundred years beakers
spread throughout much of Britain. Some types of beaker, such as those
with a long neck, may have evolved here.

The Beaker people were distinct, both in physique and culture,
from the Neolithic peoples who were already living in Britain. They
were more robust and often taller than the slightly built megalith
builders and secondary Neolithic folk, and had more prominent facial
bones and broader skulls (Fig. 18). Intermingling with the native
peoples eventually produced a mixture of physical types and long
skulls are found in some Beaker burials. But the physical characters
of the Beaker people, and their capacity for leadership and organisation, have survived in the population of Britain. Plate IX (see p. 148)
shows the typical "Mediterranean" type, characteristic of western
Britain since the early Neolithic Period, and Plate X (see p. 149) a
Beaker type.

The Beaker people were pastoralists with considerable mobility.
Some of them were prospectors: they introduced copper metallurgy
into Britain and sought copper and gold. Recent finds of beakers in
Ireland lie near to copper deposits and many traces were left en route
to Ireland, notably on or near the south and north coasts of Wales.
The Beaker people hammered out copper daggers and flat axe blades,
but only one in twenty of the Beaker graves of Britain contains metal.

Much of their prospecting must have been unsuccessful and the scarce metal was replaced by more plentiful flint. Finely chipped and shaped copies in flint of copper daggers are found in some Beaker burials. Both metal and flint daggers would be useful tools for hunters.

Although the Beaker people still inhumed their dead, they were concerned neither with elaborate burial rituals nor with months and years of tomb-building as were the builders of passage- and gallery-graves. The Beaker dead were usually trussed into a foetal position and placed, singly, as "crouched burials" in cists, and relatively small round barrows were erected over these. Beaker burials were also inserted into many of the long barrows built by earlier Neolithic peoples.

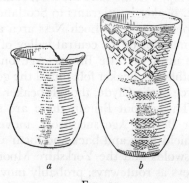

FIG. 15
a. Bell beaker. b. Long-necked beaker

The centuries from 3,000 to about 500 B.C., in the Sub-Boreal Period, were warm and became gradually drier. They were years when life on upland pastures was more agreeable than it now is. Trading and hunting by land and sea would also be affected by fewer storms. The Beaker and Bronze Age peoples were able to take their flocks and the limits of cultivation upslope into the high hills. Hunting with barbed and tanged arrowheads could be carried on extensively there. As the Bronze Age progressed, ridgeways were tramped out along the hill crests of both highland and lowland Britain and the round barrows of the Bronze Age, which often lay along them, stand out in silhouette to-day. The population steadily increased, trade routes ramified, and Wessex, at the junction of transpeninsular, riverine and, beyond them, sea routes, became in the Middle Bronze Age the magnificent centre of a flourishing culture dominated by aristocratic chiefs.

The Beaker people settled or wandered among the native peoples of Kent and Sussex, Wessex, East Anglia (especially the Breckland) and South and North Wales. Expansion and further waves of immigration from the Rhineland brought Beaker folk to the limestones of the Peak District, to the Yorkshire Wolds and Moors, and to the limestone fringes of the Eden valley east of the Lake District. The beakers of these later migrants were characteristically short-necked. Many areas along and behind the Northumbrian and east Scottish coasts were now settled and in western Scotland the new migrants frequented the coasts and islands around the mouth of the Clyde. Both ends of the Great Glen route have Beaker burials. In north Britain, long-necked beakers, developed locally, are the most common form and bell beakers are very rare. Beaker immigrants to Scotland may have sought, and found, the copper ores of the Loch Ness area and of the Ochils and Leadhills on the margins of the central valley of Scotland. Metal is, however, very rare until the late Bronze Age on Scottish sites. It is also doubtful whether the Beaker folk found the gold of the Lowther Hills around the source of the Clyde, though beaker finds occur in the area.

Throughout Britain there are signs that the Beaker people, like their Bronze Age successors, moved along ridge routes such as the Icknield Way and back and forth along the Jurassic Way between the Cotswolds and the Yorkshire Moors. They also used the larger river valleys as routeways, probably moving along the scrub-covered gravel terraces when the rivers ceased to be navigable. Several of these valleys contain their great ceremonial monuments.

In all these areas they sought pasture for flocks and land for tillage. We cannot say whether beakers were made to contain beer or milk. Barley was widely cultivated by the Beaker people; a beaker found in a round cairn on Moel Hebog in Caernarvonshire had been placed before firing on a hut floor where both barley and wheat grains were pressed into the wet clay. The huts of the Beaker people rarely survive, but those which do are round or oval; on Easton Down in Hampshire their huts were, at most, only ten feet across and were partly subterranean. Warmth, and freedom from constant rain, probably made permanent shelters less necessary for these pastoralists.

The majority of the tanged copper daggers found in Beaker graves occur in Wessex. Copies in flint are more common elsewhere. Wessex was already trading via the Avon valley through the Cotswolds and along the South Wales coast to Ireland. Copper, gold, and products made from both came from Ireland along this route. Ireland, with rich reserves of metal and a relatively dense population surviving from the Neolithic, exported to many British centres across the Irish Sea. Her exports of finished goods in the early Bronze Age included flat axes, often richly decorated, and the crescent-shaped gold collars, or *lunulae*, which were distributed in Britain and to the Bronze Age peoples of the European mainland.

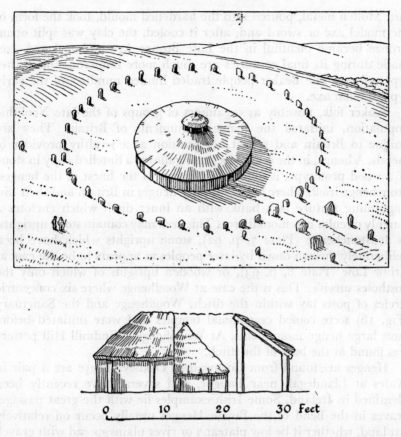

FIG. 16
The Sanctuary, Overton Hill, near Avebury, as reconstructed by Piggott

Fig. 19 shows four types of axe made in Britain during the fourteen centuries of the Early, Middle and Late Bronze Age. A similar sequence, from copper daggers through rapiers to long slashing swords, parallels this development of the less warlike axe. Whereas flat copper axes and primitive copper daggers could be hammered out, the later bronze implements demand, firstly, the correct proportions of ten per cent tin and ninety per cent copper, and then casting of the resulting bronze. The most common form of casting was *cire perdue* (wax lost) in which the bronze axe or sword was modelled in wax. Clay was then moulded around this model and as the clay was fired and hardened the wax ran out. Molten metal, poured into the hardened mould, took the form of the model axe or sword and, after it cooled, the clay was split open. Bronze became plentiful in the Late Bronze Age and socketed axes made during its final centuries are much more numerous than other types of axe. The Beaker people traded limited numbers of the early type, the flat axe.

Beaker folk, possibly as organisers of groups of the late Neolithic population, initiated the henge monuments of Britain. They are unique to Britain and reflect her position as a wealthy provider of metals. A henge, in the sense of a stone gallows, a lintelled copy in stone of a wood prototype, is found only at one of the finest of the henges, Stonehenge itself. There are about fifty henges in Britain and their distinguishing feature is a bank with an inner ditch which encloses a roughly circular ceremonial area. This area may contain stone uprights, as at Stonehenge (Plate 7, p. 92), stone uprights which have been deliberately thrown down by later peoples as appears to be the case at Arbor Low (Plate 8, p. 93), or wooden uprights of which only the postholes survive. This is the case at Woodhenge where six concentric circles of posts lay within the ditch. Woodhenge and the Sanctuary (Fig. 16) were roofed ceremonial temples and were initiated before most large henge monuments. At Woodhenge, Windmill Hill pottery was found at the base of the ditch.

Henges are found from Cornwall to Orkney. There are a pair in Wales at Llandegai, near Bangor, and several have recently been identified in Ireland. Some Irish examples lie with the great passage-graves in the Bend of the Boyne. Henges usually occur on relatively flat land, whether it be low plateaux or river plains spread with gravel. Their builders needed reasonably spacious sites, at nodal points of routeways, on land in which great ditches and banks could be readily dug by large labour forces. Henges are often close to streams to which avenues lead, suggesting that water may have played some part in the ceremonies carried out at them. Many have burial mounds around them; Stonehenge, for example, is surrounded by Bronze Age cemeteries. Other ceremonial monuments, sometimes associated with them, but earlier than the henges, are the *cursūs* monuments which take the form of long rectangles enclosed by parallel banks and ditches. They may have been processional ways and are sometimes aligned on long barrows. The banks and ditches of the Stonehenge cursūs are 400 yards apart; this cursūs starts half a mile north of Stonehenge and runs towards Woodhenge. Stukely, who discovered it in 1723, gave these

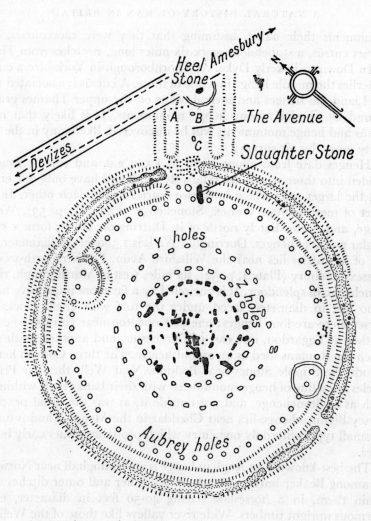

Heel Amesbury
Stone

The Avenue

Devizes

A · B

C

Slaughter Stone

Y holes

Z holes

Aubrey holes

0   50   100 Feet

FIG. 17

Plan of Stonehenge showing the circles of sarsens and bluestones and the
ditch. The latter lies outside the earth bank; in most henges it is
within it

monuments their name, assuming that they were racecourses. The Dorset cursūs, a stupendous work six miles long, stretches from Thickthorn Down to Bokerly Dyke. At Thornborough in Yorkshire a cursūs underlies the middle henge in a line of three. A cursūs is associated with the Llandegai henges and several occur on the upper Thames gravels around Dorchester among henge monuments. It is likely that more cursūs and henge monuments will be discovered, like many in the past thirty years, by air survey.

Henges date from about 1,900 to 1,500 B.C. and can be roughly divided into those which are relatively small and have only one entry, and the larger ones which have two entries facing each other. In the heart of metropolitan Wessex, Stonehenge (Plate II, p. 53), Woodhenge, and, immediately north of it, Durrington Walls, form a spectacular group of henges. Durrington Walls is 1,500 feet in diameter and one of its entries lies near the Wiltshire Avon. Farther north-west in Wessex, Avebury (Plate I, p. 52), six miles west of Marlborough, rivals Stonehenge in splendour. It is encircled by a far more impressive bank, 1,400 feet in diameter, faced under the turf with chalk blocks. In Dorset there are four henges: one at Knowlton near Cranbourne and another at Eggardon, one east of Dorchester, and another south of it which the Romans used as an amphitheatre. The three Cornish henges include the Stipple Stones near Bodmin. Near Wells the four Priddy Circles are a line of henge monuments with their banks built within the ditch as at Stonehenge, and not outside it, as was the usual practice. Gorsey Bigbury henge lies near Cheddar in the Mendips and is one of the small types with only one entry which probably comes early in the series.

The best-known East Anglian henge is at Arminghall near Norwich. Set among Beaker burial mounds, it had inner and outer ditches and, within them, in a horseshoe setting 40-50 feet in diameter, eight enormous upright timbers. Wide river valleys like those of the Welland and Trent have several henges and some Yorkshire valleys also have these ceremonial centres. Near Ripon there are three at Thornborough whose banks are coated with gypsum, possibly to imitate chalk. Two more Yorkshire henges lie on Hutton Moor, and in the Peak District are Arbor Low and the Bull Ring. From Ripon, valleyways lead through the limestones of Wensleydale past Castle Dykes henge near Aysgarth, or through Swaledale past Maiden Castle henge, into the Eden valley. Near the lowlying confluence of the Eden and Eamont lies the small henge known as the Round Table and the larger May-

PLATE 5 *a*. UNRECLAIMED FEN near Wicken, Cambridgeshire.
b. RECLAIMED MARSH near Terrington St. Clement, Norfolk.

The low-lying land, south of the Wash, includes undrained freshwater
fen and, near the sea-wall, drained salt-marsh.

PLATE 6 CAVE SHELTER, Oldbury, Kent, in which implements ascribed to the latter part of the Palaeolithic Age have been found.

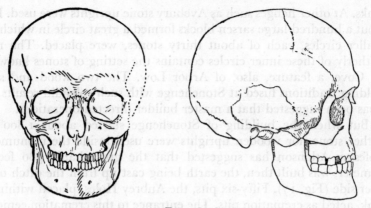

FIG. 18
Skull of Beaker man: front and side views

burgh one where, formerly, a rectangle of large stones lay within the
surviving high bank of gravel boulders.

Northumberland has two henges and in Scotland there are about a
dozen. Three of these are simple and small with only one entry, ard
lie in Dumfries, Berwickshire and Fife. The larger Scottish henges are
scattered between Dumfries (Broadlee), Lanarkshire, West Lothian,
Argyll, Aberdeenshire, Ross and Cromarty and Orkney. Among the
best-known sites is Cairnpapple Hill in West Lothian where three
huge boulders set in a circle of upright stones were replaced by a henge
containing an oval setting of stones which marked Beaker burials. The
site shows continuity of sanctity accompanied by changes in beliefs, for
the henge was replaced by a cist burial surmounted by a kerbed cairn
which was subsequently enlarged for the insertion of later Bronze Age
and Iron Age burials. Orkney retains, in the neighbourhood of the great
Maes Howe passage-graves, near Stromness, the impressive henge
known as the Ring of Brodgar where twenty-seven tall uprights survive
out of the original sixty. It lies on a low isthmus between two lochs.
Of the Stones of Stenness, not far away, only four stones remain within
the henge. The Ring of Bookan, the third in this group, lacks an outer
bank but has central stones which may be the ruins of a burial chamber
or of a cove, such as that at Avebury.

Several henge monuments embody traditions of building in great
stones; circles of standing stones were built near some of them. The
large circle known as Long Meg and her Daughters lies near May-
burgh. At henges like Arminghall huge upright timbers stood within the

banks. At other henges such as Avebury stone uprights were used. Here about a hundred large sarsen blocks formed a great circle in which two smaller circles, each of about thirty stones, were placed. The more southerly of these inner circles contains the setting of stones known as the Cove, a feature, also, of Arbor Low. The two wood and stone building traditions fused at Stonehenge with such splendid results that it has been suggested that a master builder directed operations.

But when the building of Stonehenge started about 1,800 B.C. neither stone nor wooden uprights were used inside the monuments. Professor Atkinson has suggested that the great bank, 380 feet in diameter, was built then, the earth being cast up from the ditch on its outer side (Fig. 17). Fifty-six pits, the Aubrey Holes, placed within the bank, acted as cremation pits. The entrance to this cremation cemetery led to the Heel Stone, a rough sarsen boulder. Sarsen stones used later at Stonehenge were dressed by battering them with stone hammers.

The Beaker folk, in their journeys through South Wales, may have used the ridgeway along the crest of the Presely Mountains which commands wide views over the Irish Sea, over Milford Haven and over the ridges which lead down to it. The crest of Presely culminates in natural cairns of igneous rock which weathers into columns. Columnar surface boulders are liberally scattered around. The Beaker people hauled about sixty of them down to the upper reaches of Milford Haven and rafted them coastwise up the Severn Sea, and, probably, up the Bristol Avon. Their route to Stonehenge could thence have been up the Frome River, overland to near Warminster, on the Wylye River, and down it to its confluence with the Wiltshire Avon. The bluestones could have been rafted up this river to the end of the Stonehenge Avenue near Amesbury and then hauled up the Avenue. Between 1,650 and 1,500 B.C. a double circle of bluestones was erected in the centre of the sacred area at Stonehenge and then, possibly when new leaders took over, it was dismantled.

By 1,500 B.C. the warrior chiefs of Wessex, probably descended from Beaker leaders, were wealthy traders with contacts not merely with Ireland but, over a complex network of trade routes, with the Ægean area and Egypt. These aristocrats, and perhaps their master builder who may have come from Mycenae or Minoan Crete, planned the magnificent monument whose remnants stand at Stonehenge to-day. Eighty sarsen blocks, many weighing 20-30 tons, were man-hauled by organised gangs from the gentle slopes of the Marlborough Downs, and the sarsen stones were then set up in an outer circle of

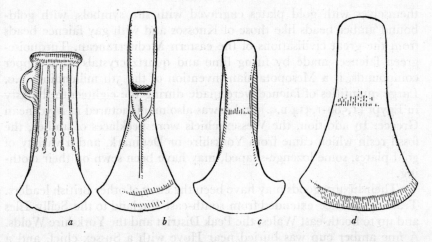

FIG. 19

Stages in the evolution of Bronze Age axes: *a*. Flat axe. *b*. Flanged axe. *c*. Palstave: the stop-ridges on each face prevent splitting of the wooden haft. *d*. Socketed axe ($\times$ 1/3)

paired uprights topped by a continuous ring of lintels. Five pairs of lintelled uprights were set in a horseshoe within the circle. The tenon and mortice technique, the shaping of the uprights and the curving and tapering of the lintels are all illustrated on Plate 7 (see p. 92). The Mycenean dagger on one of the sarsens may be the mark of the master builder. Subsequently, over twenty of the bluestones were dressed, grooved and lintelled and set up within the sarsen horseshoe. These bluestone trilithons were later converted into a horseshoe of upright pillars. Changes in ideas, and perhaps loss of wise guidance, became increasingly apparent; an intention to erect bluestones in the Z and Y holes was partly implemented and then abandoned. They were finally set up in a circle inside the sarsen circle. A great sandstone pillar was erected in front of the central sarsen trilithon. This stone, now fallen and called the Altar Stone, came from Cosheston where, near Pembroke, Milford Haven changes to an east-west course.

Much astronomical argument has raged around Stonehenge. From 1,500 B.C. the axis of the monument was aligned on the point where the sun rose on Midsummer Day, and there are other indications in their grave goods that the Wessex aristocracy were sun worshippers. Powerful leaders of the trading and religious centre of Britain, they adorned themselves with gold plates engraved with sun symbols, with gold-bound amber beads like those of Knossos and with gay faience beads from the great civilisations of the eastern Mediterranean. Turquoise-green faience, made by firing lime and quartz crystals with copper compounds, is a Mesopotamian invention of the 5th millennium B.C. Large quantities of faience were made during the eighteenth dynasty in Egypt (1,580-1,314 B.C.) and it was also manufactured in Mycenean Greece. In addition, the Wessex chiefs wore necklaces of amber, the fossil resin which came from Yorkshire or Denmark, and a variety of gold plates, some lozenge-shaped, may have been sewn on their clothing.

Their luxury goods may have been the envy of other British leaders. Trade in faience extended from south-east England to the Scilly Isles and up to north-east Wales, the Peak District and the Yorkshire Wolds. A fine amber cup was buried near Hove with a Sussex chief, and a beaker of corrugated sheet gold comparable to the gold cups of Mycenae was found in a barrow adjoining the Hurlers stone circle near Liskeard. This Cornish leader was buried with his dagger as was a Norfolk chief at Little Cressingham whose gold and amber ornaments were as rich as those of most Wessex chiefs.

After about 1,300 B.C., Wessex, like Mycenae, declined. The vigorous trade along the Atlantic and Mediterranean routes in metals and ornaments decreased as the copper lodes of Central Europe contributed increasingly to European metallurgy. But before Wessex lost its supremacy its influence was felt by Middle Bronze Age communities who lived by the upper Thames, in East Anglia and in well-drained uplands in western and northern Britain. In northern areas circles of standing stones, or isolated pillar stones, or rock surfaces ornamented with spirals or cup and ring markings are found. Ilkley Moor and the fringes of the Lake District have such ritual stones where sun worship may have been practised. On the Atlantic coast of Scotland, Galloway and Kintyre also have ornamented ritual monuments set among burial mounds.

Bronze Age round barrows in highland Britain cover a variety of grave goods. In northern Britain the native peoples placed food vessels, probably their best household pots, with the dead during the first half of the Bronze Age. The influence of Secondary Neolithic traditions, such as those of the makers of Peterborough pottery, is apparent in these heavily ornamented pots. Around the Irish Sea, Galloway, Cumberland, the Isle of Man, West Wales and eastern Ireland have a distinctive type of food vessel, while in Yorkshire and eastern Scotland these have larger rims. Necklaces of jet beads accompany the burials in east Yorkshire where jet is found and in North Wales to which it was traded.

By 1,500 B.C. cremation was the most usual funerary rite among a population which was increasing and spreading throughout Britain. Settled conditions and active trade spread the fashion of placing the ashes in an urn almost uniformly throughout Britain. Hills in central Wales, northern England and eastern Scotland were probably first peopled in these Middle Bronze Age centuries. In the fourteenth century B.C., pygmy cups, perhaps for incense, were placed in graves. Travelling tinkers and smiths circulated larger numbers of bronze axes among the farming population. The native Neolithic, Beaker and Food Vessel peoples, now welded together in the settled centuries of the Middle Bronze Age, were increasingly tied to the land which they cultivated.

Permanently occupied farmsteads can be recognised in many areas of lowland and highland Britain from about 1,000 B.C. They are found in areas where cultivation continued into the Iron Age. Small fields surrounded farmsteads, and collectively they denote extensive forest clearance by a relatively large population well equipped with metal axes. Species of snails from Neolithic sites belonged to woodland habitats, while those from Iron Age sites are snails of open grasslands.

From the twelfth century B.C. folk movements resulting from unrest in Central Europe spread outwards. Within two centuries displacement of peoples through the Rhineland and northern France pushed bands of migrant farmers into south-east England. These were people whose name comes from the Deverel and Rimbury barrows in Dorset. In their cemeteries they buried characteristic globular and barrel-shaped urns. The Deverel-Rimbury people spread throughout south-east England, avoiding clay-capped downland in Sussex and the Chilterns, and also westwards into Cornwall. In highland Britain the native urn folk continued to farm. Though their farming system is not always so clearly imprinted on the landscape as that of the Deverel-Rimbury people, they practised some arable farming and offerings of corn sheaves were sometimes placed in their graves.

In southern England square or rectangular fields, like those on the upper photograph on Plate VI (see p. 133), were laid out in these and subsequent centuries. These fields often did not exceed half an acre and were scratched out with a light plough or ard drawn by teams of two to six oxen. The plough probably lacked a coulter to cut the turf in front of the share, and turned only a shallow furrow, so that the fields often had to be cross-ploughed. Trackways link these fields to farmsteads, springs and streams. Flocks were important in the farming economy and enriched the fields with their dung. On the chalklands of Wessex, deep V-shaped ditches were dug to demarcate tribal grazing grounds or big ranch-like farms. Cattle movements could be controlled along them, and long ditches like that north of, and parallel to, the Berkshire Ridgeway may have been used for droving over longer distances. Farmhouses were both isolated and nucleated. A Bronze Age hamlet of *c.* 800 B.C. on Itford Hill, in Sussex, consisted of thirteen round huts of which four were dwellings and nine storehouses or workshops. The women dried barley and ground it in saddle querns, and wove cloth on upright looms; their loom weights and bone weaving combs have been found. There is evidence that the people lived mainly on beef and mutton, on wheat and barley bread, and on porridge, that they collected wild fruit, nuts and shellfish and hunted with slingstones. At Brentford on the Thames, however, and on the rivers of Essex, waterside villagers may have been more interested in fishing.

The hillsides of Atlantic Britain, lovely under high cloud at midsummer, must have enjoyed many more such days in the Bronze Age than they now do. By the Iron Age, days of mist and low cloud would have been common. But in the late Bronze Age, before the climate deteriorated, pastoralists set up many villages there, notably on Dartmoor and Bodmin Moor. Pastoral peoples, far more numerous than the present permanent population of upland Dartmoor, left on the landscape many ceremonial circles and avenues of standing stones and lived in stone huts which were sometimes surrounded by large cattle-pounds. Some of the huts have separate living and work rooms, and sleeping-quarters with box-beds. The fields around the settlements may cover many acres. Near Widecombe, Foales Arishes had twenty-five acres of fields which expanded and gradually coalesced in the Iron Age with those of neighbouring villages. This conversion of large areas of pasture into arable between *c.* 1,200 and *c.* 450 B.C. involved much toil with primitive ploughs and spades. The ploughs are thought to have been crook ards, similar to those of contemporary Denmark, in which a bent bough had its tip hardened by fire before being equipped with a plough-share. The farmsteads lay on the edges of the fields, and cattle from them used trackways which led up to the open moor. Villages of nearly a hundred huts had developed in Dartmoor by the Iron Age. The villagers were peaceful farmers. One or two smiths provided metal goods for farm work and some tools, such as socketed axes ornamented with rib markings, were acquired from Glamorgan.

On hillsides in northern England and southern Scotland similar villages, based on mixed farming, were built in the Late Bronze Age and in the Iron Age. Hillsides in the North Pennines, underlain by limestone, have many of them. On hillsides above the Eden valley in Westmorland there are half a dozen villages with clearly marked field systems and trackways. The fields and folds of three villages around Crosby Garrett cover 160 acres, while Cumberland and Northumberland had similar settlements. In the Southern Uplands of Scotland stock-farmers built settlements which were numbered in hundreds by the time the Romans arrived there. As in northern England, small rectangular fields were associated with them especially in Roxburgh and Peeblesshire. The farmsteads were often built on platforms cut into the hillsides and sometimes had a timber framework covered with wattle screens. Groupings of up to four round houses, built, perhaps, by a kinship group, are found within a palisade. In the Iron Age, ditches were dug round the huts for drainage. In Perthshire and elsewhere groups of round stone huts probably date from the early Iron Age. As in southern Britain, repeated ploughing of hillsides began to carry the soil downslope and lynchetted fields were formed. Thus began in Scotland the development of self-sufficient villages, set among small fields dotted with storehouses and folds, which are exemplified in St. Kilda (Plate 12, p. 113).

Iron ore, more widely distributed than tin and copper ores, was used sporadically in Mesopotamia and Egypt between 3,000 and 2,500 B.C., but the Hittites of central Turkey were the first people to work it commercially. This they did around 1,500 B.C. By 1,000 B.C. iron was in use in Greece and two hundred years later was being worked in Central Europe. By 700 B.C. iron-using Hallstatt peoples there disturbed, as did the gradually rising waters, the peaceful lake-side farmers of the Alpine valleys. They set in motion waves of migration, accompanied by warfare, which reverberated in Britain; Hallstatt invaders, equipped mainly with bronze swords, reached south-east England about 500 B.C. when the cool wet Sub-Atlantic Period was beginning. They brought with them the Iron A culture which was succeeded, in centuries of deteriorating climate which caused migration to lower and better lands, by Iron B and, shortly before the Roman Conquest, by Iron C peoples. Later Iron A immigrants came in smaller numbers up the Atlantic route, Iron B (La Tène) immigrants came from both north-east France and Brittany, while the Belgae of Iron C came mainly from north-east France to lowland Britain.

Iron is more malleable than bronze and does not require casting. It can be reheated after smelting and, while red hot, hammered into shape on an anvil. It can be repaired more readily in the forge than bronze. Furnaces, forging pits and quenching pits for purifying iron, and anvils, have been found in Iron Age smithies in southern England. Much heavier tools could be made, including coulters and ploughshares, and heavier land could be cleared and cultivated. Earlier Iron Age ploughs are shown on Figs. 20 and 30, A and B. They were probably

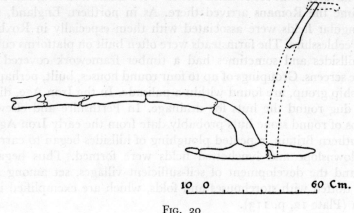

10 0   60 Cm.

FIG. 20
Remains of Iron Age plough

drawn by pairs of oxen, four being sometimes yoked abreast. The equipment brought to Britain by successive Iron Age immigrants made possible advances in the standard of living, and, because of the greater variety and efficiency of iron weapons, particularly swords wielded by horsemen, it also increased the mortality rate.

Iron A settlers of the fifth and fourth centuries B.C. were, however, more interested in tillage than warfare. They intermarried with the Bronze Age farming families and added field to field. Many of their farmsteads were bigger than the Bronze Age huts but, like them, they were round, timber-framed on stone footings and had wattle-and-daub walls and thatched roofs. Little Woodbury near Salisbury is typical of isolated farmsteads. All Cannings Cross and Boscombe Down settlements typify the Iron Age villages of the chalklands. With more rain

PLATE 7   STONEHENGE, Wiltshire. Note the tenon on the vertical stone in the foreground.

PLATE 8 ARBOR LOW, Derbyshire. A henge monument with stones thrown down.

falling on its arable and pastures, a chalkland settlement like Boscombe Down could expand to cover seventy-six acres in the eight centuries between Iron A and the end of the Roman Period. The dampness of the Sub-Atlantic Period so favoured cereal cultivation in the chalklands that the Romans were able to take them over as a productive granary with an exportable surplus, and they carved out large estates there.

Wheats (emmer and spelt) were grown and sheaves of both were hung on corn-drying racks. Spelt grains are so tight in the husk that they can be satisfactorily threshed only after the grain is loosened by baking. Grains of wheat and six-rowed barley were baked in clay ovens and were either then ground in saddle querns or stored in clay-lined pits, but when these became too damp they were used as rubbish pits. There were about three hundred and sixty of them at Little Woodbury. Herding and hunting were carried out with horses and dogs, and slings and iron spears were used in the chase.

In Atlantic Britain, Bronze Age villagers continued to farm from their round stone huts with little disturbance, but a few Iron A migrants came up the Irish Sea and settled the more fertile coastlands. Here, for example in the Vale of Glamorgan, they built stockaded farms and tended cows and sheep. Huts were clustered inside low banks on the hills of North Wales and there are similar settlements in Cornwall. These are not the heavily fortified camps of Iron B but, rather, cattle corrals. In northern England existing villages and fields expanded on the limestone hillsides, notably those of the Yorkshire Dales, such as Wharfedale, near Grassington.

During the third century B.C., continental disturbances pushed Iron B intruders into Britain. These were Celtic tribesmen and when their chiefs were not leading them into tribal skirmishes, they tended their flocks and fostered craftsmanship in metal. Their culture originated in the Alpine heart of Europe and one of their tribal centres was La Tène, between Lake Bienne and Lake Neuchâtel in Switzerland. The warrior groups which came to south-east Britain were from the Marne basin of France. These Marnians sought similar country here and, taking native women as wives, they became dominant in East Sussex, Surrey, Kent and Essex; by 150 B.C. they were working the ores of the Weald. They also settled the Yorkshire Wolds where they founded the Parisi tribe, and on dying, were buried with the two-horse chariots which they had brought to Britain. In western Britain, west of the Isle of Wight, La Tène invaders who had been in contact with the Marnians in France came in along the Atlantic route. This seaway was well-known in the classical world, and Mediterranean merchants like Pytheas, who came up it to Britain about 330-325 B.C., brought wine northwards and took back tin ingots from Cornwall. The Veneti of Brittany were among the mariners who used the route and their trade links embraced Britain and Iberia. Trade and invasion brought in fine metalwork, debased classical motifs on pottery, and new forms of fortification.

The distinctive western pots of Iron B have a mainly coastal distribution in Devon and Cornwall, and are found on and behind both shores of the Severn Sea. A few finds have been made along the shores of Cardigan Bay, and Forde's excavation of the great fort on Pen Dinas, which towers over Aberystwyth, produced some sherds. These pots are also found in the *castros* of north-west Spain and Portugal where a stylised duck ornaments them. In British pottery this duck, as imitated by native women, has been reduced to an S-shaped scrawl. Mediterranean coinage, too, suffered the same fate as classical bird ornament and coins founded on those of Philip II of Macedon (Fig.22) show a similar decline in skill when Iron B peoples attempted to imitate them in their mints.

These were household goods, or coins, which perhaps had to be reproduced quickly and in quantity. La Tène objects which were designed for the adornment of warrior leaders and of their horses and chariots show much more skill and beauty. They were often in bronze and included elaborate pins to fasten clothing, shields with brilliant enamel inlay, of which Fig. 21 is a late example, bronze bridle and harness pieces, horse armour like the pony's cap from Torrs, in Kirkcudbright, and Bronze furnishings for two-wheeled chariots. By the time the Romans invaded, such objects were circulating throughout lowland and highland Britain. Groups who were either fleeing from the Romans, or making votive offerings to Celtic gods, cast La Tène metalwork, their most precious possessions, into lakes. The Torrs pony cap was such an offering, and the rich hoard from Llyn Cerrig Bach, in Anglesey, was another. La Tène metalwork has been found along several North Wales routeways. It includes the Cerrig y Drudion bowl and the Capel Garmon firedog, from the Dee-Conway route. Oxheads on this firedog remind us of the basically pastoral economy of the La Tène peoples. The Clwyd valley and its hills have also produced a few of their fine pieces. For seasonal feasts, held perhaps after autumn cattle killings, they made sheet-bronze cauldrons and tankards. The

FIG. 21

Bronze shield found in the Thames at Battersea. Its ornament is in La Tène style

tankard from Trawsfynydd in Merioneth has their characteristic curvilinear ornament. The remains of a later shield, from Cader Idris in the same county, may have been hidden under a rock by a smith who meant to melt it down. North-west Wales had obtained gold torcs from Ireland for adornment in the Late Bronze Age and some of the La Tène goods also came from across the Irish Sea. Several of the Welsh finds may have been lost by itinerant craftsmen from lowland Britain, the area in which their beautiful products are most num-

FIG. 22

Macedonian coins which were feebly imitated by British Iron B peoples

erous. But it was western Britain which supplied the copper and tin for the craftsmen, and some of the iron for objects like the Capel Garmon firedog.

Iron B peoples left stronger imprints on the British landscape than any other prehistoric people, in the form of great hill-forts, often still marked by a series of grass-grown or dry-stone ramparts. Originally stockaded, much higher, and flanked by deeper ditches, they are still impressive features of the hilltops, hill-brows and promontories of Britain. Some of the smaller forts with weak ramparts may have been built by Iron A people for defence against the Iron B invaders. But the largest hill-forts are the tribal capitals of the Marnians, Veneti and the British peoples with whom they intermarried. Some, like the Llanbedr-y-cennin fort above the Conway valley, or Craig Gwrtheyrn above the Teifi, near Llandysul, are surrounded by a *chevaux de frise*, a fringe of protruding sharp stones to halt attackers outside the ramparts. This is a feature of Iberian *castros*, or fortified camps, and of forts built by the slingsmen of Brittany. It antedates by two thousand years the iron "horses," spikes which were set similarly by Frisian infantry to deter cavalrymen. Heaps of waterworn pebbles, placed ready for slingsmen, are often found behind the ramparts of hill-forts. Over twenty thousand were found at Maiden Castle in Dorset (Plate V, p. 132).

Early Iron B invaders probably threw up single defensive ramparts to make small camps when they arrived in Britain. They and succeeding settlers multiplied the banks of later forts. Both types are scattered throughout English uplands south of the Pennines. Iron B peoples built relatively few forts in northern England, though there are some large tribal fortresses there, like Stanwick in Yorkshire and Yeavering Bell in Northumberland. The largest forts, with close-set multiple ram-

PLATE 9 TRE'R CEIRI. Iron Age B fortress, probably of Roman times, on the lesser of the two summits of Yr Eifl, West Caernarvonshire. A rough stone rampart skirts the hill brow, steep steps lead up to the entry.

PLATE 10 HIGHLANDER teaching boy to play the pipes; Aviemore.

parts, like Maiden Castle in Dorset, Hembury in Devon, Carn Brea in Cornwall, Bagendon in Gloucestershire or Tre'r Ceiri in Caernarvonshire (Plate 9, p. 96), became the *oppida* (tribal capitals) which imitated the defended towns of Celtic Central Europe. They expanded until the Romans invaded Britain and were often centres of resistance. To-day their ramparts survive in areas which the Romans were sometimes forced to hold only lightly.

Other types of enclosure in southern and western Britain are set on hill-slopes and have widely spaced ramparts. Commanded from the hillsides above them, they have little defensive value, but they could have been built by villagers who rounded up their cattle there and kept them temporarily between the ramparts. Iron B peoples also sought steepsided spurs or coastal promontories which could be defended with the minimum of fortification. These promontory forts are common, for example, on the South Wales coast, and were defended by isthmian lines of banks and ditches. The fortified entrances of promontory forts, and those which are encircled by multiple ramparts, often have elaborate outworks and are incurved to form a tunnel, while within them are the foundations of the villagers' huts. Here they lived, either permanently or in times of war. Huts are also found outside the ramparts.

The settlement pattern represented by Iron B forts suggests occupation of coastlands by people who kept their links with the seaways, and were reinforced by immigration along them. Expansion up major valleys followed in the west. It may have been in full swing about 100 B.C. Hill-brows above the Severn, Usk and Wye valleys, for instance, then provided sites for many large and heavily defended forts. East of the lower Wye the iron of the Forest of Dean was made into currency bars, trade goods from which a sword could be made. Several have been found in the hill-forts of the Cotswolds and were traded southwards from them. There are about a thousand hill-forts in western Britain. Their distribution suggests that the stormier climate had forced people and flocks to desert the high hills, occupied in the Bronze Age, for hillbrows at medium heights. Their pastures may have been upslope of the forts but their arable fields were probably downslope nearer the valley bottoms. Lowlands and cliff-tops were also occupied where sites could be readily defended.

Not all Iron B peoples lived in hill-forts. There must have been many isolated undefended farmsteads, as in Iron A, and there were also groups which relied on water defences. Because of the preservative properties of peat, we get the best impression of an Iron B culture from the lake villages of Somerset. The Meare and Glastonbury villages were crannogs built on timber platforms linked with dry land by log causeways, and were communities of prosperous traders and craftsmen, dating from about 150 B.C. into the first century A.D. At Meare there were sixty huts and workshops on each of the two crannogs. At Glastonbury there were eighty-nine on a two-acre site. Their La Tène metalwork, glass, shale and jet ornaments, bone combs, wooden containers, and their textiles, have all been preserved. The lakes provided them with fish and fowl and nearby hillsides with land for their animals and for tillage.

The last of the stormy Iron Age centuries brought Belgic invaders into southern Britain to settle, for the most part, in lowland Britain. The Celtic-Germanic confederacy of the Belgae had resisted the romanisation of Gaul. Thrusting and resentful, they came as large bands of refugee families from north France to Kent and east Essex in 75 B.C. Here they built an oppidum at Colchester. Some of them rapidly spread to Hertfordshire where they began to build Wheathampstead town about 70 B.C. They fortified their towns with great banks and V-shaped ditches. Expansion towards Welwyn and Baldock extended their territory into the scarplands, and into the riverine sites which they preferred. The Veneti of Brittany were defeated by the Romans in 56 B.C. Soon afterwards refugee Veneti families came to West Sussex, Wessex and the south-west peninsula. In these areas, forts like Maiden Castle and Hembury were more heavily fortified. The Iron C incomers set themselves up as powerful leaders of large tribal groups. Maiden Castle became the capital of the Durotriges, Colchester (Camulodunum) of the Trinovantes, Wheathampstead (and, later, Verulamium) of the Catuvellauni, and Bagendon of the Dobunni (Fig. 24).

In the century between the romanisation of Gaul and the Claudian invasion of Britain in A.D. 43, rural life in Britain improved under the leadership of the Iron A Celts. They dominated Lowland England east of the Jurassic scarp between Lincolnshire and the Severn estuary. Belgic equipment included not only chariots but wheeled carts for trade and farming. Their ploughs had efficient coulters (Fig. 31) which cut the turf before it was turned by broad-bladed ploughshares (Fig. 30 C and D), and their ox teams were guided by iron-tipped goads. They used the potter's wheel so that potting could gradually become an industry and ceased to be entirely a household craft. Women could grind finer flour by turning the handle of a rotary quern, in which one stone pivoted on another. Excavation of their towns has produced much of this equipment. At Bagendon, two and a half miles north of Cirencester, were also found the women's spindle whorls and loom weights, their bronze brooches, bracelets and mirrors, and the nails of the men's saddles and some of their fishing tackle. These, and imported pots from Italy, were usually found in the half-timbered houses which partly occupied the 200 acres within the defences. The Bagendon mint produced coins showing a triple-tailed horse. It is usually less recognisable as a horse than the splendid galloping animal which crowns the Berkshire Downs at Uffington (Plate V, B, p. 132). This, the oldest of our white horses, also dates from the later centuries of the Iron Age.

Perhaps some of the Dobunnic coins were included in the tribute exacted by Caesar after he tested the strength of the Belgae in 55 and 54 B.C. This tribute lapsed on his death, but it must have been obvious to the Belgae that the peace which was broken by the Claudian invasion was a very uneasy one. But Belgic kings increased their splendour, and, both in life and death, were equipped with costly goods. Many burials were in elegant pedestal urns. Cunobelin, or Cymbeline, of Colchester, king of the Catuvellauni, died about A.D. 40, and the mound at Lexden may be his tomb. It was Cymbeline's heirs who, by their aggressiveness towards the Atrebates of Hampshire, precipitated the Roman Conquest.

In south-west England the Iron B tribes grouped themselves as the Dumnonii. The South Welsh were collectively known as the Silures and were led from forts such as Llanmelin in south Monmouthshire. The Demetae occupied south-west Wales, to which they gave the name of Dyfed, while the Ordovices of north-west Wales had their refuge in Gwynedd (Snowdonia), and the Deceangli were centred on north-east Wales. The Pennines and the tributary valleys of the Ouse supported the Brigantes, a warlike tribe who stemmed more from native pastoral peoples than from the displaced continental Celts who had found refuge in southern Britain. Early in the first century A.D., the Brigantes started to build their tribal capital at Stanwick, six miles south-west of Darlington. Its defences enclose 850 acres and could also have sheltered some of their numerous herds. Bones of cattle, sheep, goats, pigs, horses and dogs, and of the deer and hare which they hunted, far outnumber signs of arable farming. Only one fragment of a quernstone was found at Stanwick and querns are generally rare in Iron Age settlements in northern England.

These were pastoralists with the independence born of mobility and of a hard life in hill country. Like other non-Belgic tribes they hated the

Belgae. They also feared other non-Belgic Celtic tribes. Tacitus commented on Celtic disunity: "Seldom is it that two or three states meet together to ward off a common danger. Thus while they fight singly all are conquered." Some tribes defied the Romans with great bravery. Some made alliances with them, though they may later have revolted. In Wales the Demetae and Deceangli submitted readily to Roman control, while the Silures and Ordovices separately resisted fiercely. South and North Wales have often dealt differently with intrusive cultures.

Scotland, where the good lands are also separated from each other by mountain masses, was also occupied by diverse peoples. The peoples of the Southern Uplands shared the pastoral economy of northern England and lived in similar villages of round huts. Beyond the Forth-Clyde isthmus were the groups of tribes who became the Picts. Hill-forts had been built in Scotland since the third century B.C. They show the same range of size as those of England and Wales, and were also built on hilltops, hill-brows and promontories. But they were often timber-laced, a special feature found only occasionally outside Scotland. The timber-laced walls of Scottish hill-forts are from ten to forty feet thick and would have meant considerable forest clearance in their localities. When their timber gate-towers and lean-to houses caught fire they must have burned fiercely on the windy hilltops or coasts. Firing of the interlacing timbers produced great heat, and vitrification of the stone in the ramparts. The vitrified forts of Scotland occupy the south-west coastlands and the islands and peninsulas off the mouth of the Clyde and are found near the south-west end of the Great Glen, though they are more numerous at its north-east end. There are other groupings of vitrified forts round the Tay and Forth estuaries. These are all lands which had been singled out by Bronze Age farmers. On Traprain Law and Eildon Hill North are large forts comparable to the oppida of southern England. Traprain Law lies two miles south-east of East Linton, in East Lothian, and was the capital of the Votadini (Fig. 24). Eildon Hill North, the oppidum of the Selgovae, is situated a mile south-east of Melrose in Roxburghshire. The capital of the Damnonii of Strathclyde may have been on Dumbarton Rock.

The defended settlements of pre-Roman Scotland had numerous lean-to or round huts and excavation suggests that the people's wealth lay mainly in their herds. But saddle querns denote a limited amount of tillage, and La Tène ornaments indicate native craftsmen or trade, or, like the Roman material from abandoned bases, pillage. Beasts and men were hunted with swords, spears and slings. Several Scottish forts show occupation into the fourth century A.D.

In the south and east of the Southern Uplands the Iron Age farmers previously described seem to have continued their peaceful life on the hillsides. Beyond the Great Glen, the frontier zone of the builders of vitrified forts, the Iron Age peoples began to build, in the first century B.C., the fortified farmsteads known as brochs. A few outlying brochs are found in southern Scotland where they may have been built by mercenaries rewarded with land by the Romans. One is in Votadini territory, and a few lie in the uplands south of it, but nearly five hundred brochs lie north of the area in which hill-forts were built. Brochs are usually found on the best patches of coastal land and their density increases on good farmland as one goes northwards. There are forty-four in the Western Isles, 239 on the northern mainland, mostly in Caithness and Sutherland, 102 in Orkney and ninety-five in Shetland.

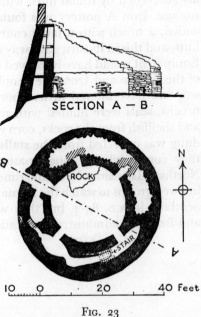

SECTION A — B

FIG. 23
Section and plan of a broch

Brochs are stone towers whose walls were twenty to forty feet high and up to eighteen feet thick at their base (Fig. 23). Cattle were stalled on the ground floor and work like threshing, corn-grinding, weaving and metalworking was carried on there. The broch people fished and hunted seals and would store their tackle there too. The living-quarters were on the upper floor in mural chambers in the thick wall which was penetrated by one entrance passage, flanked by guard chambers, on the ground floor, and by a staircase between the floors. Many brochs were still occupied in the first century A.D. but, after Agricola's penetration, and in the relative calm of the second century, many were dismantled, and their stones were used to build undefended wheelhouses, often on the same site.

Many broch-builders farmed land by the sea which had been tilled by Neolithic and Bronze Age peoples. At Jarlshof on Sumburgh Head, the southern tip of Shetland, successive villages and farms, separated by layers of blown sand, span the three thousand years between the Late Neolithic and the Viking Periods. Oval Neolithic and Bronze Age huts are succeeded by round huts, with radial partitions and souterrains for storage. Iron A pottery was found in them. As the first century B.C. ended, a broch with a large courtyard was built on top of the earlier huts, and this in its turn gave way to wheelhouses built in the courtyard. Equipment would have improved over these centuries, but the economy of the Bronze and Iron Age peoples, tied to their windswept land and sea, can have altered little. Shorthorns were stalled in the huts and brochs, seals were hunted with massive clubs, fish came from the sea and shellfish from the rocks, corn was ground in large trough querns and dung was collected from the stalls and spread on the sandy soil. Thus they continued the rough pastoral life which had persisted in the Northern Isles since Neolithic times. Broch-builders may have gathered in awed groups to watch the Roman fleet as it circumnavigated northern Scotland in A.D. 83-4, but they were happily a long way from Rome and from the administrative headquarters of Roman Britain.

CHAPTER 5

ROMANS AND BRITONS

S O MUCH has been written by specialists concerning Roman Britain that it would be inappropriate to go into great detail in a general survey such as this book attempts. Attention will therefore be concentrated mainly on some general features of relationship to environment.

Whereas pre-Roman social life in the west seems to have been dependent very particularly on the occurrence of a strong personality as leader, on the transmission of oral tradition, on rather rudimentary specialisation of crafts and trade (if we may judge from the feeble development of urban life), and on engineering still in a preliminary phase, Roman rule altered all this. It brought in on a larger scale the ideas of the city, of written tradition and institutional law of general application, of a standing army with hierarchical organisation, of road engineering based on systematic surveys, and of trade in greater bulk than had been previously thinkable with the limited communications of older times. It seems that indigenous peoples who were prepared to adopt Roman ways and language were soon treated as Romans, a feature that has to some extent characterised several of the peoples of Latin tradition in their contacts with some non-Europeans in modern times. It was the pre-Christian Roman tradition to tolerate most religions that did not claim exclusive allegiance, and this helped the process of Romanisation.

A considerable element in Celtic languages that was cognate with Latin made the introduction of new words to a Celtic-speaking people easier and facilitated the melting of Celtic into Latin, at any rate among the peoples of the cities attracted by Roman culture. In addition to elements cognate with Latin, Welsh has direct borrowing such as *pont, ffenestr* and *colofn (columna)*, features widely used by Roman engineers and architects, and *llyfr (liber)* the book which brought the written word to a land which had imaginative sculptors but no pre-Roman, or inscriptions of the Roman Period in the Celtic languages. During and after the Roman occupation, Latin would be mainly an urban language. In the countryside and throughout highland and Atlantic Britain, Celtic tongues were used. Even the Romans retained some Celtic names, particularly for rivers. The town of Exeter was Isca Dumnoniorum and the legionary fortress of Caerleon, bordered by the Usk, was called Isca (water). A legionary who died there was commemorated by his wife Flavia Veldicca; her household is likely to have been bilingual. St. Patrick, writing in the mid-fifth century, apologises for the quality of his Latin, a foreign tongue which was not the language of his home near the western sea; his father was a member of a Romano-British town council. Celtic tongues survived in the post-Roman west, while in eastern Britain, after A.D. 450, large-scale Anglo-Saxon immigration brought in the English language and cut off the more densely settled parts of Britain, linguistically and culturally, from the Mediterranean world.

Roman power was old-established when, in one of its last drives to expand the Empire, it thrust into Britain. The productivity of the lowlands occupied by Iron C peoples, and the mineral wealth of western Britain, were known to the Romans. Strabo wrote in 24 B.C. of "corn, cattle, gold, silver and iron, these are brought from Britain, also hides, slaves and clever hunting dogs." Coins of the Trinovantes bore an ear of the corn yielded by their rich Essex lowlands. Surplus corn which had been exported by British tribes would henceforth fill Roman granaries and nourish the legions. Within fifty years of the Claudian invasion of A.D. 43, lowland Britain was taken over as the productive zone of civil occupation. Its frontier was roughly the line of the Severn and Trent, backed by the Jurassic scarp and the Fosse Way, a major strategic route. Beyond the two Midland rivers lay thinly peopled forested lowland and, west of it, highland which produced poor corn crops and was the home of turbulent pastoral peoples. The Midlands were later absorbed into the civil zone, but the uplands remained under military control. Much of highland Britain was contained rather than occupied, and Roman legionaries never ventured into parts of Atlantic Britain and the land north of the Highland Fault in Scotland. The minerals of western Britain were State property and their mining was directed by Roman military engineers.

Fig. 24 shows the pattern of major roads which the Romans cut through the Celtic territories and the fortresses and towns to which these roads led. South-east of the Fosse Way, which runs from Dorset to Lincoln, major roads in the civil zone were linked by a mesh of minor roads. It was particularly intricate between London, St. Albans

Forts ■
Towns ○
Roads ——
(Course doubtful) - - - -
Canals ▭▭▭

Carpow

ANTONINE WALL

VOTADINI

DAMNONII
Springhill
Crawford
Newstead
SELGOVAE
NOVANTAE
Wallsend
HADRIAN'S WALL
Carlisle
Chester-le-Street
Maryport
Brough
Ravenglass
Catterick
Scarborough
BRIGANTES
Lancaster
PARISI
Ribchester
Doncaster
Holyhead
Manchester
Buxton
Lincoln
Brancaster
Caerhun
Chester
Car Dyke
Caernarvon
ORDOVICES
CORNOVII
Caersws
Wroxeter
Leicester
Caistor
St Edmunds
Burgh
Castle
CORITANI
ICENI
Droitwich
Godmanchester
Fosse Way
Watling St.
Cambridge
DEMETAE
Brecon
Gloucester
SILURES
Colchester
Walton
Castle
Carmarthen
Caerwent
Cirencester
CATUVELLAUNI
St Albans
TRINOVANTES
Caerleon
DOBUNNI
Cardiff
ATREBATES
London
Recuiver
Bath
Silchester
Stone St.
Richborough
BELGAE
CANTII
Canterbury
Winchester
Dover
Ilchester
DUROTRIGES
Old
Sarum
REGNENSES
Lympne
DUMNONII
Pevensey
Exeter
Dorchester
Carisbrooke

0   50   100 MILES
0   50   100 KILOMETRES

FIG. 24
Main Iron Age tribes and Roman roads, forts and towns

(Verulamium) and Cambridge. West of the Fosse Way, a few strategic roads ran through the forests, linking up military bases or towns occupied by army veterans. These supply lines ran to troublesome highlands west and north of the Midlands.

During the occupation of lowland Britain, the harshness of Roman occupation aroused opposition. Boudicca's revolt in A.D. 61 expressed the opposition of the Iceni, and the massacres which followed it must have reduced and dislocated the farming economy of East Anglia. Beyond the Welsh highlands, the Druids of Anglesey fiercely and vainly defended their island, a granary which provisioned the Ordovices, in A.D. 59.

The military occupation of western and northern Britain began with the subjection of the Brigantes whose large territory centred on the Pennines. The base for this operation was York (Eboracum), founded in A.D. 71 on the navigable Ouse. West-east roads, built on the York moraine, met there and linked York with the major north-south roads which were built to contain the Brigantes. South of York the Parisi were interested in trading down the Humber and appear to have co-operated when the continuation of Ermine Street, which ran up from Lincoln along the Wolds, was extended north of the Humber. The numerous Brigantine communities of the Pennine hills and valleys were brought into subjection by operations based on south-north roads on both sides of the hills. After their queen, Cartimandua, allied herself with the invaders, linking roads, like the rungs of a ladder, were laid out across the mountain spine.

In South Wales fierce resistance by the Silures prevented Roman penetration of their hilly terrain in A.D. 51-52. Their conquest, which was completed in A.D. 75, began with landings from the sea in southeast Wales, where relatively well-settled lowlands provided food supplies and riverside sites for forts. Caerleon, on the tidal Usk, became the legionary base and from it the armies penetrated up the Usk and Wye valleys and along the Glamorgan coastal lowland. Caerleon eventually covered forty-nine acres and it has been estimated that 6,000 troops were housed in sixty barrack buildings there (Fig. 25). Carmarthen marked the westward limit of military occupation. The Demetae of the Pembrokeshire peninsula, like the Dumnonii of the peninsula across the Bristol Channel, appear to have shown no hostility to the Roman forces.

Road- and fort-building in South Wales aimed at containment of the hill areas from coastal plains and major valleys. After the Ordovices

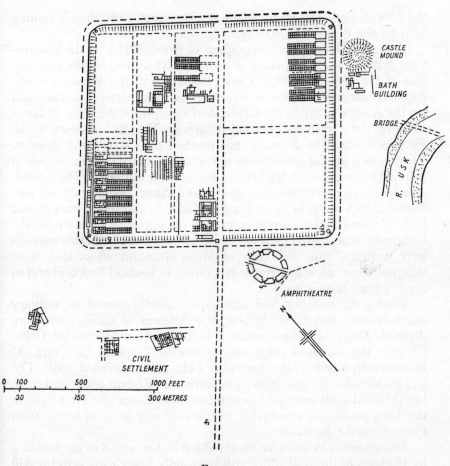

CASTLE
MOUND

BATH
BUILDING

BRIDGE

R. USK

AMPHITHEATRE

CIVIL
SETTLEMENT

0	100	500	1000 FEET
30		150	300 METRES

Fig. 25

Caerleon legionary fortress and the adjoining amphitheatre and civil settlement

of North Wales were defeated by Agricola in A.D. 78, the network of
roads and forts which enmeshed Wales was completed. Its major bases
were at Caerleon and Chester, which were linked by a military road up
the Welsh Marches, and the western points of the containing rectangle
were at Carmarthen and Caernarvon (Segontium). The resistance of
the Ordovices from their intricate mountain stronghold was broken by
penetration up the Dee and Conway valleys and by encroachment from
mountain forts like Pen-y-gwryd. Snowdonia bred fiercer warriors than

the hills of north-east Wales where the Deceangli were already mining lead for the Romans by A.D. 74.

Agricola followed up his conquest of North Wales by the penetration of the Southern Uplands of Scotland. This involved the pacification of the Selgovae of the Tweed basin and of the Votadini of the eastern coast and hills. Roads were built northwards from Carlisle and up the Annan valley to the Clyde, and north from the Tyne to Newstead on the Tweed and beyond it through Votadini territory to the Firth of Forth. The Romans thus reached the Clyde-Forth isthmus. There was a partial penetration of Galloway, but the main interest of this first reconnaissance lay beyond the Scottish Midlands. The formidable highland barrier which walled in the Pictish peoples was not surmounted in A.D. 84, or later, but a line of forts and signal stations was laid out along Strathmore to command the gateways to and from the highlands. It was from forts in Strathmore that the highland warriors were provoked into the battle of Mons Graupius where they were slaughtered or made ineffective as a threat to lowland Scotland and to the Brythons farther south.

During the conquest and subsequent consolidation of the military zones of west and north Britain, the defences of native forts were slighted. Many of them continued to be used as undefended Celtic villages: the Votadini continued to live in Traprain Law fort. At Dinorben in North Wales huts were built on the levelled walls. The fort builders learnt new skills as labourers on Roman roads and forts, but their old skills were used to build hilltop villages like Tre'r Ceiri in the Llŷn peninsula, where they also introduced ideas of fortification learnt from the Romans.

Disturbances in southern Scotland led in A.D. 122-8 to the building by Hadrian of the wall which still splendidly bears witness to his skill as a strategist. In its completed form it ran from the mouth of the Tyne to the lowest ford on the south shore of the Solway. The defensive line is continued southwards by a line of forts along the Solway shore of Cumberland. A great ditch fronts most of the wall, and from its milecastles the defenders could sally forth and pin attackers against the wall. Supplies came through sixteen large forts on the south side of the wall. After the Southern Uplands were reoccupied, a similar line, the Antonine Wall, was built across the Firth-Clyde isthmus. It was of turf, not stone, and more deeply ditched than Hadrian's Wall. Closely spaced forts replaced milecastles on it. But it could be outflanked by attacks across the Firth of Forth from Fife, and Strathmore had to be held to defend this land between the Tay and Forth estuaries. Hadrian's Wall temporarily became an almost deserted second line of defence until the Brigantian revolt of A.D. 155-8 brought a withdrawal to it. In the third century the Picts were still being contained north of the Antonine Wall and the Brythonic tribes of the Southern Uplands were controlled and protected by the Roman power. As in northern England and in Wales, they lived as pastoralists in undefended villages and scattered farms set among the pastures.

Towards the end of the third century sea-raiding by Saxon pirates from across the North Sea, and by Irish and Pictish pirates coming over the Irish Sea, caused the Romans to secure the coasts of both the lowland and Atlantic Zones. The forts of the Saxon Shore, begun between A.D. 287 and 296, ran from Norfolk to the Isle of Wight. In the west, forts were built at Cardiff, Holyhead and Lancaster, and signalling stations were set up on the Exmoor coast to watch for Irish pirates using the Bristol Channel. Signal stations were aligned along the Yorkshire coast, where Scarborough had one on its headland. Regular sea patrols were made along the coasts, though these did not prevent a joint attack by Saxons, Picts and Scots in A.D. 367, in which the Count of the Saxon Shore was killed. Saxon raiding was followed by settlement in East Anglia and in the East Riding where, around A.D. 400, land appears to have been given to mercenaries from Schleswig Holstein and north-west Germany in exchange for military service.

Subject tribes remote from the centres of civil power were given more authority as treaty states at this time. The Votadini of the Lothians were among them. The Romans were manœuvring tribal groups early in the fifth century, and the movement of Cunedda, a Votadini leader, with his followers from Manaw Gododdin, the area south of the Firth of Forth, to north-west Wales, may reflect a need to place a trusted ally there to oppose any invaders who might come from Ireland.

In the military zone of upland Britain the Romans imposed their power from forts. Great legionary fortresses like Caerleon attracted trade, and civil settlements which housed merchants, army veterans and camp followers grew up outside their walls. In the Lowland Zone, civil administration was carried out from towns. After pacification Celtic tribal aristocrats were persuaded to live in towns which were near or on the site of their former capitals. The military zone had few such vulnerable centres of Romano-British luxury. In Wales some Silures would have been tempted into Caerwent (Venta Silurum), near their hilltop stronghold at Llanmelin. Caerwent (Fig. 26), a town of only forty-five acres, was the only civil settlement in Wales.

The Roman occupation forces, like the British in the Indian subcontinent, dealt with native princes and confirmed them in office when they were co-operative. The native princedoms became Roman cantons and the Celtic leaders kept order and collected taxes and produce in them. The old tribal capitals acted as administrative centres of the cantons. Dorchester, below Maiden Castle, administered a large canton which was the territory of the Durotriges. It had a second capital beyond the Dorset Heights at Ilchester. The territory of the Dobunni was governed from Cirencester, and that of the Coritani from Leicester, and in both these cantons colonies of war veterans were set up, at Gloucester and Lincoln respectively, to augment the Roman power.

Most Romano-British towns were ports or route centres for the Lowland Zone which provided their trade. Richborough, the scene of the first landing in A.D. 43, Dover, Pevensey, Chichester and Portchester were ports which sent British produce to Gaul and Rome and took in supplies and luxuries from Mediterranean lands. Most towns would take about twenty years to lay out. Their rectangular grid of streets would later be enclosed within a wall whose line would be adapted to each site. The towns focused on the forum, around which lay imposing buildings like the senate house, theatre and temple. Town houses in gardens, and bath buildings, lay beyond them and there were often public water supply and sewerage systems. In A.D. 50 the Roman town of Colchester, for veteran legionaries, but also for the Trinovantes, was started at Cunobelin's capital of Camulodunum. Houseplots, and farmlands beyond the walls, were offered to settlers here and elsewhere. Camulodunum was sacked and burnt by Boudicca in A.D. 61 and though it was rebuilt, it was replaced as the administrative centre of Britain by Londinium. Although there had been no permanent pre-Roman settlement there, London grew rapidly. The Thames estuary and the Dover Road linked London with the continental heart of the Empire. Firm gravel banks supported a bridge across the river, and tributaries flowing below low hills were incorporated into the defences. Roads radiated eventually to all parts of occupied Britain. The walls of London, built in the first half of the second century, enclosed 325 acres, and though much of the town was destroyed by fire in Hadrian's time, a large merchant and administrative community rebuilt it.

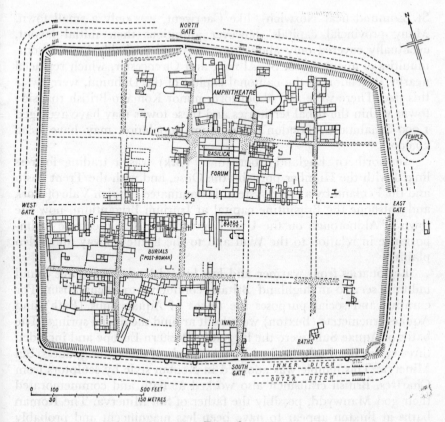

FIG. 26

Caerwent (Venta Silurum) Roman town, enclosed in walls which still stand

The initial impetus of town-building continued and many Romano-British towns were built or enlarged in the first half of the second century. Viroconium (Wroxeter) on the Severn, was built by the Cornovii and its city hall and market square were dedicated to Hadrian. It had town houses for leaders of the Cornovii, much as nearby Georgian Shrewsbury had second homes for Shropshire squires. Leicester was built and St. Albans rebuilt at this time. Leaders of the Catuvellauni who settled in the 200-acre town at St. Albans were protected by strong walls and ditches, and were well supplied from rows of shops. Silchester housed the leaders of the Atrebates and Exeter was the most south-westerly market and civil centre. The rebellion of the Iceni delayed economic progress in East Anglia, and Venta Icenorum (Caistor

St. Edmund near Norwich), like Caerwent, was only a small town. Many provincial capitals, however ambitious their initial layout, eventually covered only about 100 acres and probably housed communities of about 2,500. St. Albans, and Cirencester, which replaced nearby Bagendon as the cantonal capital of the Dobunni, were twice this size. There were also about forty minor Romano-British roadside towns within the tribal territories and these towns may have averaged 1,000 inhabitants. London's maximum population may have been 20,000.

In northern England Eboracum (York) was a trading fortress linked with the Humber ports by the Ouse, and with the Trent basin and the Fenland by a canal system. It dominated the rich Vale of York and outshone the Brigantine capital at Isurium Brigantium, now the town of Aldborough on the Ure. Luguvallium (Carlisle) rose to importance in relation to the Wall and to the fertile Solway and Eden plains.

Legionaries from warmer and less humid lands must have found military service in highland Britain conducive to rheumatism. For curative and social purposes the towns of Aquae Sulis (Bath) and Aquae Arnemetiae (Buxton) were built around medicinal springs. The baths of Aquae Sulis were the largest in Western Europe and included three swimming baths flanked by the temple of the water goddess, Sul Minerva. This temple was adorned in Roman style by sculptors from Chartres. British craftsmen also worked at Bath and commemorated their god Manwydd, possibly the father of Sul Minerva. The Roman baths at Buxton appear to have been less magnificent and probably adjoined St. Anne's Well. Arnemetia, who presided over the Buxton springs, was also a Celtic goddess.

In the third century many towns declined, although decreasing trade often sustained them for another century and even after A.D. 410 when they were left to fend for themselves. Public buildings gradually went out of use as an increasingly unsettled countryside ceased to contribute to the towns. The fourth century was cool and wet and harvests were difficult. The towns had been imposed upon tribes to whom urban life was largely foreign and the laws and taxes promulgated from them were often bitterly opposed. Medieval towns imposed on pastoral Britain by Norman and Plantagenet rulers were similarly resented. When Roman power was threatened by barbarian invasions in continental Europe, Romano-British leaders began to protect their food

PLATE II   WELSH WOMEN in "national costume", Betws-y-coed.

PLATE 12   ST. KILDA, rocks, bay, ruined village and cleitean (storehouses).

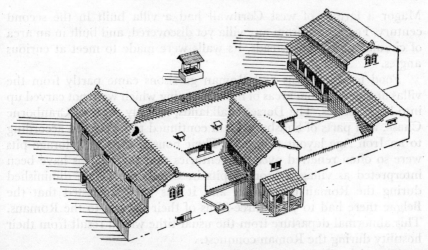

FIG. 27
Reconstruction of a Roman villa (after Davey)

supplies. The dykes around Silchester are thought to delimit the farm-lands which then supplied the town.

Before A.D. 43, many of the scarplands, major valleys and coast plains of lowland Britain provided arable and pasture land for Iron Age farmers. Tribal leaders had larger farms and these men, and those who profited from the Roman occupation, built villas on their estates (Fig. 27). Villas were farmsteads, and like all farms varied greatly in size. The dwelling house was flanked by barns, servant and slave quarters, and by customary functional features like threshing-floors, granaries and wells. Simple bath-houses are found in later villas and occasionally, as at Chedworth in the Cotswolds, farming was abandoned for manufacture. Local fuller's earth and wool, and iron which probably came from the Forest of Dean, were used there for fulling cloth and making farm tools. The villas of Romano-British farmers are numerous along the Jurassic scarp and in the scarplands and valleys east of it. A few were built on the plains east of the Pennines and others in valleys along the Welsh Marches. About a dozen occur in south-east Wales and two have been found as far west as the Towy valley. Beyond the Towy a hybrid embanked farm with primitive baths, and a corn-drying kiln, has been found south of Carmarthen. This Cwm-brwyn farmer was perhaps the first Welshman to add a bathroom to his cottage. There are many villas on the good lands of Somerset, and at

Magor a farmer of west Cornwall had a villa built in the second century. Far distant from any villa yet discovered, and built in an area of circular native farmsteads, its walls were made to meet at curious angles.

Food for the towns and Roman garrisons came partly from the villas and partly from areas of native farming which were not carved up into large estates. The Dorset chalklands, notably those of Cranborne Chase, and parts of Salisbury Plain continued to be farmed according to an Iron Age layout (Fig. 28). Their houses, corn and storage pits were so often renewed over the centuries that these farms have been interpreted as villages. Storage pits in Cranborne Chase diminished during the Roman occupation and it has been suggested that the Belgae there had to yield three-fifths of their harvest to the Romans. This abnormal departure from the usual tithe would result from their hostility during the Roman conquest.

The rich silt and peat soils of the Fenland soon attracted the Romans who drained them into the rivers and into a series of canals. The best-known canals were the Car Dykes. The Lincolnshire Car Dyke led northwards to Lincoln, from which it was later extended by the Foss Dyke to the Trent. Corn from Fenland farms could be carried to northern garrisons along this canal system. It seems to have been initiated before A.D. 70 and rebel Iceni families, displaced from their Breckland and other Norfolk homes, were probably enlisted to work the reclaimed land. The pattern of farms and fields which they laid out was a Celtic one. The Roman overseers appear to have controlled only the canals, dykes and collection of tribute. After a period in which harvests were difficult, and attempts were made to dry the corn in kilns fired with coal from Yorkshire and Durham, the Romano-British farmers were flooded out of the Fenland about A.D. 400. A minor rise in sea-level caused the drained land to revert to fen.

In Atlantic and highland Britain native farmsteads were rebuilt or enlarged, but they differed little from those of the pre-Roman Iron Age. In the Land's End peninsula houses like that at Chysauster were built with a series of rooms around a courtyard. Here and elsewhere, work and living rooms were differentiated, and there were also separate underground food stores or *fogous*. Some farmsteads included smithies where farm implements could be forged and repaired. Several Anglesey farms of the second to fourth centuries have smithies. Roman pottery in them suggests contacts with the garrison at Caernarvon. The thick-

FIG. 28

Romano-British villas and what are now interpreted as native farmsteads on the Wessex chalklands

walled houses with their low roofs gave shelter from the high winds of Atlantic Britain and some were occupied throughout the centuries of occupation with little interference from Romano-British administrators.

Small cornplots and more extensive pastures sustained farming families in Cornwall, West Wales and in many of the valleys and on the hillsides of northern Britain. The better land of valleys like those of the Aire, Wharfe and Ure appears to have supported considerable Brigantian communities. As the climate deteriorated in the late Roman Period, cattle would become more important than corn in the farming economies of both highland and lowland Britain. On the Dorset downlands large enclosures bounded by dykes were laid out, and the sheep and cattle of these and other ranches, and British cloth and hides, were well known to the Roman world of the fourth century. Among the wool products were the *Birrus Britannicus*, a felted waterproof cloak, and the *Tapete Britannicum*, a plaid blanket. In the Highland Zone a hill village like Tre'r Ceiri, enclosed by a wall with a parapet walk in the Roman tradition, has yielded no querns, but Dinorben, which adjoins better

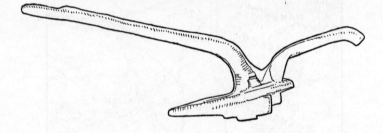

FIG. 29
Bronze model of a Roman plough from Sussex (original in British Museum)

land in Denbighshire, has produced ploughshares. Both settlements were occupied or re-occupied from the second century onwards. In northern England, and in the Southern Uplands, farmsteads and paddocks can still be seen, notably in the Yorkshire Dales, along the Stainmore Gap and in the Eden basin. In Scotland pastoralists lived in isolated farms, in hamlets aligned along hillsides, and the Votadini built farmsteads downslope from their capital on Traprain Law.

The Romans took over the metal resources of Britain as State property and were interested particularly in iron and in galena, the sulphide of lead which contains silver. North-west Iberia supplied copper ore and in the early years of the occupation Roman mining prospectors were not interested in the copper deposits of Anglesey. The classical world produced its silver from lead, as the modern world still largely does, and British lead was worked in the Mendips from A.D. 49, in Flintshire from A.D. 74 and in the Yorkshire Dales from A.D. 81. Opencast workings were often used at first. Mining of Derbyshire, Shropshire, Cardiganshire and Glamorganshire lead ores followed. In many of these areas, small forts like Cae-gaer, in the valley south-east of Plynlimon, suggest military supervision of operations.

Copper for bronze manufacture was mined in Shropshire at Llanymynech, in Caernarvonshire on the Great Orme's Head, and at Parys Mountain in the north of Anglesey. Caer Gybi fort (Holyhead) was built to secure Anglesey's copper supplies from Irish raiders. Its walls were carried down to low-water mark, like those of a Rhine-bank fort, giving free access to its harbour on the open side for the crews of patrol boats. Cornish tin was most actively worked after the mid-third

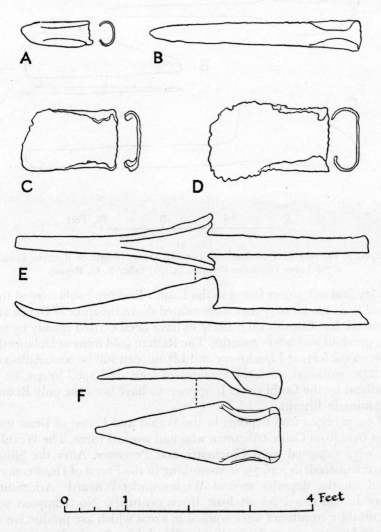

FIG. 30
Iron Age and Romano-British ploughshares: *a*. Caburn. *b-c*. Bigbury. *d*. Eckford.
e. Box. *f*. Moorgate Street, London. *a-c* are Iron Age and *d-f* Romano-British (x 1/6)
(after Payne)

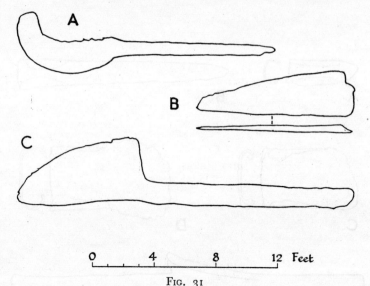

FIG. 31

Coulters: *a*. Bigbury (? Iron Age). *b*. Twyford Down (Belgic or Romano-British). *c*. Silchester (Romano-British). (x 1/6) (after F. G. Payne)

century and milestones found in the Land's End peninsula suggest that a road from Exeter may then have existed down the spine of Devon and Cornwall. But Cornish tin is likely to have been carried mainly by sea, as in previous and later centuries. The Roman gold mine at Dolaucothi, between the forts at Llandovery and Llanio, can still be seen. Adits and opencast workings, and the remains of leets and spoil-heaps, lie in woodland by the Cothi river. It appears to have been the only Roman gold mine in Britain.

Less precious iron deposits in the Weald and Forest of Dean were taken over from Celtic tribesmen who had worked them. The Wealden ores were exported from Chichester and Pevensey. After the Silures were conquered, in A.D. 75, iron-working in the Forest of Dean concentrated on the deposits around Weston-under-Penyard (Ariconium) where it continued for at least three centuries. Northampton and Lincolnshire ironstones were worked in areas which are productive to-day, and what are now the coalfields of Yorkshire, Nottinghamshire and Durham yielded coal for corn drying, heating of forts on Hadrian's wall, and smelting. Somerset cannel coal was burnt on the altars of Sul Minerva at Bath.

Clay was widely used for tile-, brick-, pipe- and pottery-making and tileries like that at Holt in Denbighshire, producing for the legionary fortress at Chester, are well attested. The best-known potteries were those of Castor, where Ermine Street crosses the Nene at Water Newton, and the New Forest potteries which produced a wide range of household ware. Most legionary forts and Romano-British towns had their own potteries, and imported wine and olive oil came in amphorae which were copied in Britain. Pottery and glass circulated widely and reached remote parts of Atlantic and highland Britain. Kimmeridge shale from Dorset was carved into plaques and furniture, and Purbeck marble from the same area was quarried for ornamental use. Whitby jet was in demand, as it was in prehistoric and Victorian times. The Romans took over the saltpans worked by the Trinovantes in Essex, and brine-working was extended from this coast to that of the Channel. Droitwich and Middlewich had brine pits and clay-lined furnaces to evaporate the brine.

Both Romans and Britons had many religious cults. Official Roman religion centred on emperor worship, bound up with the security of the Roman State, and on many gods, such as Minerva and Jupiter, who were severally commemorated in Romano-British cities. Tribal gods like Brigantia were tolerated and many other gods were worshipped in northern Britain. The sculptors of communities in the Aire valley carved numerous portrait busts which were set up as household gods. The Celtic gods of regions with Celtic farming systems suggest that the veneer of romanisation was a thin one in the hill country. At Lydney a temple adjoined by baths and guest-houses for pilgrims was set up in honour of the water god Nodens in the late fourth century— from the hill at Lydney the Severn bore can be seen surging up the narrowing Severn estuary. This pilgrim centre lies inside an Iron B fort which was sporadically occupied by Romano-British iron miners, and it flourished long after the legions left Britain in A.D. 410, possibly because Irish raiders, who then lurked in the Bristol Channel, also honoured the Celtic god Nodens as their Nuada.

While official religious cults were observed in the legionary forts, more private religions flourished outside their walls. Mithraism, the cult brought by the army from Persia, had its temples on the fringes of Caernarvon, at St. Albans, and at forts behind Hadrian's Wall. The only civil shrine, possibly erected by merchants, was the Wallbrook temple of Mithras in London. Deliberate desecration of Mithraic shrines in the fourth century suggests that some army officers had become Christians.

Christianity became the official religion of the Empire in A.D. 325, but before this date there are many traditions of its introduction into Britain. Legend connects Glastonbury with Joseph of Arimathea: it was certainly inhabited in his time. Romano-British towns had bishops as heads of local clergy (*epi-scopus* means overseer) and some of them attended the Councils of Arles (A.D. 314), Nicaea (A.D. 325) and Ariminum (A.D. 349). Excavation has revealed a Christian church at Silchester, a doubtful one at Caerwent, and Christian wall paintings and mosaics in villas. But country folk must have continued to worship tribal gods, and the term *pagani* came to mean heathens rather than peasants.

Christianity was brought to the countryside by Celtic missionaries who used the Atlantic route. Cultural and trading contacts, as well as piracy, were maintained along the old route throughout the Roman Period. Migrations from Wales to Brittany, and of the Deisi from Ireland to Pembrokeshire, followed the trade routes. St. Ninian, who studied under St. Martin of Tours, and dedicated several early Celtic churches to him, founded Candida Casa (Whithorn Priory) in Galloway in A.D. 397 (Fig. 33). As a centre of learning it attracted Irish and Brythonic monks for at least a century after Ninian's death. Another early missionary was St. Patrick, a Romano-Briton who studied at Lerins off the Mediterranean coast of France and under St. Germanus of Auxerre. He preached Christianity in Ireland in the mid-fifth century. Celtic Christianity flourished after Roman control ceased in Britain. When it was deemed necessary to suppress Pelagianism in Britain (a creed which denied the total depravity of the new-born as a result of Adam's sin), St. Germanus came from Auxerre in 429 to confer with British Christians at Verulamium. Dedications to St. Germanus in Cornwall, and in the Isle of Man, suggest that he too may have preached at centres along the Atlantic route. Celtic monasteries were widely dispersed in western Britain during the Anglo-Saxon occupation of the lowland zone.

Christianity was part of the legacy of ideas which the Romans left to the Celtic peoples. Their early writers recall the splendours of Roman material culture and look back to the Roman Period as a golden age. Both Geoffrey of Monmouth and, in 1188, Giraldus Cambrensis, refer to the golden roofs of the legionary fortress at Caerleon. One of the tales of the Mabinogion concerns Maxen Wledig, Magnus Maximus, who served as an officer in Britain and usurped the throne of the Western Empire. He is associated with the re-occupation of Caernarvon between A.D. 367 and 383, probably to safeguard copper-working in Anglesey. In the Mabinogion he comes in a dream ship to Caernarvon and enters the Roman fort, finding gold walls and furnishings there. The rigours of a harsh administration would be largely forgotten and memories of an orderly and often peaceful existence as an outpost of the Roman Empire would become paramount as less disciplined raiders and settlers came into Britain over the North Sea.

CHAPTER 6

THE EARLY ENGLISH AND THE CELTIC WEST

THE ROMAN forces, who finally abandoned Britain in 410, left behind a decaying system of towns and a road network which focused on London and on the shortest sea routes to the Continent. The peoples of Atlantic Britain were communicating with each other at this time along the western sea routes. In Highland Britain local tribal leaders rose to power as what had become a light Roman yoke was finally removed. In the Lowland Zone, after a century of sporadic Saxon raiding, there were already some Frisian settlements along the North Sea coast. These settlers, in contact with their homelands across the narrow seas, were the spearhead of penetration of what was now a vulnerable and disunited land.

A century of migration by Anglo-Saxon peoples started in the mid-fifth century. These folk movements brought in families from Jutland (Jutes and Angles), north-west Germany (Saxons) and the Low Countries (Frisians). They were Teutonic folk, speaking closely related tongues, who brought in the cattle-rearing and corn-growing economies of their largely coastal and estuarine homelands and, at first, sought similar lands in the lowlands of Britain. They settled coast plains and broad river valleys and the lower slopes of the downlands, grouping their farmsteads together and forming hamlets and villages. At first they moved by sea and river and had little need for the Roman roads and towns, which continued to decay. Some Romano-British families and tribes may have moved into the Highland Zone when they were displaced by the Anglo-Saxons. Others may have become slaves and serfs and other Romano-British groups could have peacefully co-existed with the new settlers in the lowlands. Some intermarriage would have occurred, but the English tongue of the dominant tribes soon displaced Celtic and Latin in the Lowland Zone. Celtic river- and hill-names survive there, and another small group of place-names, which includes those of several towns, are Romano-British in origin.

A great deal of dense forest and marshland still covered Sub-Roman Britain. Forests like Epping, Sherwood, Arden, Savernake, and those of the Chilterns and Weald, were then far more extensive than they now are. A ninth-century author described Andredswald, the Weald Forest, as extending for 120 miles, with a breadth of thirty miles, from Hampshire to the Kent coast. River valleys and coast flats were often marshy and could not be tilled unless they were drained. The early English settlers occupied many valley sites and, with their heavy iron axes, made ever-expanding clearings in the forests and along their margins. The shares of their heavy ploughs turned the rich and deep alluvial soils, their cattle grazed the valley meadows and their sheep the hillsides; their pigs, seeking mast in the forests, hindered their regeneration.

The early Anglo-Saxon settlers sought good farmland near their landings and at first pioneered lines of settlement, running inland from them, similar to those of their descendants along the coasts of North America. Kent, the Thames and adjoining estuaries, and East Anglia were settled first. Angles and Saxons from south-west Jutland and the lower Elbe and Weser basins, and Frisians from the Low Countries also settled Sussex and penetrated up the Thames valley to Wessex. The estuaries and areas such as the Sandlings of East Suffolk must have been reminiscent of their homelands. East Anglians still claim descent from the Angles, while Essex men, born south of the Stour estuary, boast of their Saxon ancestors. As the flow of migration increased, Jutes became numerous among the families who settled in Kent, the Isle of Wight, south Hampshire and parts of East Anglia. Penetration from the Hampshire estuaries brought another stream of Anglo-Saxons into Wessex. From the Thames valley the Anglo-Saxons spread to the scarp-foot of the Chilterns, forcing British families to retreat upslope into the Chiltern forests. Celtic elements lingered in the Chiltern Hundreds for centuries. Once regarded as a wild area, its stewardship is now merely a sinecure.

Iron, and salt for preserving meat and fish, were commodities which had already been circulating in Britain for a thousand years before the early English arrived. Saltpans, and salthouses, where the brine was evaporated, continued to multiply. Both inland and at the coast small trading centres gradually developed. Southampton and Ipswich are both seventh-century foundations. By about 600 the Anglo-Saxons had occupied the Lowland Zone and the demands of their leaders for luxuries and jewellery spread trade more widely. Royal and noble families thus acquired and traded fine brooches (some of the finest were made in English kingdoms like Kent), and silverware, pottery and wine from

Mediterranean lands. Some wool appears to have been exported and King Offa of Mercia sent Charlemagne some of the felted cloaks for which Britain had been famous in Roman times. Families captured in times of war went into slavery in both early English and Celtic households, and slaves were also exported to Carolingian Gaul and to the Mediterranean. "Not Angles but angels" could reflect a wish to convert lively pagan children who might be sent home to spread Christianity among their own people.

Groups of Anglo-Saxon families often gave their chief's name to their cluster of farmsteads, its fields and pasture land. The word -ing (plural ingas), meaning "followers of," widely used for early settlements, is found, for example, at Goring (Domesday Garinges, people of Gara), Hastings and Reading. It was also used in the sense of "people," for example at Avening, the dwellers by the Avon River. Fig. 32, showing the ingas names of south-east England, suggests an early occupation of good soils which were already largely free from dense forests and an early recognition of what are still highly productive farmlands.

Ingham, and later -ington, "the homestead of the people of," are common names of Anglo-Saxon settlements. Ham went out of use in later centuries and is rare beyond the Jurassic scarp. It is most common in East Anglia, Essex, Cambridgeshire, Surrey and Sussex. The commonest Anglo-Saxon suffix came to be -ton. It is possible that -ing and -ham were used by kinship groups who immigrated together and that -ton was used to describe the neighbourhood unit of less closely related families as settlement expanded and the population increased.

English place-name elements often reflect the cattle-rearing economy of the Anglo-Saxons. Names like Cowley, Oxton, Swindon, Shepton and Shapwick are obvious examples. Pastures, especially for swine, were given the name -den, a common element in Kentish place-names. Tenterden, the swine pastures of the men of Thanet, would be initially a temporary settlement of swineherds who took pigs up to the Weald Forest. It is one of many names for outlying lands which supplemented those around settlements. Marshlands yield good grass for summer grazing, and Burmarsh, on Romney Marsh, is a seventh-century name which is thought to mean "marsh of the people of Canterbury," sixteen miles away. Somerton and Winterton denote seasonal movements with herds and flocks seeking pasture suitable to the season. Transhumance took herdsmen and animals not only upslope to sweet upland pastures but also to bogs and marshlands which

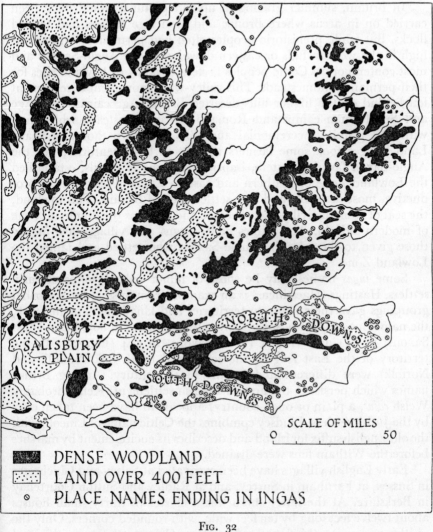

DENSE WOODLAND
LAND OVER 400 FEET
○ PLACE NAMES ENDING IN INGAS

FIG. 32
Distribution of place-names with the old suffix -*ingas*

would literally not support cattle in winter. Both the Celtic and, later, Scandinavian settlers also practised transhumance. It was, and still is, widespread in most regions of the Old World where animals have to be moved off the valley hayfields in summer to green hillsides which may be snow-covered during the winter half-year.

In Britain, summer grazing of upland pastures would have been carried on in areas where Bronze and Iron Age settlers had tended flocks. But while prehistoric peoples often had permanent settlements high in the western hills or eastern downlands, the Anglo-Saxons and most contemporary Celtic peoples preferred valley or lowland sites for their permanent homesteads. This valley-ward movement of settlement left behind on the higher hills deserted Bronze Age cairns, Iron Age and Sub-Roman camps and Romano-British farmsteads which had witnessed primitive ceremonial and tillage for two thousand years. Land hunger took some farmers upslope in later centuries, but the Anglo-Saxon farming system, imprinted on the lowlands, established the Lowland Zone of southern and eastern England as the most productive, most desirable and best-settled part of Britain. This lowland, the seat of Roman civil power, became and remains the dominant zone of modern Britain. The names of its towns and villages are mostly those given to them by the Anglo-Saxons who settled and tamed the Lowland Zone.

Some *ingas* names may be those of minor tribal groups of early settlers. Hastings (Haestingas) is an example from Sussex. Larger tribal groupings gave their name to territories and kingdoms. For instance, the name Sussex (South Saxons) was already in use in 607, Essex (East Saxons) in 604 and Wessex (West Saxons) in 514 (Fig. 33). In the territory of the East Angles, the south and north folk (Suffolk and Norfolk) were differentiated by the ninth century. Among British names which persist in the area of English settlement, Kent (probably Welsh *caint*, a plain or open country) appears to have been taken over by the Jutish settlers. Lindsey combines the Celtic name of Lincoln with the old English suffix for island and describes its encirclement by marshes before the Witham fens were drained.

Early English villages have been excavated at Selsey and Chichester in Sussex, at Farnham in Surrey, and at Radley and Sutton Courtenay in Berkshire. At the latter there was a cluster of thirty small houses about twelve feet long by ten feet wide, with rounded corners. Only the smithy was twice this length. At Sutton Courtenay the smith's and carpenter's tools, and the women's looms, were recovered. At Canterbury Jutish and Frisian burials have been found and there are signs that most Romano-British settlements in Kent were frequented by the immigrants. At Southampton a lively trade with Gaul and the Rhineland produced a more substantial trading settlement which had brick huts rather than timber or wattle-and-daub hovels. Glassware came to

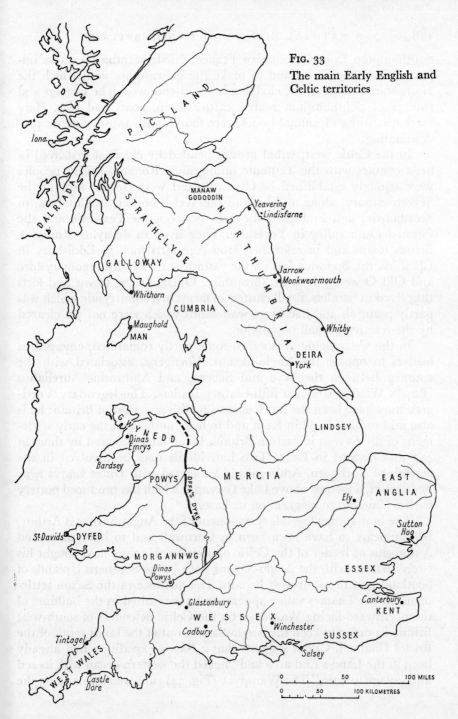

FIG. 33
The main Early English and
Celtic territories

PICTLAND

Iona

DALRIADA

STRATHCLYDE

GALLOWAY

Whithorn

MAUGHOLD
MAN

CUMBRIA

MANAW
GODODDIN

Yeavering
Lindisfarne

NORTHUMBRIA

Jarrow
Monkwearmouth

Whitby

DEIRA
York

LINDSEY

GWYNEDD
Dinas
Emrys

Bardsey

POWYS

OFFA'S DYKE

MERCIA

EAST
ANGLIA

Ely

Sutton
Hoo

St Davids DYFED

MORGANNWG
Dinas
Powys

ESSEX

Glastonbury

WESSEX

Cadbury

Winchester

Canterbury
KENT

SUSSEX

Tintagel

WEST WALES

Castle
Dore

Selsey

0   50   100 MILES

0   50   100 KILOMETRES

Southampton from Carolingian France. Niedermendig lava was imported from the Rhineland to make the quernstones with which the Hampshire basin and the chalklands are ill-endowed. The farmers and traders of Southampton reared cattle, sheep, goats and pigs. Here large quantities of animal bones were found, with those of cattle predominating.

In the Celtic west, tribal groups headed by chiefs at first lived in little contact with the Teutonic immigrants. Romano-British peoples were strongly established in Cornwall and west Devon, around the Severn estuary, along and beyond the Welsh border, in Cumbria, in Strathclyde, and in Elmet, the area between the Pennines and the forested Ouse valley in Yorkshire. They lived in decaying Romano-British towns and in refortified Iron Age forts such as Eddisbury in Cheshire, the Breidden fort on the eastern border of Montgomeryshire and Old Oswestry in west Shropshire. Outside these towns and forts they lived in hamlets, small clusters of farms in a countryside which was partly pastoral, and had large wastelands which were not yet cleared by the relatively small population.

In the west, Celtic aristocrats, some partly romanised, emerged as leaders to oppose the Anglo-Saxons. Vortigern, associated with the country between the Wye and Severn, and Ambrosius Aurelianus (Emrys Wledig) are two fifth-century leaders. The legendary Vortigern may have been the last Romano-British governor of Britain; he is also said to have lived in Kent and to have authorised the early settlement of the Saxons in eastern Britain, being later defeated by them in 457 at Crayford in Kent. Two individuals may be involved in the legends of Vortigern. Ambrosius is associated with Dinas Emrys near Beddgelert, a fortress above Lake Gwynant which has produced pottery with a Chi-Rho monogram on its base.

The best-known legendary opponent of the Anglo-Saxons is Arthur, who appears to have been born in Cornwall and to have succeeded Ambrosius as leader of the Celtic opposition. He may have fought his twelve battles with the Anglo-Saxons both in the Southern Uplands of Scotland and in south-west Britain. The advance of the Saxon settlement up the Thames valley appears to have resulted in the building of the northward-facing Wansdyke by the Celtic defenders of south-west Britain in order to keep the Anglo-Saxons out of the lands south of the Bristol Channel. Gildas suggests that a Saxon expedition had already been in the Land's End area and "licked the western ocean with its red and savage tongue." The Wansdyke (Fig. 34) runs westwards along the

PLATE 13   LAVENHAM, the Hall of the Guild of Corpus Christi.

PLATE 14   REED THATCHING, Hickling, Norfolk. An old country craft.

FIG. 34
The Wansdyke, Marlborough Downs

chalk downs from Savernake Forest and from them across the Avon valley to Bath. It angles sharply southwards on the hills south of Bath and then continues westwards along Dundry Hill towards the Severn Sea. On the hills south of Bath, Arthur probably defeated the Saxons at Mons Badonicus about 500. His Camelot, or one of his strongholds, may have been the refortified Iron Age fort at South Cadbury, between Ilchester and Wincanton in Somerset. He may also have fortified or refortified a frontier line of camps on the scarps between Badbury Rings in Dorset and Badbury Hill, a name given to hills in both Berkshire and Northamptonshire. This frontier, if it existed, was pushed westwards by the advancing Anglo-Saxon settlers, as they established the kingdoms of Wessex and of Mercia.

Wessex, the metropolis of Britain in the peaceful Bronze Age centuries, lost its leadership in the unsettled Iron Age and in the Anglo-Saxon Period, though in the face of Danish and Norse invasions it was again to lead England. During the Anglo-Saxon settlement, consolidation of Wessex, by groups coming in from landings on the Channel coast, or up the Thames, eventually gave it a south-western boundary with the Celts of Cornwall. Its western boundary, after the death of Arthur, was the Bristol Channel, and in the east it extended into Sussex.

Mercia became, in the ninth century, the most powerful of the English kingdoms. Centred at first on the Trent basin, its leaders

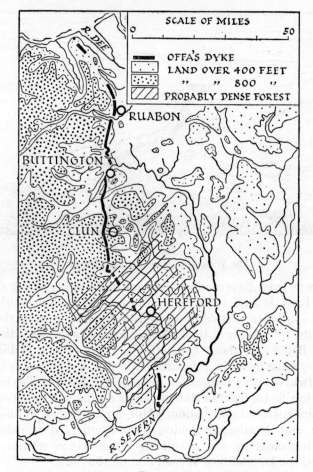

Fig. 35
Offa's Dyke (after Fox)

conquered the Middle Angles of the south-east Midlands, the Hwicce of the lower Severn basin, and the Magonsaete of the middle Wye. They had then reached the Welsh Marches where the hills rise, often sharply, from the good pastures of the Midlands. To emphasise the function of this natural bastion of Wales, a frontier was agreed and demarcated along the hills (Fig. 35). The dyke built by King Offa of Mercia in the second half of the eighth century is a boundary which uses the lie of the land well. Dense forests in major valleys like those of the Severn and Wye, which break the hill barrier, were regarded as adequate barriers in themselves and Offa's Dyke does not continue through them. The dyke is a boundary or line of confrontation which had no military function. As in some sections it runs close to the modern boundary of Wales, some Welsh politicians still refer to Clawdd Offa as a divide between England and Wales.

In Northumbria and its sub-kingdom Bernicia, the first settlers who came in across the North Sea appear to have been Frisians. They were followed by Anglians who built Bamborough as their stronghold. The great fortress on Yeavering Bell may have been adapted by them and Old Yeavering was inhabited until the seventh century. Celtic Elmet, the forested and partly marshy area around the lower Wharfe and Ouse, separated Northumbria from Mercia until it was taken over by the Anglo-Saxons in the late seventh century. The Roman Rig earthwork in South Yorkshire may have been built as part of the Northumbrian frontier with Mercia. West of the Pennines Celtic-speaking groups survived in Cumbria, as they must have done in remote Pennine valleys.

The tide of Anglo-Saxon immigration did not come in as an overwhelming wave which wiped out the British population, or cast it as jetsam into Highland Britain. Many British hamlets, hidden away behind barriers of forest or marsh, retained their identity and continued to practise their self-contained economy. When the Anglo-Saxons eventually took over these hamlets and their lands, many of their Celtic inhabitants would be forced to become serfs. The Anglo-Saxons recognised many of these British communities as *Walas* or *Wealas*, or *Brettas*, and the names of these hamlets of Welsh, serfs, or Britons, are widespread in England. Some of the numerous Walton, Walcot, Walbrook, Walmer, Walpole, Walden, Bretton and Brettenham names denote British settlements. In areas like Elmet, west Cumberland and west Lancashire, they point to a recognition by the immigrants of distinctive communities firmly established on relatively good land.

The Early English of Northumbria extended their settlement across Hadrian's Wall in the seventh century, taking over former Votadini territory and forming a kingdom which stretched from the Humber to the Forth. Celtic peoples continued to hold the kingdom of Strathclyde. Beyond them in Argyll the Scots had come from Ireland in the late fifth century to found the kingdom of Dalriada. The Picts continued to occupy the Highlands of Scotland, and the lower land east of them, where many of their mysterious Pictish stones occur. The symbols on these stones may be the insignia of Pictish leaders commemorated by illiterate followers.

Around the Irish Sea the lands which jut out into the Atlantic sea-way formed a cultural province. Seaborne migrations occurred here too. Before the Scots went to Argyll the Deisi had colonised Pembroke-shire (Dyfed) from eastern Ireland and their princely dynasty lasted there for five centuries. The Deisi lived in Pembrokeshire in raths, homesteads enclosed by earthen banks. Raths were built in Ireland from the third century B.C. until the Middle Ages. Cornwall, then known as West Wales, was not conquered by the Anglo-Saxons until 838. There was a fifth-century migration from Cornwall to Brittany in face of an earlier Saxon threat. The distinctive nature of both Wales and Cornwall was acknowledged by the Early English who gave the Britons of both areas the name *Wealas*, foreigners, Celts who had been under Roman rule. The Welsh call themselves *Cymry* (compatriots) and Cumberland, which still retains remnants of Celtic speech, was also recognised as the land of the *Cumbras* or Britons. The county appears in the Anglo-Saxon Chronicle's record for 945 as Cumbraland.

In their social organisation the Early English and Celtic peoples had much in common. Kings and chiefs, with bands of aristocratic followers, formed a court which was rarely based on a settled capital. The court moved frequently around the countryside and depended on hospitality offered by nobles and, later, by monasteries. Nobles were probably more numerous in Anglo-Saxon than in British society. In both of them freemen held lands in the communally tilled fields, and farmsteads in the villages; bondsmen had cottages to which small crofts were attached. Slaves, often captured in tribal wars, were the drudges of both systems. In both societies priests and smiths ranked as freemen and both English and Britons honoured their bards and minstrels, for these men knew the traditions of their peoples and sang of the heroes of former wars and those of their own days.

Some farmsteads in Celtic Britain were merely larger versions of Iron Age round huts, stone-built and thatched, with sleeping-benches around the walls. Small groups of such huts, surrounded by a wall, were still being built in Anglesey in the sixth century. Rectangular tim-ber houses, with the thatched roof supported by a ridge-pole, became common where timber was plentiful. In the west, and in many early Anglo-Saxon villages, houses were simpler than the homestead shown on Fig. 37. Celtic bards sang of the glories of their lords' halls and sug-

PLATE V.   a. MAIDEN CASTLE, Dorset. The greatest earthwork fortress
of the pre-Roman Iron Age in Britain

b. WHITE HORSE, UFFINGTON, Berkshire Downs. Below an
earthwork of the pre-Roman Iron Age the chalk has been laid
bare by cutting away the turf, giving a representation of a
horse

Old fields and field patterns. VIa shows Iron Age fields and VIb, the ridges and furrows of medieval common arable fields in the Midlands

Fig. 36

Distribution of Ogam-inscribed stones in the British Isles

gest that they were the equal of those of the Anglo-Saxons (Fig. 38).

At Dinas Powys, on the Glamorgan coast plateau south-west of Cardiff, a Celtic chief refortified an Iron Age camp. Set on a spur of limestone, it was reoccupied during the fifth and sixth centuries. The two rectangular houses on the hill at Dinas Powys were stone-built and had rounded corners. They probably represent the chief's hall and a dwelling for his herdsmen and metalworkers. The area is well wooded and cattle and pigs were reared and killed off each autumn. Corn was grown and three rotary querns were found in the settlement. The metal-

FIG. 37
Tentative reconstruction of the homestead of an Anglo-Saxon chief

workers used fragments of glass and bronze which were imported as scrap, perhaps from Gaul, or acquired when broken, from the Anglo-Saxons. The Dinas Powys folk melted down the scrap metal and glass and made bronze brooches with vitreous inlays, using small clay crucibles. At Garranes in County Cork a similar industry was carried on in a more strongly defended rath between 450 and 550.

There was no pottery-making at Dinas Powys. Most Anglo-Saxons appear to have used wood, leather and horn containers rather than pots. Organised manufacture of wheel-made pottery lapsed after the Romans withdrew. Kilns found in late seventh-century Ipswich suggest that the pottery industry was then beginning to be resumed, after three centuries. The people of Dinas Powys, and other settlements along the Atlantic route, imported their pots from Mediterranean lands. They included amphorae, containers for wine and oil, which can be matched in Sicily, spouted *mortaria* for mashing fruit to make purées, a method inherited from Roman kitchens, and fine red bowls, one adorned with leopards, which were being made in Antioch on the Orontes after 425. One or other of these types of pottery has been found at sites on both

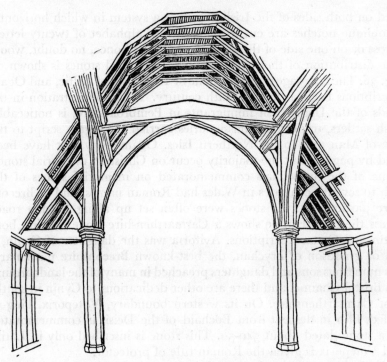

FIG. 38
Diagrammatic cross-section of an Anglo-Saxon hall

sides of the southern Irish Sea, including Dinas Emrys and a cave near
Tenby in Wales, Cadbury in Somerset, Tintagel and Gwithian in
Cornwall, and Bantham in south Devon. More are likely to be found.
These were important religious and secular communities which brought
in their supplies up the long Atlantic seaway to maintain feeding and
drinking habits which were remembered from the days of the Romans.
The well-known story of the Egyptian merchant ship which relieved a
famine in Cornwall, and exchanged its cargo of corn for tin, dates from
about 614 and is part of the trading tradition of this period. This old-
established trade with the Mediterranean became much more difficult
after the eighth century when the Moors occupied both shores of the
Straits of Gibraltar, Iberia and southern France. Coarse locally made
pots then replaced imported Mediterranean pottery in many homesteads.

The Ogam alphabet, which originated in southern Ireland, was used on both sides of the Irish Sea. It is a system in which horizontal or oblique notches are cut to represent an alphabet of twenty letters across or on one side of the edge of stones, and once, no doubt, wood. The distribution of the surviving Ogam-inscribed stones is shown on Fig. 36. The language is the Goedelic or Irish form of Celtic, and Ogam inscriptions begin before the fifth century. Their concentration in the lands of the Deisi, Irish immigrants in Pembrokeshire, is noticeable. Irish settlers, traders and missionaries carried the Ogam script to the Isle of Man and to the Northern Isles. Ogams may first have been used by pagans, but the majority occur on Christian memorial stones. Some of the individuals commemorated on memorial stones of the fifth to seventh centuries in Wales had Roman names, and in Breconshire particularly, the stones were often set up along Roman roads across the hills. Fig. 39 shows a Carmarthenshire stone bearing both Latin and Ogam inscriptions. Avitoria was the daughter of Cynin, a son or grandson of Brychan, the best-known Breconshire missionary. His numerous sons and daughters preached in many of the lands around the Bristol Channel and there are other dedications to Cynin in southwest Carmarthenshire. On its western boundary, Voteporix, king of Dyfed, fifth in descent from Eochaid of the Deisi, is commemorated on a stone dated about 540-50. This stone is inscribed only in Latin, and Voteporix is given the Roman title of protector.

In Roman Britain, Christianity was the faith of townsfolk and of families who lived in Romano-British villas, and the rural folk of Highland Britain were not converted in large numbers until the fifth century. Traditions of fourth-century conversions centre in Wales round Helena (Elen), who had been converted by St. Martin of Tours, and several churches are dedicated to her. Saints Aaron and Julius are said to have been martyred near the legionary fort of Caerleon. The evangelisation of Atlantic and Highland Britain was carried out by Celtic missionaries, often recognised as saints, during the fifth and sixth centuries. From monastic cells in the deserts around the Fertile Crescent, Christianity was taken to the Mediterranean islands, including Lerins off the south coast of France, and thence through France to Britain. St. Martin of Tours trained missionaries like St. Ninian, and St. Patrick studied at Lerins and under St. Germanus of Auxerre. St. Ninian and St. Patrick played a large part in the conversion of the Irish Sea coastlands, St. Ninian founding Whithorn Priory at the end of the fourth century, and St. Patrick later converting Ireland. Both trained missionaries to succeed them.

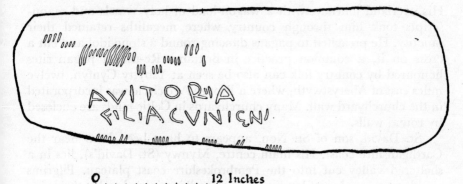

FIG. 39

Inscribed stone from Eglwys Gymyn, Carmarthenshire, with both Latin and Ogam inscriptions

The Celtic Church was essentially monastic. The mother church, or *clas*, was served by a monastic community headed by an abbot, and hermitages were built on islands or on remote coasts. Ynys Seiriol (Puffin Island) off Anglesey, was the retreat of St. Seiriol and a small group of monks whose material needs were catered for in small fields around their cells. Bardsey, often isolated by storms, was a saints' retreat off the Llŷn peninsula. In Orkney, the Brough of Deerness has monks' cells around its small church and St. Ninian's chapel near Jarlshof in Shetland and in Bute were similar hermitages. Tintagel hermitage was in use from the fifth to eighth centuries and here the separate monks' cells were placed around springs on the headland with the abbot's cell lying apart from them. On the cliffs were the library, sweathouse and corn-drying kiln. The chapel was later replaced by a Norman church. Wine and oil were imported from the Mediterranean for use in Tintagel monastery. St. Perran's oratory, also in north Cornwall, survives from this period because it was buried by drifting sand. Similar chapels are more numerous in western Ireland.

The records of missionary journeys, such as the seventh-century life of St. Samson of Dol, make it obvious that sea travel was commonplace. The more difficult journeys were the overland ones and it is these which are recorded in some detail. St. Samson travelled between Brittany and St. Illtud's monastery at Llantwit Major (Llanilltud Fawr) in Glamorgan. Using the sea route from Llantwit Major he came to Padstow and used one of the Cornish transpeninsular routes, probably that to Fowey.

His overland journey, with a wagon-load of holy vessels and manuscripts took him through country where megaliths retained their sanctity. He preached to pagans dancing round a stone idol and cut a cross on it, a common practice in Brittany. Re-use of pagan sites honoured by country folk can also be seen at Ysbytty Cynfyn, twelve miles east of Aberystwyth, where a Bronze Age circle was incorporated in the churchyard wall. Many churchyards in Celtic lands are enclosed by round walls.

St. David, son of St. Non, appears to have been born near the Cardiganshire coast. His main centre, Mynwy (St. David's), lies in a sheltered valley cut into the Pembrokeshire coast plateau. Pilgrims could use a number of landings before walking inland to his shrine, as they frequently did after St. David's began to rank with Rome as a pilgrim centre. At Porth Mawr (Whitesand Bay) and Porth Stinan, both west of St. David's, and at St. Non's Bay south of the little cathedral city, there are old chapels where pilgrims went when they landed. They were using creeks frequented by travellers since the time of the megalith builders, who buried their dead on the headlands of the St. David's peninsula. In the lowlands of England some monasteries were built in deserted Roman forts when the Early English became Christians —Reculver and Dover are examples. At Canterbury sites outside the Roman wall were usually chosen.

The dedications to native Celtic missionaries along the Atlantic coasts of Britain show them to have often worked in provinces which were already well defined culturally. Dedications to St. David, now the patron saint of Wales, are confined to the southern half of Wales and to a few localities across the Bristol Channel and in Brittany, to which there were folk movements in the fifth century. St. Teilo, St. Cadog, St. Illtud and St. Padarn also belong to South Wales, where all established monasteries. St. Deiniol and St. Beuno are the best-known North Wales Celtic saints, and a small building below the floor of the chapel of St. Beuno's monastery at Clynnog Fawr, in Caernarvonshire, may have been built in his day.

Dedications to St. Mungo (Kentigern), and his followers, link North Wales, Cumbria, and the lands of the Votadini in the Lothians and the Southern Uplands. St. Mungo, who later became the patron saint of Glasgow, may have followed in the steps of the Votadini who had already moved from Manaw Gododdin, the land south of the Forth estuary, to North Wales. Dedications to St. Chattan of Antrim are found on the Irish side of the North Channel and in Argyll and the

Western Isles. Here again the fifth-century movement of the Scots of Ireland, to found the kingdom of Dalriada, provided a field for evangelisation among closely related tribes. In 563 St. Columba came from Ireland to Iona, off the west coast of Dalriada, and set up his first monastery there. He is said to have converted the Pictish king Brude at Inverness soon afterwards. Iona was a refuge for dispossessed Anglian kings and princes, and the temporal and spiritual reconquest of Northumbria occurred from this western isle.

The early English settlers were pagans who worshipped gods like Woden, apparently in sacred groves and temples. His name is perpetuated in Woodnesborough in Kent and in names like Wednesbury, Wednesfield and Wednesday. Earthworks were attributed to him, hence Wansdyke. In 597 the Roman Church sent St. Augustine to Canterbury to convert the English, and the wife of King Ethelbert of Kent, who was converted with his court, was a Christian Frankish princess who had her own bishop. He had been assigned a church of St. Martin which had survived from the fourth century. Pope Gregory, at this time, advised missionaries to convert pagan temples into Christian churches "in order that the people may the more familiarly resort to the places to which they have been accustomed." A tradition lingered in Canterbury that St. Pancras' Church there was on the site of a pagan temple.

A princess of Kent who married King Edwin of Northumbria took Christianity there and initiated great gatherings for baptism, by rivers like the Swale at Catterick and the Glen at Yeavering, where warriors had more frequently congregated. Northumbria was St. Cuthbert's mission field, and the Angles there called the see of the bishop of Durham Cuthbertsfolk. St. Cuthbert's body, carried to and fro during the Danish invasions, was eventually enshrined in Durham Cathedral.

The differing views of Celtic and Roman Christianity on, for example, the date of Easter, were resolved at the Synod of Whitby in 664 and, when the Welsh Church was persuaded to conform, both lowland and highland Britain became more firmly linked with the Roman ecclesiastical tradition, and through it, with the imperial Roman heritage. Pope Gregory may have visualised England as a united Roman province rather than as a land of differing pagan kingdoms, and the archbishops who were to be appointed by his mission of 597 were to have had their sees at London and York. But Ethelbert's power had spread outside Kent, and the southern archbishop was appointed to Canterbury, then his chief city. London was unimportant at that time, and its see, like that of York, was a later creation. In the late seventh and early eighth centuries bishops were consecrated at London, whose see included Essex; at Dunwich and Elmham in East Anglia; in Lindsey; at Lichfield (whose see extended north to the Ribble valley), Worcester, Hereford and Leicester in Mercia; at York, Lindisfarne, Hexham and Abercorn in Northumbria; at Winchester and Sherborne in Wessex and at Selsey in Sussex. These are all large sees where it would be necessary to appoint priests to serve churches and from this, and the need to endow them, parish churches and the tithe system gradually spread.

Few of the small churches built by the Anglo-Saxons survive. Their walls have characteristic "long and short work," stones set alternately upright and horizontal, often between pilaster strips. Arcading and doorways are sometimes triangular-headed. Five of these churches can be seen in the valleys of Mercia, at Bradford-on-Avon near Bath, at Brixworth and Earls Barton in the Nene basin near Northampton, at Deerhurst on the Avon near Tewkesbury, and at Great Paxton on the Ouse near St. Neots.

Pagan Anglo-Saxons were buried with their weapons, jewellery and pottery, as were the prehistoric peoples in Britain. Converts to Christianity, however, were buried without grave goods. As late as 630 a king was buried at Sutton Hoo with his ship and magnificent jewellery and weapons. This famous burial, by the Deben estuary in East Suffolk, indicates splendour in personal ornament and skill in craftsmanship, especially in inlay and filigree work and armour. It also shows that pomp and ceremony surrounded Saxon kings, and that music was often performed around well-furnished tables in Saxon halls.

Some converted Anglo-Saxons adopted the monastic life introduced by Augustine, himself a monk, who founded the abbey of St. Peter and St. Paul outside the decaying walls of Canterbury. Reculver and Dover monasteries were built soon afterwards. The life and layout of the first Northumbrian monastery, Aidan's foundation at Lindisfarne, was Celtic. The cells of the monks and that of the abbot were encircled by a wall, as they had been at Iona where Aidan was trained. Other Northumbrian monasteries were set up at Melrose, Tynemouth and Whitby, and later, Benedictine houses were set up at Monkwearmouth, in 674, and at Jarrow, where Bede worked, in 681. Benedictine monasteries in Mercia included Peterborough, and those of East Anglia Bury St. Edmunds.

PLATE VII. a. THE DANCE OF THE DEERMEN at Abbots Bromley, Staffordshire

b. THE MORRIS DANCERS giving their annual performance on Whit-Monday at Bampton, Oxfordshire

PLATE VIII.
J. JAMES, from the
Plynlimon district,
showing features akin
to those of man of
the later
Palaeolithic age

The churches and monasteries of both Anglo-Saxon and Celtic Britain were richly endowed. The beautiful eighth-century silver bowl and brooches buried under the floor of St. Ninian's chapel, near Jarlshof in Shetland, show that the churches were regarded as sanctuaries where the community's wealth might be deposited during Viking raids. The hanging bowl of St. Ninian's may have had a liturgical use. Irish styles of ornament influenced the makers of the St. Ninian's treasure and, with some Saxon traditions, they flowered richly in the illuminated manuscripts of the period. The Lindisfarne Gospels, now in the British Museum, date from about 700 and are adorned with rich and elaborate detail. Across the Irish Sea, the Book of Kells, in Trinity College, Dublin, is the finest surviving illuminated manuscript of this period. These are the works of craftsmen who loved colour and decoration, who finely schematised native animals and plants, and who were in contact with the lands where vines grew more successfully than they did in Britain. These craftsmen and their pupils prepared many manuscripts for monasteries which made a major contribution to West European scholarship. Bede's *Ecclesiastical History of the English Nation*, based on wide reading and exchange of ideas with other scholars, continues to inspire historians. Alcuin of York was a scholar who fostered learning both in England and at the court of Charlemagne. Many centuries of learning were destroyed by Viking raiders, but the Vikings were eventually converted to Christianity, as were many of the peoples across the North Sea, in the homelands of the Anglo-Saxons, by monks such as Willibrord and Wynfrith (St. Boniface), who went out from British monasteries.

Farming economies such as those of the Early English and Britons used three types of land. Arable land was needed for crop-production and pasture was necessary for herds and flocks. If the plough oxen and the breeding stock of cattle were to be sustained over the winter, hay had to be produced on meadowland. In the broad valleys of the lowlands, meadows could readily be laid out, though in the narrower valleys of Celtic Britain meadowland was more restricted. Where mountains rose sharply from the coast, as in the Highlands of Scotland and North Wales, arable patches were also small, and, if the soils were thin, soon lost their fertility. Here tillage was shifted to other arable patches to rest the corn patches. Forests provided grazing for cattle and leafy twigs and undergrowth were recommended as cattle fodder up to the eighteenth century; pigs reared in the forests were important in Anglo-Saxon farming. Herds which ranged widely were liable to be stolen and penalties for cattle-lifting loom large in Anglo-Saxon law.

Co-operation in farming was inevitable in lowland, highland, and Atlantic Britain. Incoming and often related families of Anglo-Saxons, and kinship groups in the west, lived in villages and hamlets and together cleared the forests, laid out and tilled the fields, and co-operated in the struggle against the hostile elements to win harvests and increase their flocks. In thinly peopled and difficult terrain in western Britain, small kinship groups tilled such arable patches as they could dig and their herds grazed a much larger area of moorland which might encircle the arable and have poorly defined mountain limits. So long as the economy was based on oats and cattle the population of these western areas was relatively small. The later introduction of the potato fostered population increase and land hunger.

The better lands of lowland Britain, tilled by an Anglo-Saxon population which quickly increased by immigration and by natural increase, were occupied by about 800 in well-defined parishes whose boundaries were natural features such as streams and ridge crests. The valley and scarplands were often laid out in strip parishes. For shelter and water supply the village might lie on a gravel terrace above the flood plain of the river, or it might be on the spring-line where the porous chalk or Jurassic limestone escarpment met the impervious clays of the valley.

The arable fields were laid out around the farmsteads and usually lay on the lower hillsides or above flood-level in the valley. The meadows would lie along the river and its tributaries, and on the swiftest of these, or by a millpond, there would be a watermill for grinding corn. The upper hillsides and the woodlands would provide pasture for cattle and sheep and pannage for swine. A line of villages on spring-lines or valley margins would have its lands in strips stretching from the scarp crest to the river. For larger villages with greater demands on land, the strip might stretch across the river and up to the top of the scarp beyond it. Groups of strip parishes are frequently found to-day stretching, for example, from the Vale of White Horse to the crest of the Berkshire Downs, or from rivers which flow through the Fenland up into the adjoining heathlands. Beyond the Jurassic scarp, in the great plains of Mercia, in northern England, and in the more limited lowlands of Wales and south-west Britain, strip parishes are less common, but similar demands for arable, meadow and pasture had to be met and parishes came to have a variety of shapes within boundaries which were again well defined by physical features.

This well-planned system depended for its success on communal working of the lands of the village. Joint effort on the land to produce food for a community is world-wide and antedates the Anglo-Saxons. All the ox teams of from two to six oxen, shown in prehistoric carvings on rocks in the Maritime Alps of Italy, are unlikely to have belonged to rich individuals. Prehistoric farmers must have contributed one, or a pair of oxen, to such plough teams, and this was the custom of Anglo-Saxon and medieval farmers. In remote parts of Atlantic Britain the soil was more often turned by the spade or breast plough (*caschrom*), which depended on human motive power. Much of the Highland Zone had ploughs in prehistoric times and in the Dark Ages, and there, as in the lowlands, holdings were often awarded according to the farmer's contribution to the communal plough teams.

These holdings were strips of arable and meadowland grouped in common fields, which were enclosed only by hurdles along their outer margins while they were under corn or hay. They were thrown open after harvest and the herds grazed on the stubble or aftermath. The common arable fields were cultivated under a rotation in which one-third of the land was in autumn-sown corn (wheat, winter beans or rye), one-third in spring corn (barley, oats, spring beans or peas) and the remainder was rested in fallow. This is the basic pattern of the so-called three-field system, and it is a rotation system rather than an indication of the number of the fields of a village. These varied from one huge field worked in thirds to such numbers as were dictated by relief and drainage. Many villages had five or six fields. The size of the strip holdings was similarly determined by the lie of the land. Heavy valley land was ploughed into high ridges to improve drainage. Dark Age and medieval plough ridges in the Midlands, and in the wide valleys between the Jurassic limestone and chalk scarps, can be clearly seen to-day in spite of the efforts of mechanised farming to obliterate them (Plate VIb, p. 133).

A farmer's strips were widely separated and were spread over the fields according to the quality of the land. Equality of opportunity was ensured on land both near and far from the village. As the population increased and more land was cleared for tillage, the same system was extended to it. Boundaries between the strips varied in form, but none of them was broken up by the community's ploughs. Narrow bands a furrow or more wide were left between the cultivated strips on heavy ground. On light soils such as those of the Jurassic scarp, or the chalk-lands of Wessex, and on lands underlain by limestone or gravel in

Wales and south-west England, baulks which were called *landsherds*, *landshares* or *landskers* were built up between the strips. They were low narrow banks of small field-stones and can still be seen in common fields on both sides of the Bristol Channel. Wider unploughed strips of land lay transversely to the ends of the ploughed strips and were the headlands on which the plough teams were turned. On meadowland, and on some arable land, other boundary-marks such as mere stones were placed to mark the ends of strips. These survive, if only as local names; they can still be found in Atlantic Britain and in western Ireland.

Plate VIb (see p. 133) shows a characteristic layout of strip fields at Crimscote in the valley of the Warwickshire Avon near Stratford. The inverted S-shape of the strips on the left margin is a common feature and is thought to be caused by the swing of the plough team as it came towards the headlands. This photograph also suggests that seedling trees fare better in the shelter and greater moisture of the furrows which separate the strips.

Strips in common fields were theoretically a day's work for a plough team and did not always cover an acre. In the lowlands they were long and narrow, but even here small strips occurred in field corners. These short or triangular pieces were called *butts* and *gores* (Plate VIb, p. 133). In western Britain, where communities, available arable patches and open fields were smaller, long strips are less frequently found. But bundles of shorter strips of a quarter or a half-acre, or more, were laid out and shared out in the same way here. The scarce meadowland was even more minutely fragmented. In Celtic Britain kinship groups tilled strips communally. Their common field system, known as *rundale* in Ireland and *runrig* in the Scottish Highlands, lasted until the nineteenth century. Four Welsh settlements still have common arable fields. In isolated parts of Atlantic Britain regular fallowing to rest the land, as part of a rotation system, was not practised, for the infields and outfields which were laid out there were irregular, and not necessarily contiguous, patches which were tilled in turn. The infield, nearer the farm cluster, was more often manured and tilled than the outfield. Both could be subject to a complete reallocation of strips over the years. Farmers would have a share in the arable, perhaps a quarter or an eighth according to the size of the farm cluster, and a "stint" in the large common grazings, based usually on their share of the arable land. This stint determined the number of animals which might be turned out on to the common pasture and was a precaution against overstocking.

PLATE 15 PARGETTED PLASTER between the beams of a timber frame house, probably seventeenth or early eighteenth century, Saffron Walden.

PLATE 16 *a*. COURT BARN, West Pennard, Somerset. Mediaeval manors and monasteries, dependent on dues paid in kind, had to build barns. Windows were reduced to a minimum.

b. JORDANS MEETING HOUSE of the Society of Friends, an eighteenth-century building near Beaconsfield.

In the Highland Zone herdsmen built summer dwellings on pastures which were too far from the main settlement for the flocks and herds to return each evening. In Scotland these summer dwellings in the mountains, or near coastal marshes, were called shielings, and in Ireland *booleys*. In Wales the summer settlement was the *hafod* (or the *lluest* in South Wales) and the permanent home the *hendre*.

When the benefits of resting the land were first realised in England, the first rotation which was practised was one in which half the cropped land was in winter-sown and half in spring-sown crops, while the other half was in fallow. Both "two-field" and "three-field" systems are known to have been practised in Britain, sometimes in the same area. Walter of Henley makes it clear that this was so in the thirteenth century. Though there is little difference in practice between them, the three-field system with its more economical use of the land eventually predominated.

Farming in common fields, widespread over Anglo-Saxon and Celtic England, reached its greatest extent in the Middle Ages. Piecemeal enclosure of common fields began long before parliamentary enclosure, especially where there was a demand for building land, and where there were ambitious landowners or men likely to be in touch with new ideas in farming, like those of Essex. But this communal system, with its many advantages for farmers, imprinted by Anglo-Saxon settlers and fully developed under the medieval manorial system, supported much of Britain until the Industrial Revolution and has still not entirely disappeared.

CHAPTER 7

THE SEA ROVERS

T HE COASTLANDS of Denmark and Norway are fretted with fjords
which carry salt water far inland. Whether shallow with shelving
shores, as in Denmark, or deep, flanked by steep mountains and with
flat land only around river mouths, as in Norway, they form sheltered
nurseries for seamen. Off the mainland coasts of both countries long
sandspits, or a fringe of islands, provide homes for fisher-farmers whose
life is very closely linked with the sea. Skill in seamanship and boat-
building characterised the Anglo-Saxons and Frisians both in their
homelands and in Britain. Yet from the eighth to tenth centuries the
greater skills and superiority in sea power lay with the Danes and the
Norsemen. Their seaborne raids and immigration to north-west Europe
were never countered by seaborne reprisals on the Viking countries.
Trading towns began to be set up in Scandinavia about 800 and trade
goods are likely to have been carried largely in Viking ships. When
raiding and looting were followed by trading, piracy also became a
common Viking activity.

Finds of boats in Jutland and in England show that even large
boats were being built without masts and sails until the seventh
century. The Sutton Hoo ship, buried about 650, lacked a mast.
Although longer than any known Viking ship, being eighty feet long
and fourteen feet amidships, this craft was propelled by nineteen pairs
of oars. Both the Greeks and Romans used sails, and in 560 a Byzantine
historian described the English as barbarians who depended wholly on
oars. But Scandinavian rock carvings of the sixth to eighth centuries
show that masts and keels were slowly evolving and by the eighth
century the Vikings led as shipbuilders and navigators. Plentiful
Scandinavian spruces were available to make masts. Viking leaders
were buried in their ships; these are better preserved in Norwegian
than in British boat burials. The reconstructed Oseberg and Gokstad
ships, finely housed in Oslo, are among the most impressive of the
world's museum exhibits. The Oseberg ship, a ninth-century boat built
for use in sheltered fjords, is seventy feet long and over seventeen feet

amidships. The ocean-going Gokstad ship is seventy-six feet long with a similar breadth. She was built about 950 and in 1893, a replica crossed the Atlantic in twenty-eight days. Fig. 40 shows a replica of another Viking longship.

These ships were clinker-built. Each plank had its lower edge over-lapping that below it, and to which it was fastened by clinched nails, although originally sinews were used. If the planks had to be flush along the boat's sides, they could be mortised into each other. This was a feature of carvel-built boats, which were used later by the Vikings, but were more common in the Mediterranean. Fast Tudor ships built there were called caravels. The Vikings used iron nails, rivets and plates on ocean-going craft, cows' hair and sheep's wool were used for caulking, and the hull was tarred. Warships might be brightly painted above the waterline. Shields were sometimes carried along the gunwale, though on the Gokstad and other ships they covered the holes for the oars and had to be placed elsewhere when the ship was being rowed. The Vikings were not the first, or last, seamen to place animal heads on the prows and sterns of their ships, but their gilded dragons with gaping mouths made their dragon-ships fearsome craft. Faroe islanders' boats still carry vestiges of high Viking prows. The Oseberg ship, which was not a warship, has a splendidly carved and curled prow which matches in its beauty some of the other treasures contained in this burial.

Sweden, the most advanced Scandinavian country, concentrated her efforts during the Viking Period on trade with the Baltic lands and Russia. Denmark and Norway raided and traded in north-west Europe. The Mediterranean peoples, weakened by dissension between the Orthodox and Roman Churches, had not united to confront Islam. Mohammedan warriors had crossed the Straits of Gibraltar in 711, conquered Iberia, and advanced until they were halted by Charles Martel at Poitiers in 732 and hurled back to the Pyrenees. In the early ninth century the Carolingian Empire was at its most powerful. Charlemagne had fortified his north coasts; his frontier reached the Elbe, and Godfred of Denmark had built the isthmian barrier known as the Danevirke to keep him out of Jutland. Charlemagne's Empire seemed impregnable, and finding weaknesses in Britain during sporadic raids before 800, the Vikings made their main attacks there. Twenty years after 814, when Charlemagne died, a weak and disunited France was heavily attacked.

Before the Viking Period, a few centuries of increased warmth in Scandinavia had allowed cultivation to expand northwards and upslope. In Norway farms were built in the seventh century on the high fjell, on what are now only summer pastures. These seventh-century farms were deserted in the Viking Period when permanent settlement retreated to alluvial patches by fjords and lakes, and to coastal farmlands which were usually limited in extent. The pagan Vikings practised polygamy and prided themselves on the numbers of their sons. Over-population could be partly countered by killing off unwanted babies by exposure, but because of the right of primogeniture there was still a surplus of daring and footloose young men who had to take to the sea to raid and trade. Accounts of the size of the Danish and Norse armies may have been exaggerated by those who bore the brunt of them, but the Scandinavian population undoubtedly swarmed at this time in such numbers that neither Denmark nor Norway could support it. There is no evidence that a deterioration of the Scandinavian climate was responsible for the outflow of her armies and families.

Overpopulation in Scandinavia produced a dangerous situation for Britain, which lacked the strength and unity of the Carolingian Empire. Offa of Mercia, the most powerful of her several kings, who might have halted the Vikings, died in 796. Southern England had no outstanding leader; Northumbria and Scotland were too weak to organise resistance. The Norse and Danish Vikings at first raided those British coasts which were most readily accessible to them, the Norse coming to Northumbria and Scotland, and the Danes to south-east England. Women accompanied some raiders and by the mid-ninth century families from both countries were settling in fair numbers in Britain.

The Vikings raided the Wessex coast in 785, Lindisfarne monastery in 793 and Jarrow monastery in 794. The Jarrow raid was unprofitable and the Norsemen went next to northern Scotland and eventually round it and into the Irish Sea. In north and west Scotland the Norsemen found an island-fringed land with its mountains split by fjords. It was similar to their own country, a land which also turned its face to the sea. Their own land, Norge, North Way or Norway, took its name from their western seaway which linked the scattered communities between the North Cape and Oslo fjord. A comparable seaway, the Atlantic route, existed along the west coast of Britain; they used it and established widely dispersed garrisons and communities along it (Fig. 41).

There may have been some Norse settlement in the Northern Isles before the eighth century. The Shetland Isles closely resemble many Norwegian islands while the more fertile red soils of Orkney would have been new to the Norsemen; they settled both over the centuries and

PLATE IX.   ROBERT BURNS, showing features of the dark-haired longheads,
a large element in the British population
By courtesy of the Director of the National Portrait Gallery
Portrait by Alexander Nasmyth

PLATE X.   CHARLES DARWIN, showing features similar to those of the
beaker-making immigrants of about 1900–1800 B.C.

By kind permission of Sir Charles Darwin Portrait by George Richmond

FIG. 40
Reconstruction of a Viking ship, the Hugin, which sailed from Denmark to Britain
in 1949

used them as stations on their long sea routes. When the Vikings came
to the north and west of Scotland the coasts were already peopled by
farmers who lived in decaying wheelhouses, in corbelled stone, or
beehive, huts, and in thick-walled duns or defended homesteads.
Among them lived Celtic priests from Ireland who are remembered
by *papa* place-names. Monasteries like Iona housed larger groups of
monks.

At Jarlshof in Shetland, Viking families from Møre and Trøndelag,
which lies north of Møre, around Trondheim, (many early Vikings
came from these two provinces), built the last village on a site which
was first settled about 2,000 B.C. Their descendants occupied Jarlshof
for five centuries, replacing the farm buildings, but using the Viking
farmstead until the thirteenth century when a new farmstead was built

nearby. They raised stock, grew corn and kiln-dried it, trapped wild-fowl, collected their eggs and fished. Their economy must have been comparable to that carried on from the black houses of the Western Isles (Plate XII, p. 157), homesteads not unlike Viking farms. The Norwegian for soapstone is *klebber*. It is fireproof and could be carved into household containers and loomweights (*kle* in Old Norse). Soapstone was widely worked by the Vikings in Norway and exported to Denmark. Shetland's soapstone may have been one of its attractions for the Norsemen and Kleberg and Clibberswick are among many place-names of Norse origin there.

Jarlshof, in the lee of Sumburgh Head, the southernmost Shetland promontory, was owned in the fifteenth century by Sir David Sinclair of Sumburgh. He was chief magistrate of Shetland and captain of the palace guard in Bergen. This fine west Norwegian Hanseatic city still has citizens with Scottish surnames. Orkney was as well settled as Shetland by the Vikings and the Northern Isles ceased to be Scandinavian politically only in 1468 when Christian I of Norway and Denmark pledged them to James III of Scotland as part of his daughter's dowry. The islanders' variant of the Viking tongue, the Norn speech, lasted in Orkney until the mid-eighteenth century and for a little longer in Shetland. From 1940 to 1945 Shetland was the base from which boats far smaller than the longships, but manned by Norwegians as brave as their Viking ancestors, went back to the coasts of occupied Norway.

The names given by Viking settlers to physical features and farms survive throughout the Northern Isles. Homesteads are *bister*, *setr* or *by*. Cattle folds are *quoy* or *garth*; and *brekka* (slope), *hamarr* or *klettr* (cliff or rocky bank), *eid* (isthmus), *gja* (ravine), *vagr* and *vik* (bay or inlet) can all be matched in Norway to-day.

The Norse system of odal tenure was transplanted to the Northern Isles, and although the redemption of odal rights occurred in the twelfth century largely to provide funds for the building of St. Magnus' Cathedral, it lingered there until 1587. If a man wished to sell odal land, that is enclosed arable and meadowland held by the family, he must first offer it to his own kinsmen. If it were sold out of the family, his next of kin could redeem it from the purchaser, at the selling price, within a limited time. According to the Gulathing Law this was a year in Norway. In Sark, in the Channel Islands, the custom of primogeniture in inheritance of the family farm, and the right of anyone within a stated degree of kinship to buy back a farm sold outside the

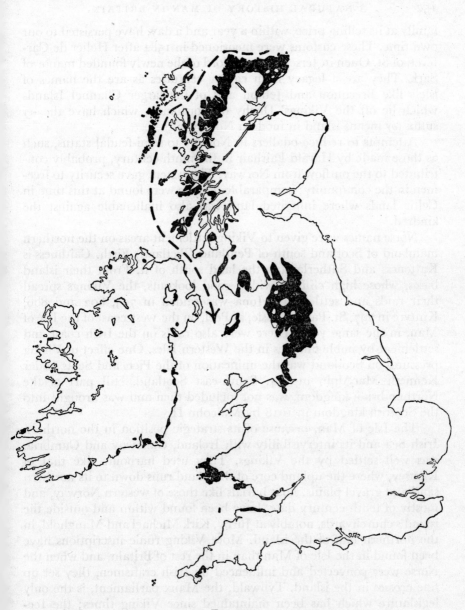

FIG. 41

Areas of Norse raiding and settlement in Atlantic Britain

family at its selling price, within a year and a day, have persisted to our own time. These customs were mentioned in 1584 after Helier de Carteret, of St. Ouen in Jersey, became lord of the newly founded manor of Sark. They are a legacy from earlier centuries as are the names of islets like Brecqhou and Jethou and of the larger Channel Islands which lie off the Vikings' Duchy of Normandy, which have the -*ey* suffix (*øy* means island in modern Norwegian).

Attempts to reduce odallers in Norway to semi-feudal status, such as those made by Harald Fairhair in the ninth century, probably contributed to the outflow from Norway. The system gave security to freemen in the community; comparable tenures were found at this time in Celtic lands where inherited land was also inalienable against the kindred.

Norse names were given to Viking settlement areas on the northern mainland of Scotland south of Pentland (Pictland) Firth. Caithness is Katteness and Sutherland is the land south of it. From their island bases, whose high cliffs provided good lookouts, the Vikings spread their raids and settlements. Iona was raided in 795, 802 and 806, Kintyre in 797, St. Patrick's Isle, at Peel, on the west coast of the Isle of Man, in the same year. There were also raids on the Irish coast and settlement by noble families in the Western Isles. One effect of Viking pressures on Scotland was the unification of the Picts and Scots under Kenneth MacAlpin in 844. South-east Scotland, still part of the Northumbrian kingdom, was not included then and was brought into the Scottish kingdom in 1018 by Malcolm II.

The Isle of Man, because of its strategic position in the northern Irish Sea and its intervisibility with Ireland, Galloway and Cumbria, was well settled by the Vikings. They used harbours like that of Ramsey, where the upland core of the island runs down to its northern sand and gravel plains. Boat burials like those of western Norway, and mostly of tenth-century date, have been found within and outside the island's churchyards, notably at Jurby, Kirk Michael and Maughold, in the northern half of the island. More Viking runic inscriptions have been found in the Isle of Man than in the rest of Britain, and when the Norse were converted and influenced by Irish craftsmen, they set up fine crosses in the island. Tynwald, the Manx parliament, is the only legislature which has been maintained since Viking times; the Icelandic Thing is a recent revival. Viking long-houses have been found in the centre of the Isle of Man.

Boat burials also occur on the west Scottish coast and in the

Hebrides. These were the Sudrøya, as distinct from the Northern Isles, and with Øya Man gave rise to the medieval bishopric of Sodor and Man. It was first under the archbishop of Trondheim, a fertile area whence many of the settlers came, then under York, and the Manx portion is still the bishopric of Sodor and Man.

Raiding by Norsemen in Atlantic Britain was followed by over-wintering, by the establishment of military bases like Dublin, in 841, and then of colonies. Fig. 41 shows the main bases and settlements of the Vikings. Around Wales their probable island bases have names like Anglesey (Ongulsey), Priestholm, Bardsey, Ramsey and Skokholm, and they would have used the great Pembrokeshire harbour which they described as Melrfjord, a fjord with sandbanks, now Milford Haven. A clinker-built longship was found in the Usk estuary in 1878; one of the last Viking raids used this river in 1087. In south Pembrokeshire, Gower and the Vale of Glamorgan, place-names suggest that some Norsemen settled as farmers and traders; among them may have been mercenaries hired from the Dublin garrison by Welsh princes. Swansea, whose medieval form was Sweyneseye, may first have developed as a Norse trading village on the Tawe estuary. Cardiff, Haverfordwest and Cardigan all traded with the Vikings of Ireland, exchanging slaves, horses, honey, corn and malt for wine, furs and whale oil. A hoard of English and Arab coins, minted between 899 and 927, was lost or hidden by a Viking trader at Bangor in north-west Wales.

In face of the Vikings the English were led by Alfred. In Wales, the same threat brought a measure of unity under Rhodri Mawr of Gwynedd, who reigned in north-west Wales until his death in 878. Well described as Great, these leaders and their sons defeated the Vikings and gave their peoples a period of peace and friendship. A grandson of Rhodri Mawr, Hywel Dda (the Good), reigned from 916 to 950 in friendship with Alfred's son and grandson. Hywel was accepted as the leading Welsh prince and he enforced loyalty to the English kings. Like Alfred he was a lawgiver and compiled the legal code which was used in Wales until the Act of Union in 1536.

Traces of Norse colonies of the tenth and eleventh centuries are numerous in the three Lake District counties and in the adjoining Pennine dales. Memorial stones fashioned by Norse-Irish craftsmen are found there. The high cross at Gosforth, near the west Cumberland coast, is the best known. The people of north-west England and Nor-way to-day use words like fell (*fjell*), foss for waterfall and gate for street. Thwait has its equivalent in the Norwegian *tveit*, a clearing, or a meadow in a wood. All are common elements of place-names in the Lake District and in the coast plains and valleys around it.

Outside the areas shown on Fig. 41, the coastal fringes and their hinterlands were unaffected by the Vikings. In Cornwall, peaceful stock-rearing communities existed on the coast in the tenth century at Mawgan Porth, four and a half miles north of Newquay, at Gwithian and other sites round St. Ives Bay, and at Gunwalloe on the west coast of the Lizard peninsula. Frisian traders coming there in search of tin brought with them bar-lip pots from the lower Rhineland. Several generations of Cornish villagers copied these pots which have two lips with a bar to protect the thongs by which they were suspended over the fire. Mawgan Porth must have been only one of many British settlements which were delivered from the fury of the Northmen. When it was overwhelmed by gale-driven sand the villagers moved inland to St. Mawgan. They might have done so earlier had the Vikings been a constant menace.

Island bases served well for the early raids by small groups of ships. By the mid-ninth century larger invasion fleets were bringing Viking armies into estuaries like those of the Thames and Seine, and penetration of the interior by highly mobile forces began. Coastal fortresses were built for overwintering, then and later. By the late tenth century large and well-engineered base camps were being built in Denmark for the armies of leaders like Cnut. Trelleborg, near the west shore of Zealand, has sixteen large barrack buildings within its main ramparts and fifteen others between the main and outer ramparts (Fig. 42). This fortress dates from 975 to 1050 and Swein Forkbeard's army could have gone from it to conquer England. Warham Camp, near Wells-next-the-Sea, on the north Norfolk coast, is possibly one of the Vikings' East Anglian base camps. The boat-shaped form of the Trelleborg barrack buildings may have originated in the days when crews hauled their boats ashore and sheltered under them. Similar Danish fortresses have been found on the shores of Limfjord and Mariager Fjord in Jutland, and in the centre of Odense, the capital of the island of Fyn.

Danish warfleets attacked the Isle of Sheppey in 835, East Anglia in 841 and in 851 the Danes wintered in Thanet. Fourteen years later they returned to Thanet, made peace with Kent, and then the Great Army wintered in East Anglia. In their campaign, from 865 to 875, their mobility, based on commandeered horses, gave them control throughout the Lowland Zone and in Northumbria. Ill-armed Saxon thegns,

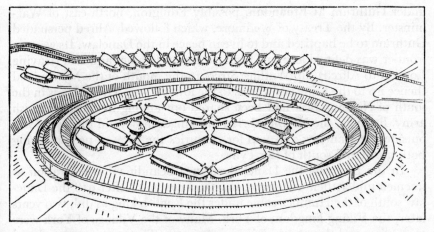

FIG. 42

Reconstruction of Trelleborg camp, Denmark, and its groups of boat-shaped houses

who gave military service to minor kings in return for lands to which they quickly returned, were no match for the Danish armies. The young and scholarly Alfred of Wessex retreated to the Isle of Athelney in the Somerset marshlands. Here he organised an army of thegns who also rode to battle (both sides fought on foot) and were versed like the Danes in surprise attacks. He later built warfleets and outmatched them on the sea.

Alfred has been compared with Charlemagne who may have been his model. As a child he was taken to Rome by his father and was well-versed in Latin as well as English. His efforts to revivify learning after wartime devastation, and to dignify the common language, were most remarkable. He codified the English laws and initiated the Anglo-Saxon Chronicle which recorded each year's events until the Norman Conquest. He made London a strong fortress. Like Charlemagne he fought successfully against the pagans, and he and his sons made England a united kingdom. The Wessex royal family provided a line of very able leaders in the ninth and tenth centuries in Egbert, Alfred (871-899), his son Edward the Elder (900-924), his daughter Ethel-fleda and Edward's son Athelstan (924-940). The last three re-conquered the Danelaw and Alfred's great-grandson Edgar (955-975) inherited a relatively peaceful and prosperous England.

Alfred's army advanced in 878 from Somerset to defeat the Danes

under Guthrum at Ethandun, possibly Edington, north-east of Warminster. By the Treaty of Wedmore, which followed, Alfred persuaded
Guthrum to be baptised and to live in peace in the Danelaw. Its western
frontier was defined as a line from the lower Thames and Lea (leaving
London to Alfred), up Watling Street to the mouth of the Mersey and
thence up to the Lune and across to the lower Tyne. There, lands in the
south of Northumbria had been shared out among an earlier Danish
army. Bernicia, the Northumbrian sub-kingdom beyond the Tyne, was
outside the Danelaw and was for centuries the prey of peoples living
both north and south of the Tyne.

In the Danelaw the Danes lived in a Scandinavian federation as
freemen under their own earls, laws and customs. After 918 the Danelaw south of the Humber came under the English king as did, two years
later, the Viking kingdom of York. Many of the Vikings of York were
merchants and the port had its own coinage. The town prospered and
by 1000 had a population of about 8,000. The walls of the port of
Chester were repaired by a Viking merchant. The functions of these
ports would have been those of contemporary trading towns which
have been excavated around the Baltic and along Oslo Fjord. The
"five boroughs" of the Danelaw, all former Roman towns, were both
military and trading centres. Lincoln, Stamford, Leicester, Derby and
Nottingham centred on their riversides and on their earthen fortresss
mounds. Other towns, like Thetford, had similar strongholds.

The reconquest of the Danelaw was carried out by establishing
garrisons similar to those in the five boroughs. Afterwards Athelstan
was secure as king of Wessex, Mercia, Northumbria, the Danelaw and
parts of Cornwall. Norwegians from Dublin menaced his brothers, who
succeeded him, but England was free from Danish raids until 980.
However, after this date southern England and Cheshire were menaced
in the reign of Ethelred the Unready. In 991, Olaf Tryggvason, later
the king of Norway, invaded with a fleet of nearly a hundred ships. The
practice of buying peace for payments of silver then started. The payments of Danegeld, which brought only temporary respite, are estimated to have increased from £10,000 in 991 to £48,000 in 1012, and
most of this silver enriched Scandinavian rather than English estates.
The inept Ethelred ordered a massacre of all Danes in England in 1002,
during which Swein Forkbeard's sister Gunnhild was murdered. Swein
Forkbeard, the Danish king, raided the Thames and made an unsuccessful attack on London, which was then well organised by her
merchants and independent of the official capital, Winchester. Swein

PLATE XI.
LORD RIBBLESDALE,
Tall, sparely built,
straight features, long
face, a "Nordic" type
By courtesy of the Trust-
ees of the Tate Gallery
Portrait by J. S. Sargent

PLATE XII. BLACK HOUSE, Uist, Hebrides. Built of unmortared stone, with smoke hole in roof

returned in 1013, to the Humber, and after reconquering the Danelaw was followed by his son Cnut.

After Ethelred's death, Cnut became the first of the Danish kings of England. Cnut did not regard England as a colony but as his main kingdom. He was as able as many of his Wessex predecessors and in his peaceful reign the English and Danes were reconciled by the recognition of the equal validity of their languages, by Cnut's appointment of Anglo-Saxons to high office in the Church and by his use of Anglo-Saxon laws. He paid off his Danish army with about £80,000 of Danegeld, rather than with confiscated Anglo-Saxon lands. Cnut made peace with all rulers except Duke Robert of Normandy. When he died in 1035, his kingdom of Denmark, Norway, England and the Hebrides was split up and England was ruled first by Hardacnut and, after 1042, by his half-brother Edward the Confessor.

Viking armies assaulted Britain in the year of the Norman Conquest and even after it. In 1066 a fleet of 250 ships assembled in Orkney and, led by Harald Hardrada, went up the Humber and Ouse. They captured York but were beaten by the English king Harold at Stamford Bridge. William the Conqueror carried out a "scorched earth" policy in northern England after 1066 which united Anglo-Saxon and Danish forces. They captured Ely and Peterborough but the Danes were bought off by William I and went back to Denmark.

The terrible energy of the Vikings was transmuted in the time of Cnut into wise administration of an increasingly prosperous kingdom. The Danelaw was becoming anglicised and the population of England was increasing. Deforestation occurred everywhere as villages and large clearings were made. When the Domesday Book was drawn up to survey property which might yield defence taxes like Danegeld, a minimum of 60,000 people lived in East Anglia. Norfolk and Suffolk had eight towns of up to 5,000 people and 1,365 taxable localities. Ipswich and Norwich thrived on trade and by the late eleventh century Norwich had a population of at least 6,600 and about twenty-five churches, many of which had Danish dedications. Thetford, defended by ditches and a great mound, was a town of about 5,000, the second largest in East Anglia. The Rhineland sent millstones to many towns in southeast England. If wood became scarce, peat was available in the Fens and in the marshes behind the Yare and Bure estuaries. The cutting of fen peat, which produced the Broads, increased until it reached its medieval peak. Coastal saltpans continued to be worked.

The Domesday Survey of East Anglia lists 84,000 sheep, 18,000 pigs and over 7,000 goats. Cattle would be numerous and draught oxen common. Oats, wheat and peas were grown, deer and wild boar hunted; fish and shellfish came from the rivers and the sea. This economy must have been widespread during the tenth and eleventh centuries and many families must have become increasingly prosperous and numerous in spite of the burden of Danegeld payments.

In the Danelaw freemen predominated. Fines for murder were imposed there according to the status of the victim; elsewhere in England it was the rank of the murdered man's master which was taken into account. Settlers from Scandinavia, if they were wealthy, kept slaves for the harder work. Slaves were bought and sold, as they were by the Anglo-Saxons, and were still being sent overseas from Bristol as late as the eleventh century. Some freemen were poor men owing service and dues to landowners, but they owned their own land. These free peasants, the sokemen, might be bound to large estates or sokes but their landholding, however small, gave them more freedom than a medieval feudal peasant. The patches of land given to free men in the Danish armies, which varied with rank and service, often took the name of the owner, with the suffix -by to denote his homestead. It often came to mean a village, and settlements with -thorp suffixes were originally dependent villages made as offshoots of earlier settlements. Both suffixes are common in place-names in the former Danelaw and in the East Midlands and Scandinavia farmers still refer to their farmsteads as their tofts.

The Danelaw was divided into hundreds, perhaps of ploughs or warriors originally, and administered from wapentakes. *Wapentake* is a Danish word and refers to the brandishing of arms when members of the Thing met. It came to mean the district from which members of the Thing were drawn and became synonymous with hundred. The hundreds of Norfolk and the wapentakes of Lincolnshire have largely Danish names.

When Alfred's son Edward and his daughter, the Lady Ethelfleda of Mercia, reconquered the Danelaw, they established a network of fortified boroughs as they pushed eastwards. Some boroughs were ruined towns which had been founded by the Romans, others, like Oxford and Wallingford, were new strategic centres. These boroughs, and the Danelaw boroughs which the English took over, became administrative and military headquarters of shires. Lincoln, Derby, Nottingham, Leicester, Northampton, Huntingdon, Cambridge and Bedford shires originated in this way. The shires of Anglo-Saxon

Wessex were also incorporated into the shire system. The boroughs were peopled by burgesses who held their tenements at a fixed rent from the king. The Domesday Survey names over seventy boroughs, but there are many omissions, including London and Winchester.

Boroughs became trading centres, and if they lay on navigable rivers and on former frontiers between kingdoms and their hinterlands containing areas with contrasting land uses, important fairs developed within or beyond their walls. St. Giles Fair at Oxford, between Mercia and Wessex, and Stourbridge Fair at Cambridge, between Mercia and East Anglia are early examples. Boroughs, furthermore, had their own mints. King Athelstan, in laying down the number of moneyers that each should have, gave one to the smallest, the ports three each, Winchester six, Canterbury seven and London eight moneyers. The dies were distributed from London.

In Bede's day London was already re-established as a busy port, and when England was peaceably linked with the Scandinavian homelands of the sea rovers, London's position gave her advantages over south-coast harbours. Danish merchants settled in London and emerged in the eleventh century not merely as traders but as kingmakers. London provided £10,500 of the Danegeld which Cnut collected to pay off his army. The Danish merchants founded churches dedicated to St. Olaf, and, outside the city wall, to St. Clement Danes' and had their own sokes granted by the king within the city. Merchants from Cologne and other Rhineland cities also settled in London, as did Frisians from Flanders. Frisians had traded to many British shores during the centuries of Viking raiding and Alfred engaged many of them to man his fleet. Nobles, and prelates such as the bishops of Norwich and Worcester, had houses in London. Such houses, in London and other towns, later came to be an investment rather than points through which supplies could go to country estates; the abbess of Barking, for example, had twenty-eight houses in London. But whatever their function, these homes of merchants were within the city walls. The movement outside the walls of London, and the beginnings of a dichotomy vital for English history, started when Edward the Confessor built his palace and his abbey west of, and beyond, the city walls.

Within the boroughs many householders had substantial crofts, and outside them they held strips in common arable fields and meadows, and shares in the common pastures. The link with the countryside would be further strengthened by street traders and by countryfolk coming to the fairs and markets. Guildhalls began to be built in the cities for men to drink their guild. In Athelstan's reign there was a peace guild in London to suppress theft; guilds existed in the late eleventh century at Canterbury, Dover and Winchester. Guilds later fostered civic unity in many boroughs.

King Alfred aided the recovery of the Church from wartime pillage and his sons created new sees such as Wells and Crediton and completed the minster which he had planned at Winchester. As the Danelaw was reconquered and the Danes there converted, the English kings granted estates in it to the Church. The archbishop of York was given lands in Nottinghamshire on which Southwell Minster was founded. Monasteries devastated by the Vikings were not always rebuilt. When Northumbria was reconquered, the see of Lindisfarne was moved to Chester-le-Street, once an important fort on the Roman road to Hadrian's Wall. This see was centred on Durham after 995.

The tenth century saw a great Benedictine revival in north-west Europe. The learned Dunstan, who became archbishop of Canterbury in 960, was mainly responsible for England's part in it. The archbishops of Canterbury and York, in contact with the reorganised monasticism, founded, with the support of the nobility, new monasteries such as Ramsey in Huntingdonshire, Cerne Abbas in Dorset, Eynsham in Oxfordshire and the abbey of Burton-on-Trent. Ruined abbeys like Thorney, Peterborough and Ely were rebuilt. Monks replaced secular clergy in these abbeys and the quality of parish priests, many of them poor men, gradually improved. Cnut, son of the pagan Swein Forkbeard, made many gifts to Benedictine abbeys, enforced the payment of tithes to support the churches and finally suppressed pagan elements which were lingering in the Danelaw. His contemporary, Olaf of Norway, who became the patron saint of Norway's young Church, was attended by English priests who were part of a missionary effort of long standing there.

The Vikings were raiders and pirates, but they were also skilled navigators who made wide conquests and established colonies far distant from their homelands. Had the longships of the Vikings been larger and more speedy, and their political organisation less liable to fragmentation under weak kings, England might have kept her links with Scandinavia across the North Sea. But the last Danish kings were inept men, and Edward the Confessor, the last Anglo-Saxon king, looked across narrower seas to Normandy and promised the succession to Duke William. England passed after 1066 into the orbit of France. The sea rovers were confined to their homelands by their Norman

PLATE XIII. PREACHER'S HOUSE, Ludlow. West Midlands timber work above an earlier ground floor in stone

PLATE XIV. A VICTORIAN ROOM, Strangers' Hall, Norwich

cousins and after some last Norse raids on England and Wales this activity ceased.

The Vikings contributed to the ethnic amalgam of Britain which in their day already had Celtic, Roman and Anglo-Saxon components. They readily adopted new ways and new skills. In Normandy the descendants of Viking settlers became great church-builders and built the splendid abbeys of Caen and Jumièges. There was also a remarkable twelfth-century phase of church-building in Denmark. The Vikings and their Norman descendants had a more lasting influence on Britain than on any other European country. The streams of experience which came together in Britain produced results far beyond a summation of their respective traditions. A certain amount of objectivity, and with it of original initiative, is apt to emerge from contacts of peoples if hostility is not too bitterly continued. Contacts of diverse traditions give a measure of liberation from the heavy hand of established and enforced custom and belief.

CHAPTER 8

THE PERIOD AFTER 1066: A BRIEF REVIEW

I N THE Norman and subsequent periods we pass into phases for which documentary and material evidence is more abundant and has been interpreted from many standpoints. Events of the past millennium will therefore not be treated chronologically but rather under various headings such as dwellings, rural settlements, towns, churches and castles, because these are outward and visible signs of the adaptations of the peoples of Britain to their environments. The brief general sketch which follows is a prelude to these chapters; there are inevitably many omissions from it.

The Norman Conquest strengthened political, economic and cultural links with continental Europe and, above all, with France. Lowland Britain, fitted by nature to bear the strongest imprint of the Norman manorial pattern, produced food for an increasing population and wool for export. Boroughs and ports multiplied; London, York, Winchester, Canterbury, Lincoln, Oxford, Thetford, Norwich and Ipswich were thriving communities before 1066, as were, nearer the Highland Zone, Chester, Hereford, Worcester, Gloucester, Bristol and Exeter. The ports of southern England prospered as medieval exporters of wool and importers of wine. Southampton and other ports took in wines from Bordeaux for the nobility and merchant class; the wines of Aquitaine and elsewhere were a desirable alternative to supplies of impure water.

The Cinque Ports, which had to produce men and ships in wartime, were Hastings, Romney, Hythe, Dover and Sandwich. Winchelsea and Rye were added later and minor harbours were affiliated to the main ports, as was Folkestone to Dover. Their privileges included the holding of a court of admiralty under a judge acting for the Lord Warden of the Cinque Ports. Continental trade connections and judicial and administrative organisation expanded. European merchants and craftsmen settled in Britain. In 1250 the Hanseatic League established Merchants of the Steelyard in London, and they played a considerable part in the city's commerce. Flemish weavers came in during the reign of Edward

III (1327-77) and were followed, in Tudor and Stuart times, by French and Flemish Huguenots. East Anglian woollen manufacturers owed much to Flemish immigrants.

Highland Britain, with meagre resources for grain-production, and disadvantages of position when trade flourished mainly along the coasts of the English Channel, at first had few rapidly growing medieval boroughs and ports. In Wales the boroughs were Anglo-Norman foundations with a military function. Aloof behind their strong walls, and dominated by their castles and English communities, they fostered mutual hostility between town and country folk. The fortress ports of Edward I in North Wales controlled the narrow coastal lowlands and aimed at containment of the interior. Their port function was initially limited to landing men and provisions from the sea (Fig. 43 and Plate XXIX, p. 272). As in other parts of Wales, these medieval boroughs played roles similar to those of the Roman forts. They were often on or near their sites.

Norman army leaders were rewarded with lands of the defeated English and, when the Domesday Survey was compiled in 1086, at least four thousand Norman knights and about two hundred barons held land in England. The distribution of land to trusted followers took into account the vulnerability of the south-east English coast, and of East Anglia, and the need to guard and penetrate the Welsh Border and the moorlands of northern and south-west Britain. The lands of the barons were often in many scattered units, thereby restricting their power and ensuring co-operation with the king. No long struggles between kings and feudal lords developed as they did in France with Champagne, Burgundy, Brittany, and with the kings of England in their capacity as lords of Normandy and Aquitaine.

The establishment of *Curia Regis*, with officials attending its assembly for lesser matters and tenants-in-chief for major problems, was an important administrative step. The smaller assemblies developed in due course into the Privy Council, and the larger ones were a germ which contributed to the evolution of Parliament. Norman knights gained experience in local government in shire and hundred courts which William I and his sons took over from the Anglo-Saxon system. Henry II established regional assizes at which twelve jurymen could testify in support of a claimant before the king's justices. In Edward I's reign inquiries into the evidence for local custom (*Placita de quo warranto*), and the granting of charters to boroughs, were further steps which gave sanction to local custom under royal authority. This recognition of local diversity within national unity was facilitated by the fact that common law (i.e. law based on custom, *droit coûtumier*) was a Norman as well as an English institution.

The Normans brought into Britain improved techniques in the designing of arches and vaults. We speak of round arches and barrel vaults as the Norman style; its continental equivalent, the Romanesque style, derives from the suggested adaptation of the round arch from Imperial Roman forms. Norman building styles were applied to the strong square keeps which replaced the wooden castles from which the Normans first maintained their power over the country (Plate XXVIII, p. 253), and to their splendid churches, monasteries and cathedrals, equally safe strongholds of their faith.

After the Conquest the Church tried to impose the rule of celibacy for the secular clergy of the parishes, as had Anglo-Saxon reformers and in the thirteenth century many efforts were made to provide the parishes with learned and celibate priests, who, in the feudal system, ranked as freemen. Celtic and Saxon saints were still honoured, but under the Normans dedications were more often made to the Virgin Mary. Lady chapels were built in many cathedrals, usually at their east ends, where they helped to support choirs and chancels raised to impressive heights.

In the late eleventh and in the twelfth century, many parish churches were erected in an increasingly peaceful and ordered country-side. Benedictine monks had settled in England before the Conquest. They usually served townsfolk. Norman lords who controlled Highland Britain from walled boroughs endowed Benedictine priories which were often built in the shadow of the lord's castle. Priories isolated in the countryside might be fortified, like Ewenny Priory in Glamorgan. Many, however, felt that the rule of St. Benedict was not being strictly observed and among them was Stephen Harding of Sherborne, sub-prior of a small group which sought the seclusion of the woods of Cîteaux. As abbot of Cîteaux from 1109 to 1122 he insisted on solitude in the countryside, and he and St. Bernard planned the system of Cistercian daughter houses. The first English house was established at Waverley in Surrey in 1118, but it was in north and west Britain that the Cistercians found solitude. The valleys of the Yorkshire Wolds and the Pennines, partly devastated by William I, and those of Wales, where thirteen Cistercian abbeys were built, attracted these monks with their simple routine (Plate 26, p. 229). They laboured in fields around the abbeys, and there, and on outlying granges staffed by lay brothers,

PLATE 17   IGHTHAM VILLAGE, Kent.

PLATE 18 BOURTON-ON-THE-WATER, showing the attractive buildings built in the
Cotswolds from local limestones for many centuries.

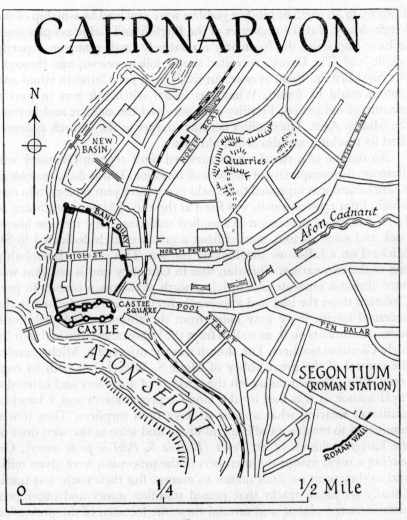

FIG. 43
Caernarvon, a bastide town founded by Edward I

which were often well-run sheep farms, they introduced better standards of farming into the uplands of Britain.

The Normans came into a Britain which, in the Danelaw, had only recently had many pagans, or, in the west, practised a form of Christianity which tolerated older beliefs. Among these had been a recognition of an earth goddess, a source of fertility in crops and animals.

Tributes to an earth or mother goddess were replaced by worship of the Virgin Mary. But the mysteries of the English and Celtic peoples seem to have impressed the Normans, a relatively small group in a partly hostile land. The Church recruited simple folk as priests, and throughout rural Britain, then, as now, survivals from pre-Christian ritual and custom could be found. What was called witchcraft was in part a mixture of old beliefs. Fertility cults survived throughout and beyond the Middle Ages. The conflict became sharper as the Church systematised its teaching and discarded old ideas.

An outline of a ritual which survived until 1837 in Guernsey will illustrate the complexity of the web of tradition. It was *La Chevauchée de S. Michel* and was supposed to be held every third year on a certain day which, from 1599 onwards, was fixed at the end of May or beginning of June. An armed procession in specified uniforms, some men on horseback and some on foot, started from a priory church dedicated to St. Michael on a hill-brow overlooking the sea. This church is probably one of the two earliest Christian sites in Guernsey and is on what was once almost a separate island, lying north of the main island. In pre-Christian times the islet had apparently been specially dedicated to the ancestral spirits, if we may judge from the abundance of prehistoric stone monuments on it, as well as from the importance attached to it by early Christian teachers. The church was the priory of S. Michel, under the control of the great abbey of Mont S. Michel, but with its own court. When the procession left the territory of the priory and entered a royal manor, it was met by the king's representatives and a band of musicians wearing what appear to have been surplices. Thus it was conducted to receive an offering of bread and wine at the west door of the harbour church of St. Peter (*Ecclesia S. Petri in portu maris*). On leaving a royal manor the members of the procession were given milk, and so they went on from manor to manor. But their route was traditionally set along tracks that passed standing stones and other prehistoric sacred places, and around these the footmen of the procession would perform ritual dances. Some of these stones became boundary stones between manors, as so often happened in medieval times. The footmen were given permission by proclamation to kiss any woman along the route, provided that no woman was to be kissed by more than one of them. These are but a few selected items from a mass of detail but they show that there are probably regal, manorial, ecclesiastical, megalithic and fertility-cult components in this conglomeration.

It was at the foot of one of the great standing stones that, until modern times, the people of the parish concerned burned the old year in effigy in November. The effigy was called *Bout de l'an*, i.e. the end of the vegetation year, and was burned on what became the festival of All Souls; the day was later adjusted to 5th November as in Britain. One district of the island, formerly rich in megaliths, was until recently supposed to be under the guardianship of supernatural animals. Indeed, it may be that the whole island was sacred to ancestral spirits and it unfortunately became notorious for witchcraft trials in the sixteenth and seventeenth centuries, probably as a result of the persistence of megalithic cults. The neighbouring island of Jersey, invaded and largely held by a French nobleman for a while in the fifteenth century, had its attention diverted from these ancient rites by military considerations.

The old traditions gave the country folk of Britain scope for dance, song and story. The Roman Church sought to direct these energies, for example by the spread of Christmas and other carols, several of which have come down to us from the fourteenth and fifteenth centuries. The Puritan middle class later frowned upon the play of fancy in them and in the stained-glass windows and frescoes of the medieval churches.

In France the long and difficult struggle between the king and the sovereign nobles led to a close political link between Church and king, whereas in England the king's stronger position led, rather, to clashes. William I, Henry II, Edward III, Henry VIII and Elizabeth I all stiffly resisted ecclesiastical claims. In France both Crown and Church were closely linked with the medieval university of Paris, and the Sorbonne attempted to give authoritative decisions on disputed theological questions. In Scotland the senior universities of St. Andrews (founded 1412) and Glasgow (1451) were associated with medieval bishoprics; they were founded during the Franco-Scottish Alliance. In England there were no medieval universities at Canterbury, York, or London and neither Oxford nor Cambridge had a medieval bishopric. Centralisation has been kept in check among us until modern times when the elaborate technique of administration and the complexity of social legislation are making local diversity more difficult to maintain. A belief that diverse areas of Highland Britain, with their special problems, are neglected by the central administration, expresses itself in nationalist movements which have not been checked by the setting up of Scottish and Welsh Offices under Secretaries of State. In both countries tenacity of tradition and an alert national consciousness are still preserved.

The English language received many additions from Norman

French after the Conquest. Beef (*boeuf*) mutton (*mouton*) and pork (*porc*) were served at feasts of Norman knights. Ox, sheep and swine are the names used by herdsmen who had to tend the animals rather than feast upon them. The victors of Senlac, and the mercenaries recruited by William I from Normandy to pacify his new kingdom, would mostly marry English girls who would teach their children the English language, enriched by new words learnt from the men. Thus, with two diverse traditions in intimate contact among non-literate folk, inflexions in both languages would degenerate. English apparently did not become the language of the court until the time of Edward I and would not therefore have become standardised. Complications of pronunciation developed, some derived from Norman and others from English usage.

Geoffrey of Monmouth wrote in Latin in the twelfth century. But Langland and Chaucer wrote in English in the fourteenth and, moreover, they described the English countryside, where feudal manors were beginning to break up, and their contemporaries who lived in it. English returned to general use and, as services were commuted for money payments, servile labourers previously tied to the manor could, if enterprising, take their skills elsewhere. Trade and crafts benefited and a written version of the common tongue had to be developed for commercial use. Written mercantile records gradually replaced tallies, and domestic accounts were kept in many households. William Caxton, who brought his printing press over from Flanders in 1477, worked until 1491 in his house near Westminster Abbey and made possible the flowering of literary English in the sixteenth century.

New medieval boroughs were often planned towns. Salisbury, by the Avon, replaced Old Sarum on its over-dry hill. In Wales Edward I built bastide towns like Conway, Beaumaris and Caernarvon (Fig. 43). These walled towns, modelled on English fortress towns in France, were dominated by their castles and their walls enclosed streets laid out in a chessboard pattern. They were garrison towns and Welsh people were not allowed to live in them or in other Anglo-Norman boroughs in Wales. In English towns Normans and English and their descendants lived side by side. Here too, a castle often towered above the town and its churches. The castle of Norwich, the second city in the kingdom in the fourteenth century, is one of many which still stand high on their castle mounds. Windsor Castle is another (Plate XXXI, p. 288). Craftsmen supplied the castle, churches and prosperous burgesses with armour, furnishings and implements. Most needs were supplied locally. Fairs held outside the walls attracted pedlars and vendors of goods from farther afield, and beggars, tumblers and jugglers came in from the countryside where, like the preaching friars, they more usually wandered.

The houses of the burgesses (Plate XX, p. 189) extended back from narrow street frontages and often included workshops. Pottery-making and weaving were among the crafts practised there. In the fourteenth century Edward III brought Flemish wool-workers to Norfolk and Suffolk and in the next two centuries the profits of the East Anglian woollen industry were used to enrich its towns with fine churches, town halls and guildhalls (Plates 13 and 28, pp. 128 and 237). Sheep with long-staple wool were reared on the local pastures and Worstead gave its name to a fine cloth made from this wool. The Cotswolds were another great wool-producing district and here too, fine churches, and merchants' houses like the Chipping Campden home of William Grevel, who died there in 1401, adorn the market towns. Sacks of wool exported by the Staplers averaged thirty thousand a year in the early fourteenth century. By the mid-sixteenth century cloth exports by the Merchant Adventurers greatly exceeded in value those of raw wool. The woollen industry moved eventually from Lowland England, with its small or slow streams, to the flanks of the Pennines where water, and, later, steam power were applied to it. The woollen industry is one of our oldest, and strongest, in persistence and quality.

In the later Middle Ages and in Tudor times the iron industry expanded in the countryside. Charcoal from the woodlands, ore supplies and water power from water dammed up in "hammer ponds," were available in rural areas such as the Weald. Hammering of iron was a step towards mechanisation. A sixteenth-century attempt to smelt iron with coal failed, and forests were increasingly felled for charcoal-burning, salt manufacture, and household use. Chimneys, fireplaces and iron firebacks, made in local forges such as those of Sussex, became more common as the domestic use of sea coal increased. Knifemaking became concentrated on Sheffield where the local sandstone could be used for sharpening knife blades. In Highland Britain, Elizabethan and later mining companies worked tin in Cornwall, lead in the Mendips, West Wales and the Lake District, and German miners also worked copper in the Lakeland Fells. Excessive deforestation led in the eighteenth century to a shift of the iron industry from the Weald to areas like the north scarp of the South Wales coalfield where woodlands were still abundant, and iron ore, swift streams and limestone were all available. After a century of further over-exploitation of raw material, this time of ore supplies, another move was necessary, and the iron and steel industry is now mainly located in or near ports. Modern metallurgical industries, with their use of alloys, are widely distributed, but around Birmingham and Sheffield, and in the Scottish Midlands, old skills have been adapted to new techniques.

Wales, a land of small farms and Tudor squires, was brought into the English parliamentary and administrative system by the Act of Union of 1536. In the same year northern England, led by the Percies of Northumberland, opposed Henry VIII's treatment of the monasteries in the Pilgrimage of Grace. The great border families, leaders of an independent people, with lawless elements who lived by cattle-raiding, were eclipsed after their revolt of 1570. The Union of England and Scotland under James I in 1603 brought peace to the border; unfortified manor houses replaced peel towers, and homes of tenant farmers were no longer burnt by raiders. Between 1603 and the Act of Union in 1707, Scotland kept its own government and parliament. After 1707 Scotland sent members and peers to Westminster but retained its own Church and legal system. Colonial markets were thrown open to the Scots, and trade, and a substantial contribution by Scotland to colonial development, was initiated. After the rebellion of 1745 the Scottish Midlands were orientated towards industry and trade. Both highland and lowland Scotland exported peoples to the Commonwealth and to the Americas, culminating in the emigration of nearly 900,000 Scots between 1900 and 1930.

Until the fourteenth century, increases in population in England and Wales led to land hunger. Cultivation of common fields persisted, though piecemeal enclosure had begun, notably in areas where common fields were small. Services on the lord's land began to be replaced by money rents. Several visitations of the Black Death, starting in 1348-9, may have halved the population. Bubonic plague, which was still a threat in Tudor times, created a seller's market in labour and allowed a yeoman class to develop. It also led to an increase of pasture, especially for sheep, at the expense of arable land, and to the abandonment of villages. The grass-grown sites of these deserted villages are numerous on the scarplands of England. For such reasons freedom from serfdom came much earlier in Britain than in continental Europe. The landlords, including monastic landlords, heeded warnings like Wat Tyler's Rebellion of 1381, which culminated in the capture of London.

In Tudor and later times, self-sufficient villages produced wheat for the gentry's bread, and barley and rye for their own. Fresh beef, previously plentiful only at the autumn killings, became more regular as improved hay crops allowed more cattle to be overwintered; mutton was eaten more frequently than in continental Europe, and was supplemented by poultry, hares, and coneys. The rabbits introduced by the Normans locally became a pest. Beer and small beer were produced from barley and herbs; cider was drunk in the West Country. Potatoes brought in from America were planted in gardens, and patches on the margin of fields were still described as "potato gardens" in the nineteenth century. Locally crops were grown for export or for industry. Wheat from its rich hinterland was sent to Scandinavia and Flanders from King's Lynn. Woad, madder and saffron were grown in Suffolk and Essex to provide dyes for the East Anglian woollen industry. Saffron, collected from the stigmas of the autumn crocus, gave its name to Saffron Walden.

Urban and rural society discarded outmoded medieval ideas more quickly than did the Church. Parishes were often badly served by priests. Preaching friars circulated new ideas among the country folk. Though they criticised the hierarchy they were not always as poor as were Franciscans in theory. Wycliffe (1320-84), denouncing transubstantiation, and voicing resentment at the influence of pope and king on the English Church, opposed the preaching friars and other orders which accumulated wealth. Wycliffe's ideas affected John Hus and others and initiated the religious reforms that so occupied Europe and Britain in the sixteenth century. English Puritanism, with its appeal to the poor, its virtues and its faults, was grafted on to old stocks. The revolt against the Roman Curia led Tudor sovereigns to claim and exercise ecclesiastical authority. Congregations in England, Wales and Scotland could, by the end of the Tudor Period, read or listen to readings from the Book of Common Prayer and the Bible in their own languages.

In the discussions of the sixteenth century there emerged, more definitely than at any other time since the death of Socrates, the idea that the truth must be sought by free inquiry. In Britain this attitude is associated with the names of Francis Bacon, William Harvey, Robert Boyle, Christopher Wren and Isaac Newton in the seventeenth century, and with the foundation of the Royal Society by Charles II. After the Civil War in England and Wales, scepticism and divergence from Church doctrines were common. Presbyterian Scotland was more orthodox. Diverse religious groups developed and persecution ceased.

Voltaire said that Britain had "a hundred religions and one sauce." The sincere conscience was thereby better safeguarded than by a scheme of one religion and a hundred sauces.

In the seventeenth century there were Independents, with each local group governing itself, Baptists believing in adult baptism, and Presbyterians with consistories governing churches and groups of churches. All were profoundly influenced by John Calvin's insistence on the omnipotence of God. The Unitarians dissociated themselves from the traditional Trinitarian doctrine. They were often intellectual groups and had to devise means of higher education because Oxford and Cambridge remained subject to theological tests until the late nineteenth century. The Society of Friends was another group which arose in the seventeenth century and has tried to promote respect for conscience.

Most seventeenth-century groups outside the Anglican Church were, on the whole, eclectic. In the eighteenth century, John Wesley, George Whitefield and their collaborators went out into the countryside and into the mining and manufacturing slums, and new religious groups called Methodists came into existence. Their name sprang from the rules of conduct laid down for them. In the nineteenth century the Anglican Church found new lines of interest and work and, outside it, toleration allowed scope to the Roman Church. A renewal of the fundamental ideas of Methodism brought into existence the Salvation Army. The twentieth-century Churches are working towards a profound re-examination of the Christian faith and a greater unity among the denominations.

Fifteenth- and sixteenth-century voyages of discovery, initiated by Prince Henry the Navigator and undertaken by Bartolomeo Diaz, Vasco da Gama, the Cabots and, above all, Columbus, stirred British sailors to adventure and exploration. Shipbuilding and commerce were vastly expanded to bridge the newly discovered oceans. The development of fore-and-aft sails made it possible to sail nearer the wind and to make more direct journeys. Bilge water, a cause of disease among sailors, diminished as design improved; better diets reduced scurvy. Regular voyages, by merchant ships of increasing size and speed, developed after raw cotton began to be imported from the Levant in the seventeenth century. Cotton, sugar and tobacco brought prosperity to ports like Liverpool, Bristol and Glasgow. In the days of sail, small ports flourished all around the British coasts. After about 1840, iron ships propelled by steam, and needing deeper harbours, concentrated shipping

PLATE 19 POLPÉRRO, a fishing and holiday village on a sheltered Cornish inlet.

PLATE 20 MARKET HOUSE, Shrewsbury (1595), showing mingled mediaeval and renascence features characteristic in Britain from about 1530 until the time of Inigo Jones.

on modern ports. Many of these have now also lost their old trades. Ports formerly geared to coal export in Durham and South Wales seek new traffic; they are too shallow for modern bulk carriers of ore or oil.

Trade with tropical lands, and the improvement of ships, led to the use of mahogany, satin wood and other woods suitable for inlay, both for ships' and household, furniture. The eighteenth century produced fine furniture, more graceful than earlier heavy oak pieces. Ships of the East India Company brought in china and lacquer-work. Elegance prevailed until, in the mid-nineteenth century, hideous and fantastic imitations of medieval styles became fashionable, and the railways circulated standardised building materials which replaced local stone, thereby producing some remarkably obtrusive buildings, particularly in country towns and in rural areas (cf. Plates XXI, XXII and 23, pp. 208, 209, 220).

The Scottish Lowlands were prominent in eighteenth-century life. After the '45, Scotland's textile, mining and iron industries, her agriculture and her overseas trade, greatly expanded. The contribution of her engineers, like James Watt, to industry, marine engineering, colonial development, and the modern technological revolution, is well known. A cultural renaissance accompanied material progress in the eighteenth century and the names of Hume, Reid and Adam Smith are associated with it. Boswell and Burns made their country internationally famous (Plate IX, p. 148). Sir Walter Scott (1771-1832), revealed the romantic aspects of Scotland to a world which has since gone there to find them in settings of great natural beauty. The outstandingly beautiful areas of Scotland, the Highlands and Atlantic fringe, are largely depopulated lands to-day. Pastoral farming on the lean hillsides and narrow valleys contrasts markedly with mechanised farming first developed in the Lothians in the mid-nineteenth century, but industry in Fort William, powered by hydro-electricity, has a finer setting than older metallurgical trades in the Scottish Midlands.

In the century after the Napoleonic Wars Britain was not involved in major conflicts. Victorian Britain accumulated wealth, rejoiced in her material prosperity and made no far-sighted national plans for the future. We became the leading industrial nation, seriously affected by German and American competition only in the last decades of the nineteenth century. In 1851, half the population still lived in the countryside. By 1901 two-thirds lived in towns, partly as a result of agricultural decline which set in in 1870; from 1871 to 1881 a hundred thousand farm labourers left the land. This loss has continued, in spite of tariff protection and farm subsidies; mechanisation has been both a cause and result of it. It is estimated that the population will number about 61 millions in the year 2,001 and, while agricultural productivity may double in the Lowland Zone, vast imports of grain, other food-stuffs and raw materials will be needed to support this population. The farming population of Britain now forms only a small fraction of the whole, but it nevertheless moulds the pattern of the larger proportion of our landscape. This landscape is a largely man-made heritage from the past, an easily damaged treasure which needs wise use and management. It can meet demands for urban and industrial expansion, mechanised farming, forestry, water storage, nature conservation and recreation only if these land uses are carefully planned and well integrated.

It is possible that, by 2,000, there may be thirty million cars available for travel during longer weekends and two annual holiday periods. Longer journeys to work will be undertaken by car or public transport. Towns will need to be redesigned to meet this revolution in transport, and the countryside will be under great pressure for outdoor recreation. The passive enjoyment of country scenes by pleasure motorists is now the major form of outdoor recreation. It is characteristic of the slow adjustment of our thinking to problems posed by rapid change that we are still trying to control motor traffic by acts framed in a period when petrol was rationed and the post-war increase of population was greatly underestimated.

The Victorians saw the decline of canal traffic and the decay of the tramroads which ran down to them. Competing companies built an intricate rail network which covered both industrial and rural Britain. Passenger traffic on roads declined and with it, in villages and market towns, bustling posting inns. Now these inns thrive once more, flanked by roaring streams of traffic, and motels, caravan and camping sites cater for the motorist in roadside fields. The web of railways which carry both freight and passengers is very much less intricate than it was in 1910 and many canals are either infilled, or are used only to supply water for industry, or for recreation.

Victorian growth of suburban rail networks initiated commuting and ribbon development around towns. At first commuters were well-to-do; only a minority of Victorian industrialists were concerned about the surroundings in which their workpeople lived (Plate XXIV, p. 225). Urban sprawl speeded up between the two world wars because of the improvement of both road and rail access to the countryside. Ribbon development spread industry as well as housing along roads at this time (Plate XXV, p. 244). Post-war planning has controlled but has not halted urban sprawl. Most townsfolk went to the seaside, if only for a day trip, in the late nineteenth century, and Brighton and the south-coast resorts, those on the Thames estuary, on the coasts of northern England, North Wales and East Anglia, had a rapid Victorian development. Blackpool became a borough in 1876. To their tourist functions these resorts have now added provision for commuters and retired folk. Small ports are busy with coastal traffic, or pleasure craft, or both, while to large ports with deep harbours come some of the world's bulk carriers of grain, oil and iron ore. But, whereas in 1885 a third of the world's sea-going ships were registered in Britain, many tankers and ore carriers which enter British harbours now fly flags of convenience. The Norwegian merchant navy is far greater than our own in proportion to her population, and oil companies charter the modern Northmen's tanker fleet.

The Victorians may have contemplated a Channel tunnel, but they can hardly have visualised British-designed hovercraft which will also take a growing flood of Britons across the narrow seas. Above all, the Victorians never took into account air travel for cheap continental holidays which would be an alternative to a week at Blackpool, air routes to remote Western Isles in Atlantic Britain which had hardly adjusted themselves to motor traffic, immigration by air with possibilities for the reintroduction of diseases whose dangers they knew well, and the potential, not yet fully exploited, of interchange of ideas among peoples as air travel reduced distances between them.

Heavy industry and engineering in the time of Victoria were largely tied to the coalfields. Modern industry, powered by electricity and gas, distributed through national grids, or by oil carried by road, rail or pipe-lines, is far more flexible and more widely dispersed. Supplies of natural gas from the North Sea will vastly increase our energy resources and further diversify our industrial pattern. New industrial concentrations are developing by the deep estuaries of the Thames, Severn, Mersey, Humber and Forth. Nuclear power stations, first built on empty coasts, are now planned for sites nearer built-up areas. Cooling-water supplies determine the locations of nuclear, oil- and coal-fired power stations, and the waters of rivers like the Trent are used and re-used by them. Use and re-use of river water for domestic and industrial consumption is increasing, and with it the need to regulate river flows nearer their sources. Some narrow valleys of headstreams in

Highland Britain will be flooded by regulating reservoirs to supply towns increasingly distant from them. Water supplies could be supplemented by reservoirs impounded by barrages thrown across the Dee estuary, Morecambe Bay, the Solway Firth and the Wash.

Post-war urban renewal has had to be carried out speedily, and unimaginative housing schemes have often resulted. Such environments, together with some forms of mass entertainment, and the monotony of mechanised work and pleasure, gradually make for a standardisation of human personality. It is not difficult to-day to lose one's sense of wonder and all contact with nature.

The environment produced for the working folk of the nineteenth century bred disease, squalor and loss of individuality (Plates 21 and XXIII, pp. 212 and 224). Cholera no longer rages in the large remnants of this environment, and the National Health Act and modern medicine have produced a much healthier urban population than the first Public Health Act of 1848. But dereliction and its evils are still features of cities and worn-out industrial areas, particularly coalfields. These areas have bred men like the Rochdale Pioneers, who in 1844 founded the Co-operative Movement and gave working people a stake in the country. By the end of the century socialism and trade unions were becoming equally important and their well-read leaders were coming to the fore. Victorian socialist leaders studied in the Mechanics Institutes rather than in the new civic universities of their day. The depression of the 1930s induced outward migration from many industrial areas. Some still have vigorous leaders whose energies go into the reshaping and renewal of their localities. The burden of dereliction in difficult environments, and the squalid modern buildings and litter which it breeds, have often stunned communities into bitter resentment rather than into purposeful activity. Scarred landscapes merit as much research as scarred bodies, and crippled communities, like human cripples, need more liberal and long-term aid, and more compassion from more fortunate people than they have hitherto received.

Industrial Britain has also bred fine women, particularly the wives of miners and others who meet dangers at work. A century ago, children, as well as women, worked in mines and factories, and they had no compulsory schooling until 1870. Women gradually began to enter the professions only after Florence Nightingale trained nurses for service in the Crimea. Now many large hospitals are staffed by devoted coloured nurses and the health services by a relatively large number of women doctors and ancillary staff. Many light industries now employ more

PLATE XV. a. MOTTE AND BAILEY earthwork of Norman times, Berkhampstead Castle. The motte (mound) had a wooden keep on it; the bailey was enclosed by a palisade and may also have had wooden buildings on it

b. THE "ROMAN" STEPS, Merioneth. This was probably a medieval packhorse route through the Rhinog Mountains

PLATE XVI. A FISHERMAN'S LANE, Looe, Cornwall. Narrow lanes with close-set houses are very characteristic of fishing villages

female than male workers and areas of declining industry seek new factories which will provide jobs for men made redundant by the reorganisation of heavy industry.

Our first eight chapters have attempted to outline the growth of Britain's social tradition in the belief that the future must build on the past. Between the accessions of Victoria and Elizabeth II there have been more rapid and disastrous changes than in any other century in our history. In replanning Britain we can learn from the mistakes of our forefathers of this and earlier periods. We may realise that unity is more than uniformity, that persecution and ostracism promote insincerity and destroy initiative, that none of us, no sect or party, should presume to claim that it has the whole truth. Milton, speaking for the Liberty of Unlicensed Printing, puts the case for liberty, against licensing, of printing, an evil of his day as well as of our own in many lands, in his finest prose:

"There is yet behind of what I purposed to lay open, the incredible loss and detriment that this plot of licensing puts us to, more than if some enemy at sea should stop up all our havens, and ports, and creeks; it hinders and retards the importation of our richest merchandise, truth."

CHAPTER 9

THE PEOPLE

IT HAS LONG been known that the British people show a considerable variety of physical characteristics. Some, especially in South Wales, are dark, small-boned, slender and rather short, others, especially those living on and behind the English and Scottish coasts of the North Sea, are tall, big-boned and often fair in colouring. In general, head-form is rather long and really broadheaded men are in a small minority in most parts of Britain. Our colouring is on the whole darker than that of most Scandinavians but fairer than that of most Spaniards. While baldness does occur in a considerable proportion of our males, it is not so common, nor does it appear so early, as it is apt to do in Central Europe. In the nineteenth century, Dr. John Beddoe published observations of physical traits in Britain that demonstrated his acuteness of observation. Since his day comparatively little work has been done on local anthropometric differences, except in respect of stature. The author, in conjunction with Dr. Elwyn Davies and other colleagues, has tried to analyse the physical traits found in the Isle of Man and Welsh-speaking Wales, because it is in fringe areas such as these, rather than in the conurbations, that the successive layers of our population may be discerned.

Local differences in the proportions of men with various physical traits certainly do occur, but one must not expect anything approaching absolute contrasts. Past history helps to interpret local differences. Physical traits may be, and typically are, inherited, so that they may persist for many hundreds of generations. We all know that "family likeness" is a topic of conversation round every baby. Particulate inheritance is the general rule, father's nose or mother's eyes, or vice versa, or both from one or the other parent. Mendel showed why this happens, and it is recognised more and more that inheritance is best interpreted on Mendelian lines.

If all the ancestors of any one of us had been separate people, each of us would be represented by 32,768 persons fifteen generations ago, say about the first Elizabethan Age, and by this number squared, or well over one thousand million persons, somewhere about the time of the Norman Conquest. The first figure is considerably greater than the total population of many an area within which intermarriage usually occurred in former times, while the second figure is greater than that of the population of the whole world in the eleventh century. The fact is that the threads of descent intertwine in complex fashion and the same thread has wound itself again and again into an inheritance. It thus happens that, at any rate in rural areas with, in the past, predominantly local intermarriage, the same gene must often have appeared several times in the ancestry of a particular individual and it is likely that similar genes will be inherited from both sides of his ancestry. In this way a particular item of physical inheritance, or a bundle of physical characteristics, may come down in whole or part along several ancestral lines and so may be reinforced in spite of crossing with other persons carrying different features.

There may also be supplementary natural selection of valuable variations or elimination of deleterious ones. Environment and food supplies may influence growth, as has been shown by the supply of vitamins and school milk to mothers and children. Changes may have occurred as the age of first motherhood increased. Very early first motherhood is believed to result in small-grown offspring. Old theories of rapid change of head-form with change of environment are nevertheless now discredited.

It is desirable to ensure that a local sample for study is composed of the normal inhabitants of a district, and to ascertain such facts of ancestry as are available, using those who can trace their four grandparents in the district. This means, in most cases, that a great deal of the ancestry is local for, until modern communications had become really effective, marriages among ordinary people nearly always occurred between partners living within about five miles of each other. A modern administrative area is rarely an ideal unit for study. The watershed of a highland may be a county boundary, but the people of that highland have often moved to all the edges of the surrounding lowland. Few lowlanders have moved up to the highland except for relatively short periods of some activity such as mining. The maritime and inland areas of any county may have very different stories of settlement. Local knowledge of traditional intercourse, of dialect and commercial relations help in the delimitation of districts for study, and rural districts provide better samples than the mixed populations of towns. Women's growth stops at an earlier age than that of men, leaving them with less thickness of bone, an advantage in child-bearing, but, consequently, with several physical characteristics less marked than in men. We have therefore limited our study to adult non-senile males.

Differences in the physical characteristics of local populations can be illustrated by reference to Wales. To take colouring first, we find that in the Gower peninsula 38 per cent of a sample are blond (fair hair and blue or grey eyes) and 24 per cent are fully brunet (dark hair and brown or hazel eyes). In the Llŷn peninsula the proportions are 33 per cent and 41 per cent, whereas in the area around the Plynlimon moorland, in north Cardiganshire and west Montgomeryshire, the corresponding figures are 18 per cent blond and 41 per cent brunet; in south Cardiganshire they are 15 per cent and 46 per cent and in the Hiraethog Moors of Denbighshire they are 15 per cent and 49 per cent respectively. In general, in and around the interior plateaux of Wales men with dark hair (but with any eye colour) form between 70 and 77 per cent of the total and the proportion of blond men is only 14 to 22 per cent (Fig. 44).

If we take head-form, we find that in the Plynlimon area 13 per cent of all pure brunets, or 5.3 per cent of the total sample, had long and very narrow heads (cephalic index below 73.6). This is thrice the average incidence of this head-form in Wales as a whole, whereas blond men with this head-form are less than one per cent. In the Plynlimon area, the Hiraethog Moors and south Cardiganshire, fully brunet longheads (cephalic index below 78.6) form 26-27 per cent and blond longheads only 6-10 per cent of the population; in the Gower and Llŷn peninsulas fully brunet longheads form 14-16 per cent and blond longheads 16-19 per cent of it. Analysing further, we find that in south Cardiganshire 38 per cent of the fully brunet longheads have head length over 200 mm. whereas in the Plynlimon area the corresponding proportion is only 22 per cent, but in this latter region 48 per cent have head breadths below 151 mm., whereas in south Cardiganshire the figure is only 26 per cent. Thus, in the Plynlimon area, longheadedness in fully brunet men is due to low absolute breadth rather than to extreme length, whereas in south Cardiganshire the opposite is the case.

There are also interesting correlations with stature. For example, the fully brunet longheads in the Plynlimon area are generally of short stature (average: 1,679 mm.) but the broader headed men (cephalic index over 78.6) are notably taller (average: 1,711 mm.). Blond men, however, are of short stature here (average: 1,682 mm.) and in south Cardiganshire (average: 1,685 mm.). In Gower, on the other hand, the

PLATE XVII. OXFORD, aerial view. St. Aldate's, Carfax (with St. Martin's tower), the Cornmarket, St. Giles' Fairground, the Woodstock and Banbury roads can be followed S–N. The High Street with alignments of churches and colleges runs W–E

PLATE XVIII. ST DAVID'S, Pembrokeshire, showing the "city", Cathedral and, in the valley, the ruins of the Palace built by Bishop Gower

blond men are markedly tall (average: 1,722 mm.) whereas in the Hiraethog area it is the fully brunet longheads who are tallest (average: 1,715 mm.).

Details of differences in the distribution of particular physical characters, and in the association of these characters with each other, could be multiplied, but these examples are perhaps adequate to illustrate the regional diversity which exists and is a matter of common, as well as of scientific, observation.

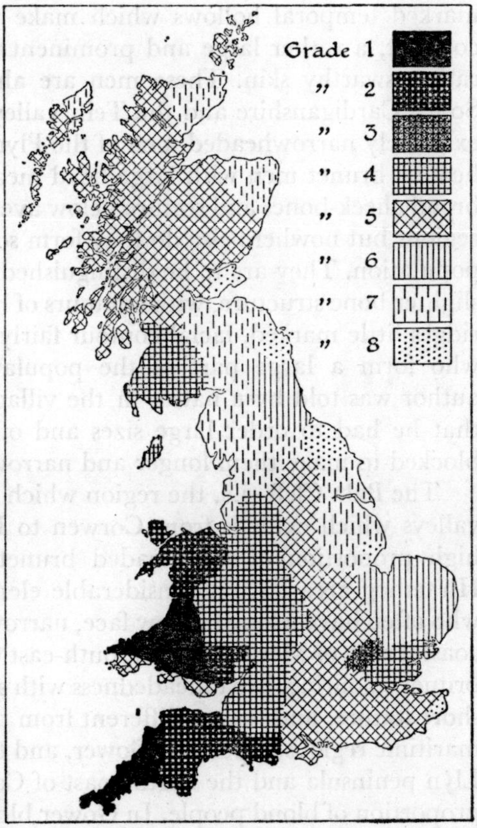

Analyses of this kind show that brunet longheads form, as it were, a general basis for the Welsh population and form the most common element in all the regions, but they constitute a preponderant part of the population in and around the interior plateaux where they form 20-26 per cent of the total and are between

FIG. 44

Tentative map of the distribution of pigmentation (hair and eye colour) in Britain

twice and four times as numerous as the blond longheads. The latter form 6-10 per cent of the total; in the maritime areas, on the other hand, their relative proportions show no great difference. The maritime areas also have large numbers with dark hair and blue or grey eyes. This combination of dark hair and light eyes is a feature of Atlantic coastlands north of the Loire estuary and perhaps nowhere is it so widespread as in Atlantic Britain and Ireland. In Wales it is almost as common as full blondness.

The Plynlimon country harbours a relatively high proportion of extremely narrowheaded brunets with prominent brows, strongly marked temporal hollows which make the cheek-bones stand out in contrast, a rather large and prominent mouth and, in a few cases, a rather swarthy skin. These men are almost always of short stature. South Cardiganshire and the Teifi valley, while they do not have the extremely narrowheaded men of the Plynlimon area, have many long-headed brunet men with large head measurements, strong and rather broad cheek-bones and stature below average. Such men occur in other regions but nowhere else do they form so significant an element in the population. They are to be distinguished from the brunet longheads of slighter bone structure, with contours of head and face far milder, brow ridges little marked, facial contour fairly smooth and features regular, who form a large part of the population throughout Wales. The author was told by a hatter in the village of Llandysul, on the Teifi, that he had to order large sizes and often had to have the hats re-blocked to make them longer and narrower.

The Bala Cleft (i.e. the region which drains into the system of fault valleys which extends from Corwen to Barmouth and Towyn) has a high proportion of shortheaded brunet men, and both it and the Hiraethog area have a considerable element of tall brunet longheads who often have a long narrow face, narrow nose and strong profile. The coastal area of Merioneth and south-east Caernarvonshire is notable for brunet colouring, broadheadedness with small head measurements, and short stature, and is thus different from the neighbouring regions. The maritime regions, especially Gower, and to a lesser extent Anglesey, the Llŷn peninsula and the north coast of Caernarvonshire, have a higher proportion of blond people. In Gower blond colouring is far commoner than in any other area of Wales, large head measurements are character-istic and tallness is more general than elsewhere and is most marked among men of blond colouring. The Llŷn peninsula and the northern coastlands of Caernarvonshire have a marked element of blond broad-heads of rather low stature, but the blond longheads who are common in these areas are noticeably taller than men of other groups in Llŷn; in the north Caernarvonshire coastlands they are of markedly lower stature. In Wales generally the blond longheads show less variety of associated characteristics than do the brunet longheads, but it is pos-sible to distinguish between a more lightly-built element with regular and rather fine features, and a more raw-boned variety with more prominent cheek-bones and aquiline features.

The Welsh population probably includes elements descended from very ancient groups which came into Britain over the land-bridge which then existed with continental Europe. These drifts of population brought genes of very early British ancestry which have survived especially among the mountains and moorlands. Such upland plateaux are areas of difficulty. They have long been mainly regions of export of men and women, especially young people, and have attracted few immigrants. They may be expected therefore to have sheltered old-time drifts. Remote and economically difficult regions tend to preserve relic populations and notable elements with very long narrow heads are known from areas such as the Dordogne, the province of Tras os Montes in north Portugal and from Sardinia. The very long narrow head is also found among jungle peoples in South India, the Australian aborigines, the Korana people of South Africa and other relic populations in remote areas at the ends of lines of human migration and drift.

It is known that if an animal species occurs in several unconnected and remote areas, it is probably an ancient species which was at one time more generally distributed but has been exterminated or replaced in several parts of its old province of occurrence. The same may be true of the people with very long narrow heads, strong brows and deep temporal hollows, in Wales.

The population of Britain in Palæolithic times was probably very small; the few surviving skulls are discussed on p. 56. Some of them, as elsewhere in Western Europe, had very low cranial indices, long heads with a median ridge, marked temporal hollows and strong brows. Similar characteristics occur among the men of the Plynlimon area (Plate VIII, p. 141). It is possible that they are the result of continuous inheritance or of a resurgence in a small inbred group. Traces of the same heritage may be seen also in the Hiraethog area of Denbighshire. The low plateaux of south Cardiganshire appear to have attracted more early settlers than its present exposed coast and this may explain the high proportion inland of dark very longheaded men with more rugged features than are general among brunet longheads.

It has long been accepted that dark, longheaded, rather short men (Plate IX, p. 148) have been an important element of the British population since the Neolithic Period. We do not know the colouring of early populations, but that they were predominantly longheaded and of medium or sub-medium stature has been well-established. We also know that among these Neolithic populations were the builders of the megaliths. Such megalithic monuments are a notable feature of the western coasts of Britain and are related to the megaliths of Brittany and the Iberian peninsula (Chapter 3). In them longheaded people of medium or sub-medium stature predominate among those buried. The importance of brunet longheads of short or medium stature on and around the plateaux of South Wales can be abundantly demonstrated. In north-west Wales, hard volcanic rocks and grits produce rugged mountains which would have afforded only limited opportunities for early settlement. These areas do not show an outstanding preponderance of brunet longheads, although they are numerous enough, and the admixture of blond longheads is considerable. Hill-brows in north-west Wales have many Iron Age forts. But the Hiraethog area of Denbighshire, open rolling moorland more like that of South and West Wales, has a proportion of brunet longheaded men which is comparable to that found there. This is also true of Anglesey, where high winds and rock exposures in a generally flat landscape would provide forest-free patches which are known to have been settled by Neolithic men.

The occurrence of tall, brunet, broadheaded men in the Plynlimon, Bala Cleft, Hiraethog and south Cardiganshire areas, and their insignificance or absence in coastal areas, may be associated partly with the westward movement of Beaker people through Wales, as they prospected and traded, and partly with the settlement of the Welsh uplands in the more favourable climatic conditions of the Bronze Age (Chapter 4).

The distribution of blond men in Wales is of a different kind from that of brunets and especially of brunet longheads. The blond men, although present everywhere, are specially characteristic of the maritime projections—Anglesey, the Gower and Llŷn peninsulas, south Pembrokeshire and the coastlands of north Caernarvonshire. Welsh folklore contains many traditions of fair people from the lowlands meeting the small, dark people of the uplands ("the fairy folk"), who sometimes had a fear of iron (see p. 37). These traditions are probably related to the incoming of Iron Age peoples to the lower lands. The same areas also suffered the incursions of the Vikings who ravaged Anglesey and Llŷn and raided and settled parts of the shorelands of the Bristol Channel, from south Pembrokeshire to Monmouthshire. The comparatively high frequency of blond colouring and tall stature, and especially of these characteristics in association with long and medium heads, in these maritime projections, indicates a relationship with immigrants who used the Atlantic route. It may be that the blond men of lighter build and finer features are to be associated with migrations of Celtic-speaking peoples and those of more robust form with Norse invasions.

The Isle of Man also shows differences in the physical characteristics of local populations. In the island as a whole, blond colouring preponderates over fully brunet colouring in the proportion of 40 per cent and 37 per cent, but whereas in the north of the island blonds formed 47 per cent of the sample and brunets 27 per cent, and in the southern lowland behind Castletown 45 per cent were blond and 31 per cent brunet, in the hilly country of the extreme south-west of the island 40 per cent were brunet and 39 per cent blond and in the area around Douglas, and in the glens behind it, 49 per cent were brunets and only 33 per cent blonds. In other words the proportion with dark colouring in the eastern glens is almost twice as great as it is in the north of the island where the proportion with fair colouring is almost half as much again as it is in the eastern glens. These differences in colouring are most pronounced among the longheaded men. For example, in the north of the island 49 per cent of all longheaded men are blond and 25 per cent are brunet and in the southern lowland the proportions are 42 per cent blond and 33 per cent brunet. In the eastern glens, on the other hand, 56 per cent of all longheads are brunet and only 35 per cent are blond; in the extreme south-west 44 per cent are brunet and 37 per cent are blond. In the north, too, longheaded men of taller stature exceed those of shorter stature by 48 per cent and in the southern lowland by 28 per cent. In the eastern glens they are evenly balanced and in the extreme south-west those of shorter stature exceed those of taller stature by 11 per cent.

The physical composition of the Manx people is similar to that of Wales except that there is little, if any, evidence of extremely narrow-headed brunets such as those found in the Plynlimon country, or of extremely longheaded brunets such as those of south Cardiganshire and the Denbighshire Moors. In the Isle of Man the north of the island, which has boat burials and many Norse place-names, has a high proportion of tall, blond, longheaded men, whereas the glens of the east and the hill country of the extreme south-west have large proportions of rather short, brunet, longheaded men. Both the latter areas have a number of megalithic and Bronze Age monuments.

Comparatively few observations of physical characteristics of living populations are available for England. Fullard found that brunet and blond were more or less evenly distributed in mid-Lancashire west of the Rossendale Forest but that fair colouring was far more marked along the through-ways from Yorkshire north and south of the Rossendale Fells. Parsons reviewed in 1920 the distribution of colouring in

England and Wales, almost entirely confirming the pioneer work of Beddoe. He found that rural folk were on the whole fairer and urban people darker; Professor E. G. Bowen has shown that short dark people take better to urban life. The people of south-west England and the Midlands are predominantly dark; East Anglia, Lincolnshire and east Yorkshire have much fairer types. The distribution of fair colouring indicates the degree to which Angles, Danes and Norsemen have contributed to our population.

In 1923, Dr. J. F. Tocher published a mass of data concerning colouring, stature and head-form in Scotland. These observations were made on soldiers of twenty years or over, i.e. on a somewhat specialised group. Nevertheless, sampling the measurements in a preliminary way, one finds that the Scottish population is nowhere predominantly dark, though a dark-haired element may form 40 to 50 per cent of a local sample. It is a little over 50 per cent in a large Aberdeenshire group, and about 50 per cent in a small Argyllshire group, but it falls to 40 per cent in most parts of northern Scotland (Caithness, Sutherland, Ross and Cromarty, and Inverness). In the south-west the percentage falls to about 33, but this sample is small. Beddoe's small sample from the same area showed a preponderance of darks. Red hair is rather more common in Argyll and in the south-west than in the Aberdeenshire sample.

In stature, taking 1,750 mm. as the lower limit of tallness, we find that Caithness and Sutherland have about 42 per cent of the sample above this height, while the percentage falls to 37 in Ross and Cromarty and to 27 in Inverness. It is only about 30 in the small sample from south-west Scotland. An estimate from Tocher's samples gives an average height of 1,715 mm., or 5 ft. 7½ in. This is a higher value than one gets for most parts of Wales except Gower and south Pembrokeshire, where, as on the east Scottish seaboard, one finds Scandinavian elements in the population. Tocher's samples do not appear to include many extremes in head-form and people whose indices are moderately low apparently form a larger proportion than in most parts of Wales. In Aberdeenshire about 25 per cent are broadheads; the percentage falls to about 17 in north Scotland, to about 7 in Argyll and to 9 in south-west Scotland.

The stature of full-grown Neolithic men averaged about 63 inches; Bronze Age men may be as tall as 69 inches. The Anglo-Saxons averaged about 66 inches and the Vikings appear to have been a little taller. Medieval clothing and armour, generally speaking, would fit modern

men of medium or sub-medium stature. Better twentieth-century feeding of children appears to have resulted in increased average height.
Many years ago, Shrubsall drew attention to the fact that men in the
Lowland Zone were generally taller than those who lived west and
north-west of the Jurassic scarp. Better food supplies, and especially
the wheat of the Lowland Zone, could be responsible. Shrubsall noted
a taller element in the Lake District and north Lancashire, areas of
Viking settlement. City populations often include more short dark
people than their rural hinterlands, possibly because of natural selection
in the crowded conditions of the nineteenth and early twentieth
centuries.

For Britain in general, we may sum up by saying that the earliest
inhabitants, hunting bands who used the land-bridge which then
existed across the Dover Strait, were mainly very long- and narrow-
headed but that they included a few moderate longheads. Both types
persist to the present day. The population would be very small and
inbred until large Neolithic groups immigrated into Britain. Neolithic
folk, coming largely from Mediterranean lands through western
Europe, included many longheaded, probably dark-haired, people.
Moderate rather than extreme longheads appear to have been preponderant among them. Peoples from Central Europe contributed to
our population from the Neolithic period to and beyond the Iron Age,
and from this area a small and distinctive broadheaded, probably dark-
haired element was contributed to our western coasts. Cultural relations between eastern Britain and the opposing shores of the North Sea
go back to Mesolithic times, though the major contribution of Frisia,
Denmark and Norway came after the Roman occupation. Anglo-
Saxon and Viking contributions to our population include tall, fair,
rather longheaded men with rather thin features, who are found in
small areas in the Atlantic ends of Britain but are more widely distributed in its Lowland Zone.

Illustrations of well-known men often give a better idea of elements
in our population than mere descriptions of types. Robert Burns
(Plate IX, p. 148) seems to illustrate some of the characters of our dark
longheads, who show a Neolithic inheritance. Plate VIII (p. 141),
showing a man carrying Palæolithic traits, was mentioned above.
Charles Darwin (Plate X, p. 149), painted before he grew a long beard,
seems to have had some of the characteristics of the Beaker people,
though these features may have been carried to his family by later
immigrants. Lord Ribblesdale, in J. S. Sargent's portrait (Plate XI,

p. 156), is a characteristic tall, thin, fair type with regular and fine features.

Investigation of blood groups has recently contributed to the story of the peopling of Britain through examination of data recorded by the Blood Transfusion Service. A detailed report on the survey of blood groups is nearing completion (1967). Human blood is classified according to its constituents into groups A, O, B and AB. Group AB is relatively uncommon and, like group B, is an expression of the B gene. It is therefore both theoretically sound and practically convenient to add together B and AB as is done below. Most individuals belong to the groups O or A but the combined B group may reach 5 to 25 per cent of a local sample, the lower figure applying mainly to eastern England and the higher to Atlantic Britain generally. In Scotland Dr. Elizabeth Brown of Inverness has shown that the percentage of B blood rises to above twenty at places on the Cromarty coast.

Persons with group O blood exceed those with A blood nearly everywhere in Scotland, Northern Ireland and most of Wales, with exceptions here and there in the South Wales coalfield and in Pembrokeshire. Group O blood is present in considerable numbers of people, especially where history hints at survivals of Romano-British life; the Colchester and Chichester districts may be mentioned here, but throughout England there are several other widely dispersed localities which show the same features. The large cities, with the partial exception of Bristol, have a marked preponderance of O blood; they have attracted large numbers of landless rural folk rather than the yeomen farmers of the surrounding countryside. The high percentage of O blood in Ireland and most of Wales, northern England and western Scotland may be thought of in connection with the immigration along the Atlantic route of Neolithic farmers before and after 3,000 B.C. It is generally thought that these early immigrants included many families from Mediterranean lands. The Mediterranean region has a preponderance of O blood though there is some B blood in the east of the region.

Pembrokeshire has a relatively high percentage of A blood, accompanied by as much as 18 per cent of B blood. South Pembrokeshire, which is often called Little England beyond Wales, has been considerably influenced by Anglo-Norman contacts and it received numbers of medieval Flemish settlers. In England there are also high proportions of A blood. They may exceed the percentages with O blood in places which were settled by Anglo-Saxons, Danes and Vikings, viz. east

PLATE XIX. COMPTON WYNYATES Warwickshire. Built largely during
the second half of the fifteenth century, it was once fortified.
Here Charles I lodged during the Civil Wars

PLATE XX. COURTYARD of the Strangers' Hall, Norwich. A medieval house of superior character

Yorkshire, Lincolnshire, Norfolk, south-east Essex, Kent and east Sussex. North of the Tees and the Ribble the percentage of A blood diminishes rapidly. The Anglo-Saxons came from a region of north-west Germany which has, and almost certainly had, a fairly high percentage of A blood; they were essentially rural, took possession of the soil and became a farming population. They displaced the Romano-British elements or converted them into landless serfs; it was the Anglo-Saxons who became the dominant element in the population.

Celtic languages, spoken throughout Britain until the Early English settled here, are now used by a majority of the population only in parts of Atlantic and Highland Britain. One branch of each of the main groups of Celtic speech has already disappeared. In the Goidelic group Manx is no longer a living language, though Scottish and Irish Gaelic survive. Breton and Welsh are still in everyday use; Cornish, the third Brittonic tongue, went out of use many years ago. All the Celtic peoples have left a legacy of place-names which usually describe topographical features and are of great interest.

The Scots who moved into western and north-western Scotland from Ireland, in the sixth century, brought in Gaelic speech; Scottish and Irish Gaelic are still closely related. Gaelic-speaking Scotland has seen nearly two centuries of migration to the Scottish Midlands and emigration overseas. It is now thinly peopled and there are more Gaelic speakers in, for example, Glasgow and Edinburgh than in some Highland villages. The greatest proportions of Gaelic speakers are now found along the north-west coast of Scotland and above all in the Hebrides. In Skye, the north-west of Mull, in Tiree and throughout the Outer Hebrides, Gaelic is the first language of over 70 per cent of the people. But only about 75,000 people now speak Gaelic and it is slowly losing ground in spite of the devoted work of Gaelic associations and the holding of the Gaelic *Mod*.

Welsh speech is also most often heard in areas along and behind the west coast of the country, and is spoken by large proportions of people who are often thinly scattered among the Welsh uplands. But it is also the first language of most of the people of Anglesey and of the lowlands of Caernarvonshire and Carmarthenshire, which are relatively well peopled. In Swansea there were 27,947 Welsh speakers in 1961, slightly more than the total of 27,775 for the whole of the largely Welsh-speaking county of Merioneth. In Glamorgan there were over 200,000 Welsh speakers in 1961, of whom 11,550 lived in Cardiff. Migration from Welsh-speaking rural areas to these and other large

Welsh towns is common, as it is to Liverpool and London. The contribution of rural Wales to London was mentioned on p. 37. Many Welsh-speakers still migrate there and meet regularly in Welsh cultural groups and chapels.

The application of the Education Act of 1944 gave educational parity, and the Welsh Language Act of 1967 gave legal parity, to Welsh. It is now taught in primary schools in nearly all Welsh counties, and in the predominantly Welsh-speaking areas it is, with English, the medium of instruction. It is also taught as a subject in most secondary schools and during recent years a number of bilingual secondary schools, using Welsh and English as media of instruction, have been established.

When the New Testament and Prayer Book were translated into Welsh in 1567 they standardised the language and invested it with a new dignity and purity. In spite of mistaken nineteenth-century educational policies, which proscribed Welsh in schools, Welsh is still the language of the home in much of Wales and there is a considerable output of Welsh literature of high merit. Over 650,000 people over the age of three years spoke Welsh in 1961. This was 26 per cent of the population. In 1951 the figure was 28.9 per cent and in 1931, 36.8 per cent. The rapid rate of decline in 1931-51 was thus slowed down in 1951-61. The survival of the language will depend on effective teaching in the schools and continued use by younger age-groups, provided that opportunities are given for them to work and stay in the Welsh-speaking areas of rural Wales. The dominantly Welsh-speaking counties are at present suffering depopulation or are maintaining their numbers largely by immigration of English speakers who retire there.

The English language suffers from the very irregular relations between spelling and pronunciation and we might adopt with advantage some of the spelling modifications used by the Americans to overcome this difficulty. But these irregular relations are the result of something that makes our language almost uniquely rich, namely its intimate combination of heritages from Anglo-Saxon, from Norman-French and from the classical sources drawn upon in many centuries, but particularly the seventeenth and eighteenth. Chaucer's tales and William Tyndale's translations of the scriptures contrast in language with the writings of Dr. Johnson so markedly as to suggest two languages, while in Shakespeare's plays the two are used with almost equal facility and felicity. The wealth of the English language in fine shades of expression may have made it less sharply defined than French, but it has helped to build up the literature of the imagination that is a major contribution of Britain to the world. And not only the literature of the imagination claims mention here. It has been a feature that leisured Britons have contributed in considerable numbers to science, history, travel-studies, philosophy and government by their writings, as well as by their active interest in public affairs. Furthermore, in all these fields of thought there are great contributors to our literature—Darwin, Huxley and Sherrington; Gibbon, Macaulay and Winston Churchill; Captain Cook and Doughty, Hobbes and Berkeley, Hume and Mill, Milton, Burke and many another. Their writings are far more than contributions to knowledge in their special fields: they have expressed themselves in finely chosen language; they are literary figures as well as scholars.

It has indeed been a great thing for Britain that she is, as it were, between the south and the north, between the Mediterranean and the Northern heritages, partaking of both and effecting combinations of varying proportions, so that variety, ingenuity, initiative and practical compromise are our better features.

CHAPTER 10

CLOTHES

FOR MUCH OF our prehistory, clothes took the form of mere coverings which protected the body and ensured survival in a hostile environment. Skins and hides were transferred to the backs of human animals. Adornment perhaps begins when lumps of fossil resin—amber—were collected and worn as rough necklaces by Mesolithic folk.

Palæolithic and Mesolithic hunters, who ranged over what became Britain far longer than any subsequent peoples, are likely to have gone naked or to have wrapped themselves in the skins of their prey. Rock paintings suggest that men ran naked in the chase, but that they also wore skins and animal heads to imitate and lure hunted animals. The intense cold of some Palæolithic periods would make fur coverings a necessity, especially for babies, who were probably carried in skin slings or bags. Holes pierced with fragments of bone would take thongs to hold skins together at the neck and elsewhere; a bone sewing needle was found in Church Hole at Creswell Crags, near Worksop. When the long retreat of the ice-sheets was finally completed, Mesolithic hunting and collecting groups made temporary camps in Britain. Their scraping and boring tools show that women were working the skins of red and roe deer, elk and beaver, as long ago as c. 7,800 B.C.

In warmer climates, around 7,000 B.C., cloth was already in use. Jarmo in Iraq was founded then and its people used cloth before they invented pottery. Linen was made in the Fayum in Egypt in 4,500 B.C. and Neolithic women in the lake-side dwellings of Switzerland wove patterned linen cloth. Spindle whorls and loom weights have been found there. Flax is abundant in the Mediterranean and Western Asia and over much of Europe. Common flax or linseed is native to Britain and here, and in Europe, it would be a common weed of cultivation; the fibres of the stem and the oily seed were both useful. Sheep's wool caught in bushes could be garnered in Europe from the Neolithic onwards. Turbary sheep were domesticated then in Switzerland, and related beasts were rounded up in the causewayed camps of Britain, which date from c. 3,200 B.C. Flax seed occurs at Windmill Hill but there is no evidence there that flax was woven. Bone awls, flint perforators and antler combs for removing coarse hair from skins suggest, rather, that hide and fur clothes were worn by the largely pastoral people of the causewayed camps, and also by later Secondary Neolithic folk, in both England and Wales. Skins would be more plentiful, and warmer, than imperfectly woven linen or woollen cloth, and they would last longer. Wool from early breeds of sheep is also likely to have contained much kemp, coarse hair which would produce harsh cloth.

Bronze Age finds suggest an increasing use of cloth, and in Wessex, where an aristocracy was sustained by a wide network of trade routes, considerable personal adornment. Pairs of buttons, perforated by V-shaped holes to take a thread, are known from the Early Bronze Age. These were probably cloak-fasteners, used like cuff-links. The chiefs of Wessex, and of outposts of their culture in East Anglia and the Yorkshire Wolds, were probably buried fully clothed. Pins, buttons, gold plates which must have been sewn on to their clothing, and gold-bound amber and faience beads from the east Mediterranean are found in graves of *c*. 1,400-1,300 B.C. Both woollen and linen clothes are likely to have been worn by these aristocrats. Over much of Highland Britain, hides, skins, and less exotic ornaments would be more common. Irish gold was sought and traded along the Atlantic route, and across the North Sea, for jewellery and ornaments. It was fashioned in the Early Bronze Age into *lunulae*, engraved crescent-shaped plates worn round the neck, and in the Middle and Late Bronze Age into torcs, twisted ribbons worn around the neck and possibly, in the case of the larger ones, around the waist.

Britain has not, as yet, produced Bronze Age clothing such as that shown on Fig. 45. Preserved by the acid waters of a Danish bog, the skirt is pleated, and blanket-stitched at the hem. The girdle is looped behind a bronze disc. Men wore fringed cloaks over a woollen shift which reached the knees, and the man from Tollund in Denmark had a cap and shoes. Bronze Age pins were disc-headed or in two pieces, forerunners of the widely dispersed *fibulae* (safety pins) of the Iron Age and later periods (Fig. 46).

In the Late Bronze Age stone and clay loom weights, to hold the threads on vertical looms, weaving combs and sewing needles become increasingly numerous in the remains of farmsteads. Cloth supplies must have improved in quantity and quality. Iron Age craftsmanship survives mainly in the form of metalwork, but it is likely that the skill which went into La Tène mirrors and other toilet articles was also

FIG. 45
Bronze Age woman's dress,
suggested by remains found
in Denmark

applied to garments. When the Romans arrived, the families of Belgic chiefs appear to have been style-conscious and well adorned. The Romans reported that the British used checked cloth, which often included bright reds, and excavation of the Somerset lake villages has revealed some of the equipment of the wool-workers, including their bone combs. They and their contemporaries produced British woollen cloth which impressed the Romans. The *Birrus Britannicus*, a cloak so well felted that it was waterproof and turned a sword, and their plaid blankets, are mentioned in a price-fixing edict of Diocletian.

Vegetable and animal dyes would have been used from an early period. Trade with Mediterranean lands would bring in many dyeing techniques, notably the extraction of Tyrian purple from the marine shell *Purpura*. Woad-staining of their bodies by Britons is well-known, and blue robes are said to have been worn by the Druids. In 1850 the body of a Romano-Briton was found preserved in peat at Grewelthorpe Moor, near Ripon. He wore a green cloak over a scarlet shift, yellow stockings and leather sandals. Many Romano-Britons are likely to have adopted the Roman toga, and the tunic, which was worn in various forms until the late Middle Ages.

The stem fibres of the nettle, and its relative hemp (*Cannabis sativa*), may have been used for sewing thread and to make coarse linen from an early date. To-day rope and twine are made from the outer layers of hemp stems, but for much of British history smocks and coarse towels were usually made from hemp, and "hempen homespun" became synonymous with peasant. It is possible that Anglo-Saxon migrants fostered greater use of hemp in Britain. Silk garments are mentioned in the wills of Anglo-Saxon nobles. Silk, because of the need to reel thread from several cocoons, and for specialised looms, is likely to have been scarce for at least six centuries after its introduction into Europe from Constantinople in the reign of Justinian. Its manufacture

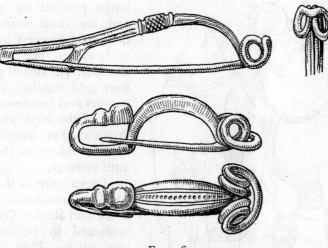

FIG. 46
British fibulae of the Iron Age

in North Italy started in the twelfth century and in France in the late fifteenth century. Huguenot refugees wove silk in England in the late seventeenth century and in the eighteenth century silk came into wide use among the fashionable. Imports of Shantung silk, made from the cocoon of the oak-egger moth in North China, and Japanese silk, made it a more plentiful fabric in nineteenth-century Britain. Its former high value is seen in the phrase "taking silk" when Queen's Counsel are appointed.

Leaders among the Anglo-Saxons wore knee-length tunics and fur cloaks (Fig. 47). The demand for highly prized furs continued to reduce the animal population. In the Laws of Hywel Dda, pine marten fur was worth thrice the price of any other skin except that of the beaver and was used for the king's robes. Anglo-Saxons wore thick stockings cross-gartered with leather thongs. Brooch fastenings were often large and beautiful and belts had jewelled clasps. Gold and silver finger-rings, armlets, swords and shields, were also treasured by their owners and were buried with them. The finds from the Sutton Hoo burial indicate the high standard of craftsmanship. Horse trappings were also beautifully made, as they had been in the La Tène period. A tenth-century necklace was said to be worth 120 mancuses of gold. A mancus was about 70 grains of gold and according to Anglo-Saxon law was the price of an ox or three acres of land. Anglo-Saxon women's

FIG. 47
Anglo-Saxon costume

kirtles reached the ground and the tunic worn over them was fastened by pairs of brooches, one on each shoulder. The richest women wore gold headbands. Their mantles and hoods were like those of the men, and children's clothes copied those of their elders, as they did until recently.

Tunics worn in the Dark Ages by missionaries of the Celtic and Roman Churches continued to be used by later priests. They became the white alb (*alba tunica*), and eventually the surplice, worn over a long gown. The cloak became the chasuble with a hood, and the gown and hood of academic ceremony derive from these garments. Franciscan friars still wear the medieval long gown and hood in its simplest form.

Armour was worn by both Anglo-Saxons and Normans. William I's knights wore long coats of mail in which flat iron rings were sewn on to leather or heavy linen. This banded armour proved inadequate as weapons improved. Steel plates and gauntlets were added to it in the fourteenth century and in the fifteenth century they became a suit which completely covered the body.

Below their long tunics Normans wore thick cross-gartered hose called *chausses*. Later in the Middle Ages stockings were separated from trunk hose and became *bas de chausses* and *haut de chausses*, hence *bas* for stockings in modern French. In the twelfth and thirteenth centuries weavers' guilds were improving the quality of cloth in the towns and both men and women there wore long tunics. Those of women reached the ground, and with them they wore a woollen or linen over-tunic or *bliaut*, with a jewelled belt, and an under-tunic or *cotte*, later divided into bodice and petticoat (*petit cotte*). Gentlemen too wore long gowns indoors but simple folk wore short garments, probably by night as well as by day. We know little about medieval underclothes or night-clothes, though kings apparently wore fur cloaks as dressing-gowns. Living conditions in the early medieval period were austere and clothing was simple, fairly subdued in colour, and as warm as the wearer's means allowed. Skins of British wild and domesticated animals would be used for the cloaks of humbler folk. Trade by Hanseatic merchants between lands around the Baltic and North Seas brought in a variety of furs for the wealthy. Later in the thirteenth century, elaboration in clothing accompanied increasing intricacy in architecture, and fashionable fourteenth-century garments were brightly

FIG. 48
Fourteenth-century costume

coloured and had some extravagant features (Fig. 48). More sober merchants and scholars wore long gowns until the Tudor Period. Chaucer wore one, with a plain hood. In 1330 Flemish weavers began to settle in Norwich and with them came ideas for making richer materials.

Fig. 48 shows that the tunic has become shorter. This fitted *cotte hardie* begins to look like a coat. The cape is largely ornamental and the felt hat has a jewelled brooch. Shoes are more pointed, although they have not yet reached fifteenth-century lengths, when their points had to be suspended by chains secured to the knees. Fig. 49 depicts the fashions of the fifteenth century, which are perpetuated on our playing cards, then newly invented. Fur is now used for trimming rather than for complete garments. Men wear full tunics, pinched at the waist, but with very full, padded sleeves. Ladies of Edward VII's day suffered similar discomforts. Fifteenth-century hose were brightly coloured and one leg might contrast violently with the other in colour. Women's

FIG. 49
Fifteenth-century costume

head-dresses were hung with fine muslin, and monstrous jewelled turbans, and horned hats, as well as "steeples," were worn. Silk, coming in from Italy, lent itself to use in this period of luxury and ostentation among the rich. Simpler folk wore more comfortable clothing.

From the sixteenth century, Highlanders have worn kilts and plaids, though after the '45 they were illegal wear until 1782. The clans, based on kinship (*clanna* means children) each developed their own tartans using vegetable dyes from the glens. Jackets replaced plaids for everyday use, but the useful length of woollen cloth was still carried by the people of the Highlands. Sir Walter Scott and the woollen manufacturers of the Southern Uplands did much to publicise tartans and to foster the wearing of the short kilt outside the Highlands. The pouch hung from the waist-belt became the ornamental sporran and various other accessories of "Scotland's national dress" were and are copied as souvenirs. The kilt, forbidden to clansmen in 1746-82 was, ironically, saved by its military use. The first Highland regiment, the Black Watch, formed in 1739, wore the kilt, as did many other regiments raised before the Proscription Act was repealed in 1782. These kilted regiments confounded many enemies; in World War I the 51st Highland Division was known as "the Ladies from Hell."

The Age of Elizabeth I was also one in which the nobility indulged in display and in "fashions from proud Italy" and France. This was the period of absolute monarchy. Its beaux were depicted by Nicholas Hilliard, the first of the English miniature painters. Henry VIII had led the fashion for the slashed, bolstered and befurred clothing worn

by the man on Fig. 50.
The farthingale, a full
skirt worn over a hoop,
and the stiff, peaked,
bejewelled bodice, are
late Elizabethan ideas.
The couple shown on Fig.
50 wear ruffs, which had
to be plaited on poking-
sticks. Ruffs came in from
Spain. There was an
alternative to them in
the form of a large fan-
shaped collar in as much
as three layers of cambric.
Laundering of this neck-
ware was made possible
by improved soap made
from whale blubber. For
the wealthy this replaced
soap made from wood
ash and the fat of dom-

FIG. 50
Elizabethan costume

estic animals. The woman's small hood, worn under the hat, had been
brought in by Anne of Cleves. Starched cambric head-gear, often very
becoming, survives among European countrywomen in, for example,
Brittany, Holland and Scandinavia, but women with skill and time to
launder it are now scarcer there.

Trunk hose separated from the stockings, as shown on Fig. 50,
became the breeches of later centuries. Shoes had begun to have heels
and to resemble modern ones. The Cavalier on Fig. 51 wears breeches,
and although lace, braid and embroidery were now often used on the
fashionable clothes of both sexes, costumes were on the whole simpler
than those worn at the Elizabethan court. Hair was worn long and
curled. Women's skirts were cut away to show richly embroidered
petticoats. It was from these fashions that the puritans recoiled and
introduced the plain and sombre styles shown on Fig. 52. The close-
cropped "Roundheads" wore no lace or trimmings and their womenfolk wore large, useful aprons. But colourful clothing returned with
Charles II and many close-cropped heads of the Commonwealth
Period (1649-60) were concealed under wigs. The French habit of

FIG. 51
Cavalier costume

wearing wigs instead of long natural hair continued into the eighteenth century when European men and women of fashion wore elaborate wigs. By the end of this century a tax on powder, and the lead of men like Fox, brought unpowdered natural hair back into favour. Wigs have, of course, persisted among European lawyers and even those of tropical lands which use European legal systems.

Sixteenth-century persecutions in France and the Low Countries, and the Revocation of the Edict of Nantes in 1685, brought in as refugees, craftsmen who greatly developed the silk industry in south-east England. In the eighteenth century, flax-growing and linen manufacture, previously best developed in Flanders, expanded in north-east Ireland. Supplies of household linen, underclothing, starched collars, cuffs and shirt-fronts became more plentiful. Industrialisation, applied to the linen, cotton and woollen trades, made it easier for the lower classes to copy the fashionable. Cotton, cheap, flexible, and easily dyed and washed, was a most useful fabric, particularly in the smoky areas which manufactured it.

In the early eighteenth century, coats and waistcoats were worn. Coats were at first full-skirted and waistcoats were long, while later in the century waistcoats became shorter and coats were cut away (Fig. 53). Hooped skirts and other extravagances of the "Age of Reason" gave way to the high-waisted dress modelled on classical lines—"the Caroline wrapper"—which was also popular in the early nineteenth century. The elegant couple shown on Fig. 53 are typical of visitors to Bath, the fashionable spa of Beau Nash and Jane Austen. The Napoleonic Wars deprived English travellers of their grand continental tours, and Highland Britain, "picturesque," strange and old-fashioned, was

much visited by them. They discovered "national costumes" peculiar
to both Wales and Scotland. In the
latter the Highlander's kilt was
dubbed typical of all Scotsmen. In
the eighteenth century both sexes
wore plaids, fashionable ladies wearing silk or silk-lined ones draped
around their shoulders, while the
common people wore red or tartan
worsted plaids over homespun dresses
or suits. Well-to-do women replaced
their plaids by silk and velvet cloaks
in the mid-eighteenth century when
French and Italian materials were
imported into Edinburgh and other
towns, and by the end of the century, better wages paid for English
broadcloth for Sunday clothing outside the Highlands, and sometimes
within them. Warm clothes and
bonnets replaced tartan plaids even

Fig. 52
Roundhead costume

for smallholders' wives, and ploughmen were found to be copying the
fashionable coats, linen shirts and cravats of their betters.

Eighteenth-century topographers and travellers found that Welsh
farm wives wore old-fashioned open-fronted gowns cut back to show
the petticoat, which was protected by an apron. Wide collars were
characteristic, as were caps worn under beaver hats (Plate 11, p. 112).
The latter were less tall than those added to the "Welsh national costume" later in the nineteenth century. This serviceable costume,
homespun and often home-made, could also have been seen throughout rural England by eighteenth-century travellers in search of the
picturesque. More flannel, woven in cottages or in small woollen mills
which then existed in many valleys, was worn in Wales than in England.
Lighter fashionable garments were, of course, worn in Welsh towns.

Bemused by their strange surroundings, the travellers not only
made the working dress of Welsh countrywomen into a national costume, but also invented regional variations of it. Here they were
assisted by Lady Llanover, the forceful wife of Benjamin Hall, who gave

FIG. 53
Late eighteenth-century costume

his name to Big Ben. Lady Llanover's water colours of peasant costumes of the South Welsh counties in fact show little variation in style around 1830, except that the skirt is not always cut away. She and her friends tried to foster "Welsh costumes" and Welsh flannel manufacture. Later in the nineteenth century, postcard manufacturers, and the tourist trade, produced the fancy dress shown on Plate 11 (see p. 112), complete with tall beaver hats and accompanied by suitably oldfashioned occupations such as spinning and the knitting of stockings. To-day, when the wearing of the "national costume" is limited to eisteddfodau, and to the fancy dress of small girls on St. David's Day, a vestigial half-knitted stocking may be seen pinned on to the dress. Plate 11 shows how, for the benefit of tourists, the white bonnet became a picturesque frill under the brim of the beaver hat, the blouse and skirt replaced the cut-away gown, the serviceable sleeves of working clothes acquired frills, and the plain collar was replaced by further frills or by a paisley shawl. As it is now realised that the last-named nineteenth-century feature is a rather anachronistic element in a "traditional" costume, the shoulders of small girls are now covered on 1st March by red or checked flannel.

The costumes which were really worn in Welsh towns and in the countryside in the eighteenth and nineteenth centuries may be seen in the Welsh Folk Museum at St. Fagans, near Cardiff. In the towns they differed little from those worn in Edinburgh or London. In the countryside they were plainer and heavier garments suited to work in windswept farmyards and stone-flagged kitchens. In 1970, British women do not work in their farms in mini-skirts, though their daughters who work in market towns may wear them.

Victorian clothing was staid, often ugly, and long-lasting; Edwardian fashion was as extravagant as that of the court of Elizabeth I. Class distinctions were obvious in clothing until after World War II when cheap well-designed clothing became available in multiple stores. Frock coats, silk hats, morning coats, and even evening tailcoats, though still symbols of social stratification, have become almost a fancy dress worn on great occasions. Factory work for women, followed by service in the First World War, produced shorter clothing and short hair. These and subsequent changes are well portrayed by *Punch*. The Second World War, with square-shouldered clothing for both service and civilian women, had been followed by an acceptance of slacks for women, and by some becoming and some extreme styles of both male and female gear. These have been designed by a fashion industry whose wholesale trade is centred in the decaying remnants of Georgian London. British fashions, especially those based on wool, are widely copied, and the industry is a big employer of labour. Clothing factories, though still most common in Yorkshire, have often been dispersed through development areas to provide work for women.

In 1883, Hilaire de Chardonnet invented rayon thread and the Courtauld family later developed the artificial silk industry in Britain. Another synthetic fibre, nylon, was used mainly by the services in World War II. Nylon and other man-made fibres derived from coal and mineral oil, such as Terylene and Orlon, now rival natural fibres and are often interwoven with them in fabrics. Textile factories have spread beyond the older cotton and woollen manufacturing regions and now outwardly resemble chemical plants. Man-made fibres, often flame-resistant, drip-dry, "easy care" and crease resistant, have many advantages over traditional materials. Many are hard-wearing, though this is often the last quality demanded of them. The fashion industry's need for constant changes has now reached its peak with the invention of dresses made from reinforced paper. As some grades of paper are made from the rags of clothing, the wheel of fashion may be said to have come full circle. Because of our changeable climate, paper clothing is unlikely greatly to displace warmer sources of rags.

The Anglo-Saxon and medieval garments shown on Figs. 47-9, including leather shoes and straps, and furs, could all now be reproduced in man-made substitutes. A great variety of fabrics is now available at competitive prices, and well-designed mass-produced clothing has made it possible for almost everyone to be fashionable, for a wide range varying from the extravagant to the sensible to be available, and for children and younger people to look gay and often decorative.

CHAPTER 11

DWELLINGS

THE MAIN preoccupations of Palæolithic and Mesolithic hunters were to find food and some form of shelter for their families. Drawings in caves in south France and north Spain suggest that some groups used tents supported on poles. Nomadic peoples who have succeeded them have used many forms of tent, including wigwams and gipsies' *tans*. In their simplest form the latter have a framework made of two rows of curved willow wands. Caves would provide prehistoric hunters with winter shelter, and fires near their mouths would give warmth, and security from wild animals whose lairs they may have been. Plate 6 (see p. 85), shows one of many caves used in Britain. Roof height within the shelter could be increased by hollowing out the ground below it. This practice began in Mesolithic Britain, and children can be seen making such *dens* (and tree-houses) to-day. At several Mesolithic sites in Surrey there are artificial hollows near springs. At Star Carr in Yorkshire, Maglemose folk used their axes to fell trees and to make platforms (see p. 54). Their marshy lake-side site made necessary a firmer foundation for their shelters and they reacted as do beavers in building their lodges.

Some Neolithic peasants may have constantly moved with their herds. At autumn round-ups at the causewayed camps they slept and feasted in hollows between the banks. But most Neolithic Britons would have needed more permanent houses near their corn plots. Few of these flimsy structures have been found and excavated (see p. 64). They may have developed from lines of stones placed round the bases of tents, or from walls built across the mouths of caves. Some, like Clegyr Boia, near St. David's, were "lean-to" structures built against rock faces. Most British Neolithic dwellings are rectangular, and even at this early date their corners may be rounded to reduce wind resistance. In some huts stone foundations supported wooden uprights and the spaces between them were filled with wattle-and-daub. Stone, wood, mud and some form of thatch (reeds, rushes, straw, heather or turf), the basic building materials of Britain, were all used in Neolithic dwellings.

The houses of the Secondary Neolithic farmers of Orkney and Shetland are discussed on p. 66. Preserved by drifting sand, their thick walls, box-beds, dressers, keeping-holes and fish tanks show how, with good building materials (in this case thin stone slabs), primitive fisher-farmers could construct homes well adapted to a difficult environment. Many similar Neolithic dwellings must have disappeared in Britain. The basic thick-walled rectangular house, with rounded corners and thatched roof, often housing both a family and its animals, continued to be built from Neolithic until recent times. The black house of the Atlantic coast and West Highlands of Scotland was built on a Neolithic plan (Fig. 54 and Plate XII, p. 157). With walls up to nine feet thick, and a central hearth, it was so dark that work would have to be done out of doors when possible, but it was warmer and more wind resistant than the bijou cottages which began to replace it in the nineteenth century.

The Beaker people appear to have been semi-nomadic and to have used tents and temporary dwellings. A few oval hut-foundations survive from this period. The round stone huts of later Bronze Age people are more common, especially in western Britain where surface stones are plentiful. On Dartmoor many hut-circles built of granite boulders, and formerly covered by thatch or turf, and the fields and pounds of their builders, can be seen (see p. 90). These dwellings would be larger versions of the round store-houses (*cleitean*) found on St. Kilda (Plate 12, p. 113). Corbelling, the practice of building roofs with projecting and overlapping slabs, was used by the builders of the megaliths, and may have been employed for roofing small huts then, as it was in later periods. The huts shown on Fig. 55, from the Hebrides, and the corbelled pigsty on Fig. 56, a type still surviving in South Wales, represent primitive dwellings which originated in Neolithic times, and, for thousands of years, provided poor folk with rudimentary shelter. Until Tudor times many British peasants lived in one-roomed hovels, and on unproductive marginal land in the highlands, remote from new styles which spread through the lowlands, old forms of dwellings like beehive huts and black houses lingered until the nineteenth century and even later. A time-lag of as much as a century in the spread of building styles from south-east to north-west Britain can be detected until recent times, even in the more productive western areas.

Late Bronze Age farmsteads in England and Scotland are described on p. 91. Many of these round huts, set among walled or embanked fields, continued to be used in Romano-British farming systems, while larger huts, or groups of round huts, either of stone or timber-framed, were probably occupied by kinship groups. Isolated farmsteads for single families are likely to have been less frequent than they were subsequently. In the Yorkshire Dales, the limestone fringes of the Lake District, the Cheviots and Southern Uplands, there are remains of hundreds of round huts which housed pastoral groups for many of the

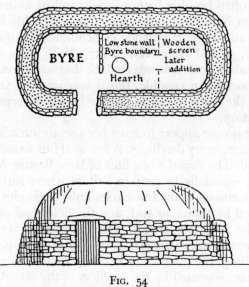

FIG. 54
Ground plan and elevation of a Hebridean black house

centuries between the Late Bronze and Dark Ages. Hillsides were often steep in these areas and flat bases for the huts were obtained by "cut and fill" methods. The round or oval hillside platforms thus obtained can be easily identified. Rectangular platforms of later centuries can also be seen in upland Britain and when dwellings are built on such slopes to-day, "cut and fill" techniques are still used.

Iron A settlers in south-east England built round, timber-framed, wattle-and-daub dwellings. Little Woodbury (see p. 92) is typical of many huts which would then have been scattered over the chalklands. Iron B farmers lived within or around stockaded camps in round huts which, in their largely stony territory, were dry-walled. They may also have lived in farm clusters downslope, on better sheltered sites, and retreated to the hill-forts in wartime. The lake villagers of Somerset used

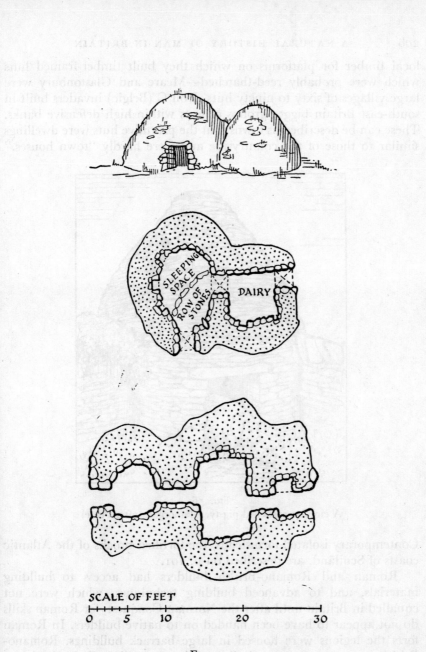

SLEEPING SPACE

ROW OF STONES

DAIRY

SCALE OF FEET

0   5   10   20   30

FIG. 55
Corbelled beehive huts in the Outer Hebrides

local timber for platforms on which they built timber-framed huts which were probably reed-thatched—Meare and Glastonbury were large villages of sixty to ninety huts. Iron C (Belgic) invaders built in south-east Britain bigger groups of huts within high defensive banks. These can be described as towns, but the primitive huts were dwellings similar to those of the countryside and were hardly "town houses."

FIG. 56
A circular corbelled pigsty, Glamorgan (after Peate)

Contemporary isolated farmsteads, the fortified brochs of the Atlantic coasts of Scotland, are described on p. 101.

Roman and Romano-British builders had access to building materials, and to advanced building techniques, which were not equalled in Britain until after the Norman Conquest, for Roman skills do not appear to have been handed on to native builders. In Roman forts the legions were housed in large barrack buildings. Romano-British town houses were similar to country villas. Only the lower courses, in stone or brick, of about 600 Romano-British timber-framed villas survive. They were farmsteads with outbuildings (Fig. 27) and

PLATE XXI.   THE BALLROOM of the Lion Hotel, Shrewsbury. Built by the
            Adam brothers (1728–92)

PLATE XXII. RODNEY STREET, Liverpool. A street with typical late
Georgian buildings

only about a tenth of them had luxuries like mosaic floors, baths and hypocausts. Native people sometimes attempted to copy them (see p. 113) but most Britons continued to inhabit round huts. They might be grouped around a courtyard, and have separate living and work rooms; underground storage chambers, like the Cornish fogous, were built near some homesteads.

The Romans introduced brick- and tile-making into Britain, though manufacture lapsed after their withdrawal. Roman bricks varied in size according to their purpose and were not fired so hard as modern bricks; they were re-used, but not imitated, by the Anglo-Saxons. Bricks were reintroduced from Flanders about 1220 and their use was advocated in Stuart times to replace diminishing timber stocks. William III fostered the use of bricks from his native Holland and they spread rapidly from the towns to villages placed near suitable supplies of clay. Diapered brickwork, using "Flemish bond" bricks whose black ends made a patterned wall, spread through south-east England.

Roman tiles, such as those produced in the tilery at Holt, on the Denbighshire side of the Dee, for the legionary fortress at Chester, were made for many purposes. Flat and ridge tiles, box tiles for water pipes and hot-air ducts, and *tesserae* (cubes of tile or brick for flooring), were typical Roman products. In mosaic floors coloured stone was also used. Large-scale reintroduction of roofing-tiles to Britain came in the sixteenth century, and, in London particularly, pantiles from the Low Countries were used to cut down the frequent fires caused by ignition of thatched roofs on timbered houses.

The Anglo-Saxons mainly settled on well-timbered lowlands and built in wood and wattle-and-daub. A few of their stone churches survive to witness their skills, but excavations of their villages suggest that ordinary farmsteads, or the houses of traders at such villages as Hamwich (Southampton), were very primitive. Sutton Courtenay, one of their villages near Oxford, was occupied in the fifth and sixth centuries and consisted of about thirty squarish hovels with rounded corners. The huts were of wattle-and-daub, with thatched roofs, and their floors were sunk two feet to give more height. After the Norman Conquest, dwellings with vaulted basements, which sometimes rose above ground level, gradually replaced these "sunk houses." Basements were useful for storage and in farmsteads often became the byre. Similar Anglo-Saxon dwellings of the ninth and tenth centuries have been excavated at St. Neots. Timber, stone wall-footings, hazel wands for wattling, and mud for covering it, would be used according to their availability. The

Vikings did not apparently introduce into Britain the "block-work" dwellings of the North European coniferous forest belt. The early European settlements of North America had many of them and "log cabins" played a great part in American history. In Britain deciduous timber lent itself less readily to their construction.

In western Britain, in the Dark Ages, round stone huts enclosed by stone walls, as in Anglesey, or by earthen banks, as in the raths of Pembrokeshire, continued to be built. The village at Mawgan Porth in Cornwall, inhabited from the ninth to eleventh centuries, is in the Dark Age tradition. Here too the dry-walled rooms are set around court-yards.

The Anglo-Saxons, contemporary Welsh and, later, the Vikings, built for their leaders, and their retainers and military followers, aisled halls which contrasted markedly with homes thrown together by the peasantry (Figs. 37 and 38). The seventh-century palace of the Anglian kings of Northumbria at Yeavering was a hall 100 feet long and had rooms screened off at each end. The free retainers lived in a second hall half as long, the serfs in huts. All these buildings had sunken floors, central hearths and were windowless. At South Cadbury, which may be Arthur's Camelot, the postholes of a large timber building have been discovered on the summit plateau; others may be revealed there. The Laws of Hywel Dda, who died in 950, describe rectangular aisled halls constructed for the Dark Age and early medieval princes of Wales. The values of their timbers are set out in the Laws and the main supports of a king's hall seem to have been three pairs of crucks (see p. 214). Smaller houses for freemen and serfs, constructed of timber and wattling, are also described. The permanent houses were long-houses, the abodes of both humans and animals. The Laws mention the more flimsy *hafdy* (the *hafod* was a summer dwelling), built on the mountain pastures as summer shelters. Such summer dwellings were used until recently throughout Highland and Atlantic Britain.

The seaborne invaders who came across the North Sea buried their great men in their boats. Where they found no homes to dispossess on landing, they may well have upturned their boats on the beaches and used them as temporary shelters. Some of their houses were boat-shaped and their roofs resemble upturned longships. Fig. 57 recon-structs one of the thirty barrack buildings at Trelleborg in Zealand (see p. 154 and Fig. 42). The stone footings of similar boat-shaped buildings have been found at Jarlshof in Shetland and at the Braaid in the Isle of Man. At Thetford, an Anglian hall fifty feet long and fifteen feet wide

FIG. 57
Reconstruction of one of the boat-shaped houses at Trelleborg

was divided into five rooms by cross-walls. The rooms contained sleeping-benches and may have housed separate families.

The practice of housing cows in milk, and their calves, under the same roof as the family, lasted from prehistoric until recent times in Britain. Many reasons have been given for it; among them are the warmth generated by the cattle, the belief that the milk yield increases if cattle can see the house fire, and the convenience of milking without leaving the house during winter storms. Throughout Atlantic and Highland Britain cattle and humans had their own halves of the house, and basement byres are still common under mountain farms in Europe. Early medieval farmsteads excavated on Welsh hillsides, such as those which overlook the mining valleys of South Wales, are rectangular "platform" houses with the "house-end" cut into the bank and the end occupied by cattle built on the "fill," and thus draining down the protruding bank of the platform. These long-houses had stone sleeping-benches along the walls of the "house-end" and a pair of doors opposite each other in the long walls. A gutter usually runs between the doors. These groups of platform houses can be matched today in Slievemore, a derelict village in the centre of Achill Island.

A wooden partition, often with feeding-racks, would lie on the byre side of the gutter, and, in later long-houses, a wooden cupboard or dresser provided a partition on the house side of it. Many variants of this basic plan developed (Figs. 58 and 59), and reconstructed examples can be seen in the Welsh Folk Museum at St. Fagans. Long-houses occurred throughout Highland Britain, though many of them were later reconstructed. One of the Mawgan Porth houses measured thirty-three feet by fifteen feet and was divided by a wooden partition. Its house-end had a central hearth, sleeping-benches and a door in the gable-end. The side walls also had a pair of doors joined by a passage. The byre drained through a corner hole and its floor was lower than that of the house-end. At Jarlshof a house built in the fourteenth century had cattle in its lower half.

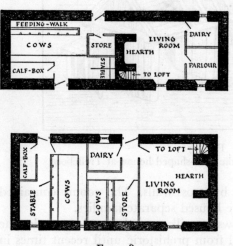

FIG. 58
Ground plans of Welsh long-houses (after Peate)

Simple long-houses such as the black houses of the Scottish islands were in common use until the nineteenth century in the Scottish Highlands. Like the hovels of medieval serfs, or of the common folk of later centuries, they invoked the horror of travellers who were more familiar with the amenities of English towns, or less austere rural environments. The "houses of sticks and dirt" were reasonably healthy so long as their owners lived and worked out of doors. Their furniture comprised only the basic necessities of existence, for the common folk of the Middle Ages rarely possessed more than beds, rough stools, cooking- and other pots, and tripods and andirons to support their cooking-pots over an open fire.

Long-houses and other primitive dwellings were most numerous where the land was unproductive or was isolated from new building techniques and materials which came in from continental Europe. Even in the English lowlands, the majority of the population lived in primitive huts until the Tudor Period. The golden age of the English cottage came in the century after 1550 and left its strongest impact in the lowlands and scarplands of south-east England. When the peasantry began

PLATE 21   CWM-PARC, Glamorgan, leading into the main Rhondda valley. The
concentration of pits, roads, railways and ribbons of houses in narrow
valleys poses problems of rehabilitation.

PLATE 22   MORAY PLACE, Edinburgh. A fine example of Georgian planning erected *c.* 1822 from designs by Gillespie Graham.

to move to the coalfields of Highland Britain in the eighteenth century, and were housed in terraces of small cramped cottages, their living space, if not their environment, was usually better than that which they had left.

The nobility, townsfolk, freemen and yeomen fared better. From the Anglo-Saxons to the Tudors richer folk built raftered aisled halls. The single-story halls of the Dark Ages, some of which were "sunk houses," were replaced in the Middle Ages by "tower-houses" in which

FIG. 59
A Welsh long-house, Ty'n-dolau, Llangeitho, Cardiganshire

the hall was on the first floor. It might be approached by an outside staircase and the lower floor could be used as a byre. Tower-houses had open hearths, smoke escaping through roof-holes, and partitions to provide privacy for the different generations of the lord's family. Many retainers would sleep with the cattle or in separate huts. The hall was the main living-space and the living-room was for long known as "the hall" in the Lowland Zone. Northern England called the living-room "the house."

Norman keeps, built first in wood and replaced in stone, were tower-houses (Plate XXVIII, p. 253). At their simplest they had a hall built over an undercroft or cellar. Medieval castles became more elaborate as they fulfilled their function as military strongholds for local armies and their domestic apartments continued to centre on the hall or solar. Additional private rooms multiplied in castles and great houses. Chimneys were added in the thirteenth century and separate kitchens were afterwards included in the house. Stokesay Castle (Plate XXX, p. 273), shows many stages in the evolution of the manor house. Its earliest structure is the twelfth-century tower-house. In the thirteenth century a rich Ludlow cloth merchant built the halled house at Stokesay. It has more private rooms than were usual at this time. Tower-houses were being built as late as the fifteenth century near the Scottish border. Fortifications were permitted there in the fourteenth century and peel towers began to be built. During raids cattle were rounded up into the ground floors of peel towers while the flimsy homes of the herdsmen were usually burnt. South Scotland has many tower-houses, such as those near Peebles and Kelso.

Moats formed another form of medieval defence. Between three and four thousand moated settlements are known in England; they include moated castles, villages and monasteries, but most of them are moated manor houses, large farmsteads of the twelfth to fourteenth centuries. Although many moats were filled in by agricultural improvers, hundreds may still be seen in East Anglia, the Midlands, the Welsh border counties, and in the lowlands of Lancashire and Yorkshire. The moat provided a defence for cattle against wolves, as well as during warfare. Moats are often found in claylands and clay cast up from them provided a firm island on which to build. They provided fish for fast days and, in centuries when dwellings were often built of timber and thatched, water for fire-fighting.

The valleys and hillsides of the Lowland Zone, the Midland plain, and the Welsh border, had plentiful hardwoods, especially oak, for the construction of timber-framed houses. Durable oak timbers were often removed and re-used by medieval serfs when they left a manor. Where timber was so scarce that builders depended on logs cast up on beaches, as in the Western Isles of Scotland, the roof-timbers of black houses were usually taken away with the rough furniture when a family left a derelict house. In the Middle Ages the use of curved timber, or crucks, became general in southern Scotland, east Wales and in England west of a line from Flamborough Head, through Sheffield, to Southampton Water. Cruck-building was common until 1700 in these regions. Some of the best surviving examples of crucks, and of elaborate timber-framing, can be seen in the Welsh Marches, on both sides of Offa's Dyke. Pairs of crucks were obtained by splitting a tree-trunk and were erected with their bases on the ground or on the outer wall. They curved at the same angle and met at the ridge, where their crossed upper ends supported the ridge-pole. This in its turn supported the roof framework. Two pairs of crucks, with additional timbers, enclosed a one-roomed house, the space between the crucks being known as a

FIG. 60
Timber-framed house, Abernodwydd, Llangadfan, Montgomeryshire

"bay." A house "of one baye's breadth, a silly cote," could be extended lengthwise, as the family increased in wealth or numbers, by adding further pairs of crucks.

Henry III (1216-72) had glass in the windows of his palace at Westminster, but windows (*wind-eyes*) were unglazed in most medieval houses. Straw or heather would be stuffed into windows in the most primitive houses at nightfall. Others would be hung with oiled cloth or would be shuttered. The house called Abernodwydd, from Llangadfan in Montgomeryshire (Fig. 60), now in the Welsh Folk Museum, has sliding shutters. Windows on its longer walls could be shuttered according to the direction of the wind. This house from the Welsh uplands has a stone gable on its exposed western end. But it was near a well-timbered tributary valley of the Severn and the remaining walls are half-timbered. The house is of the central chimney type with a thatched roof and an earth floor. Such floors were hard and long-lasting and continued to be laid down for centuries. Many mixtures were used and were rammed down after careful spreading. Where coal was burnt, a third of the floor material might be coal ash, a third lime, and a third loamy clay and horse dung.

House-builders then, as sometimes to-day, sought shelter for upland dwellings. Plate 3 (see p. 48) shows a small mountain farmstead tucked into the shelter of the rocks from which it is built. But it was not thought desirable for medieval housefronts to face into the sun. It was believed that the south wind brought the plague; it certainly brought the heaviest rain to percolate through weak walls. Devonshire farmsteads were often built around courtyards and walled off from the wind on the south side.

It has been suggested that the practice of "jettying-out" the upper story of a house, which lasted from the Middle Ages to the late seventeenth century, arose because the lower story would be protected from rain by the overhang. Jettying-out used the cantilever principle and strengthened the frame of the house. It also provided corner-posts in which the owner's pride and the carpenter's skill could be expressed (Plates 13 and 15, pp. 128 and 144).

The Tudor Period was more settled, so that it made fortified dwellings unnecessary, while increasing trade and prosperity allowed rich merchants and nobles to build or rebuild both country and town houses. Great houses were first built around courtyards which often had a fortified gatehouse (or embodied part of the old castle). Gradually fortifications and courtyard walls disappeared and manor houses with large windows replaced them (Plate XIX, p. 188). The building styles of the Renaissance are seen in houses like Montacute in Somerset or Audley End, near Saffron Walden.

Tudor peasants and yeomen, now that their dwellings were no longer fired in wartime, built more durable cottages and farmsteads. Where coal replaced wood for household fires, chimneys had to be built to carry away the unpleasant smoke. It had mainly been medieval London which had suffered "the stench of burning sea coal." Lofty halls were replaced by smaller one-story rooms and the rich had separate dining- and withdrawing-rooms. Houses were often half-timbered and even farmhouses began to have window-glass made in the Weald and in Staffordshire. Yeomen farmers and wool merchants used the profits of the wool trade to build fine houses in the Cotswolds, East Anglia, London and the main ports. In the Lake District Elizabethan "statesmen" and mine captains built the houses of stone, with rubble cores and flagstone roofs, which still adorn the Lakeland dales. They were rough-cast or limewashed later. During the Civil War of 1640-60, there was little building, but afterwards manor houses and farmsteads multiplied and large villages usually had a shop where rural householders could increase their stocks of pots and ironmongery. Jacobean panelling and portraits, instead of tapestries, appeared in great houses. Carpets replaced the rushes which had harboured plague-bearing fleas, and chairs slowly began to replace stools. The first wall-papers were flock papers which came in during the mid-seventeenth century and replaced the painted cloth hangings of the sixteenth.

The Great Fire of 1666 destroyed most of the medieval and Tudor city of London. Timbered and thatched houses were replaced by brick and tiled dwellings—much of the medieval city had been built of timber and mud. John of Gaunt's Savoy, between London and Westminster, was one of the earliest stone dwellings. Dutch and English bricks were, however, widely used for London houses before the Great Fire. Tile roofs, because of their weight, could be supported only by substantial build-ings, and thatch continued to be used on most half-timbered dwellings. Pantiles, imported from the Netherlands in the sixteenth and seven-teenth centuries, were made in England from the mid-eighteenth century, and were laid so that a continuous groove led the rain down to the gutter. They form the attractive roofs of the sturdy cottages of the Yorkshire and East Anglian coasts. St. Peter Port in Guernsey, set on a steep and broken hillside, is made still more attractive, in views from the sea, by the pantiled roofs of an old section of the town, Quartier Beauregard.

The replanned and rebuilt London included terraced houses which replaced dwellings built by individuals. In the eighteenth century, as land values and urban populations increased, terraced houses were built higher and narrower to save space (Plate XXII, p. 209). Georgian houses needed fanlights over their doors to give light to dark halls. In that century artists like the Adam brothers gave beauty to house in-teriors (Plate XXI, p. 208). Squares and crescents were also laid out in London and in towns like Bath, Brighton and Edinburgh in the eighteenth and early nineteenth centuries (Plate 22, p. 213). Bow-windows, introduced at the end of the eighteenth century, and cast-iron balconies, adorned many Regency housefronts. Resorts which were developing in the early nineteenth century have or had fine Regency terraces.

The development of the rail network in the mid-eighteenth century meant that building materials could be circulated to areas distant from their place of extraction or manufacture. Bright red or pale yellow bricks from the Midlands were used to build spas like Llandrindod Wells in Mid-Wales, where houses had previously been stone-built or half-timbered. Victorian ostentation expressed itself in many ways and there often appears to be no limit to the mixture of building materials used (Plate 23, p. 220). In the first half of the twentieth century, too, brick, stone, contrasting slate and ridge tiles and half-timber were commonly applied in the same building. Reinforced concrete, introduced late in the nineteenth century, is now widely used and the steel in it allows buildings to be almost "moulded" by architects. Glazed or cladded walls are common even in dwelling-houses, though they are most strikingly used in office, flat and factory blocks.

But for most of our history regional building styles have reflected the availability of local raw materials from which dwellings could be constructed. The Jurassic scarp has the most beautiful building-stone in Britain. Cotswold stone, happily still used, if only for facing house walls, is a warm honey-coloured stone which produced attractive buildings often roofed with flagstones (Plate 18, p. 165). Its heyday was the period between the fifteenth and eighteenth centuries when the Jurassic scarplands supported sheep and profited from them. East of the scarp there is little good building-stone; timber and wattle-and-daub often replaced it. In East Anglia, clunch, or hard chalk marl, was used for house walls, and flint was a common building material, especially in north Norfolk. Cob, a mixture of mud, hair, moss or straw, was widely used and often contained street sweepings. Its use declined after the seventeenth century, but good examples of cob-work can still be found in the villages and farmsteads of Devonshire and Somerset. With their tarred stone footings, "good hats" of thatch, and white-washed walls with rounded corners, such cottages and farmhouses add gaiety and charm to the landscape of south-west England. Cob and, later, brick, were used to build the ovens of cottages and farmsteads, often outside the house wall.

Timber-framed houses, with wall-spaces filled with clay strengthened by hazel wands, are common east of the Jurassic scarp and throughout the formerly well-wooded Midland plain. From the West Midlands they extend, like the pedunculate oak (*Quercus robur*) from which their timbers are mainly derived, up the middle valleys of the Wye, Severn and Dee. West Wales, the country of the smaller, branching, sessile oak (*Quercus sessiliflora*), formerly built in stone. It is interesting to observe "black and white" houses petering out as one nears the main watershed of Wales when travelling westwards. Only one or two examples are now found west of the watershed. Fig. 61 shows a timber-framed cottage with a stone footing from Warwickshire. In the

south of some Midland counties both stone and timber were plentiful.
Timber-framed houses were often at their most ornate in the Welsh
Marches where market towns like Ludlow have examples of "magpie"
houses in which the wood was painted black (Plate XIII, p. 160). In
contrast are the Kentish styles in half-timbering, one of which is shown
on Plate 17 (see p. 164).

FIG. 61
Timber-framed cottage, **Leek Wootton, near** Kenilworth, Warwickshire

Wall-spaces both indoors and outdoors were often covered with
plaster and the timber frames of houses were often completely concealed by white or colour-washed plaster. The Romans used this on
walls and ceilings and frequently painted over it. Lime plaster kept in
the warmth of the house and insulated ceilings, but it is not waterproof. In the late eighteenth century more durable "cement plaster,"
i.e. stucco, came in to cover stone and brick walls. In East Anglia

TWO ROOMED
WITH OUTSHOT EXTENSIONS   TWO GABLED WITH DORMERS

FIG. 62

Cottages at Farnham, Suffolk, and Stanton, Gloucestershire (after H. Batsford and
C. Fry, *The English Cottage*, Batsford 1938)

plaster was often moulded into patterns by pargetters—housewalls at
Saffron Walden retain some good pargetting. As bricks spread throughout the country in the seventeenth century, spaces between structural
timbers were infilled with brickwork but this brick-nogging was often
used only for the lower story of a half-timbered house.

Other methods of weather-proofing dwellings included weather-
boarding, which can be best seen in Kent and Essex, and tile-hanging.
Kent and Surrey have many cottages in which walls are hung with
overlapping tiles, sometimes in the shape of fish-scales. In the eighteenth
and nineteenth centuries schooners carried slates from the quarries of
Cornwall and West Wales to many western and southern ports. Slate-
hanging can be seen in ports like St. Ives and Looe (Plate XVI, p. 177)
and in Regency houses which turn their backs to the sea winds in Tenby
in Pembrokeshire. The purple slates of North Wales, which roofed
many industrial towns, are still used as roofing-slates, but slate-hanging
is no longer necessary. Slabs of North Wales slate are used for cladding
modern buildings. Mass-produced tiles, first of asbestos and now of
clay, and varying in colour and suitability for the localities in which
they are used, have partly replaced more expensive roofing-slates. The
greenish slates of Borrowdale, more varied in colour than purple ones,
were formerly more widely used in northern England.

Until the late eighteenth century, English towns and villages were
seemly groups of dwellings. They included dignified Georgian terraces
in the towns, and cottages and farmsteads built by craftsmen from local

PLATE 23   VICTORIAN HOUSE (1887), showing the love of display in the period of the first industrial revolution. A meaningless tower is a frequent feature.

PLATE 24   a. LLANRHYCHYWN CHURCH, Caernarvonshire. In moorland Britain a village church is often a simple rectangle with a low roof and small belfry.

b. CRAIGWEN CHAPEL, Caernarvonshire, showing two doors, originally one for men and one for women.

raw materials in the villages. Cottages varied from modest dwellings with outshots to larger two-story houses (Fig. 62). Stone, brick and tile were replacing mud and thatch. The last phase of enclosure of the common fields spread some newly-built farmsteads among their re-grouped enclosed fields. New cottages, often in pairs, were built near these farms for farm labourers' families. Other farmers built "tied cottages" in the nineteenth century to house workers who might otherwise be tempted into new industries, and unmarried servants slept in the farms in attic rooms, and sometimes above the cattle in the byres.

Victorian wealth, improved communications and mechanisation combined to produce dwellings which varied from dull terraced houses for working folk to ostentatious middle-class houses and upper-class mansions. The former, however inadequate, were at least plain box-like structures; the two latter combined the more ornate building styles of many centuries. Norman arches, Gothic windows and Scottish baronial turrets, all based on coal exports, are incongruously combined in suburban mansions around some nineteenth-century ports. This was a period which found St. Pancras, a Gothic railway station, not in-congruous. Pinnacles and towers with no function were widely used (Plate 23, p. 220). Round *tourelles*, introduced into Scotland during the Auld Alliance, which were meant to contain staircases and can be seen with this function in towns like Stirling, spread across the Border and were attached to large Victorian villas.

The Victorians also discovered cast iron as a building material, and conservatories, miniature versions of the Crystal Palace, were built on to their larger houses. Plate glass replaced the smaller panes of Georgian and Regency windows in the mid-nineteenth century. Gas-lit rooms, increasing at this time, had high ceilings because of the fumes from this form of lighting. Electricity has allowed ceilings to be lowered. The interiors of prosperous Victorian and Edwardian dwellings were usually as cluttered and ugly as their exteriors (Plate XIV, p. 161), and the good workmanship which went into details and into individual pieces was marred by the overall effect.

Twentieth-century architects have repudiated Victorian ostenta-tion and unsuccessful combinations of Gothic and other styles. The inter-war period, like that of the Victorians, was often imitative, and produced Neo-Georgian houses and a wealth of half-timbered gables on suburban brick houses. The coast fringe of Britain, with dwellings ranging from bay-windowed, flat-roofed, reinforced concrete villas to the cheapest of bungalows for holiday use or retirement, probably suffered most from the faults of inter-war building. Dwellings are now better designed for their functions, and more care also goes into the design of their furniture and fittings. In the early eighteenth century, tropical woods like mahogany replaced oak for furniture-making and veneering became common. The cabinet-maker's art flowered in the workshops of Chippendale, Hepplewhite and Sheraton. To-day a greater variety of tropical and temperate hardwoods is available to good designers.

The Parker-Morris building standards of room size and equipment, laid down in 1961, are being adopted by local authorities in their house-building schemes. Prefabrication of house units, which started when prefabricated bungalows replaced bombed houses, is likely to increase. New dwellings, built in the heart of the countryside, especially bunga-lows, are often identical with those of the towns. In these there is a vast programme of replacement of worn-out dwellings.[1] In the finest rural landscapes great care is taken to preserve old dwellings and to build new ones in material appropriate to the locality. Even in the country-side, gardens are smaller because of high land values. Owners of country houses lack labour to maintain pleasure-grounds which they have in-herited and which may include Elizabethan herb gardens, Renaissance "canals" which were ornamental fishponds, orchards, box-edged flower gardens once filled with species introduced from the Low Countries by Huguenots who taught the English their love of colourful gardens, kitchen gardens in which newly introduced potatoes and tur-nips were first grown, and conservatories which produced hot-house fruit, flowers and ferns.

---

[1] Because of high urban land values tower blocks of flats often replace two-story houses, but these blocks need to be surrounded by adequate play-space and, ideally, by well-landscaped gardens.

CHAPTER 12

VILLAGES AND HAMLETS

PREHISTORIC VILLAGES, in their sites and defences, demonstrate the relative stability or insecurity of the periods in which they were founded. The groups of farming families who built the Late Bronze Age villages of the chalk downlands, of Dartmoor, and of the limestone uplands of northern England, laid out their fields and cattle-pounds around undefended hut clusters (see p. 90). Iron B groups, involved in the defining of territories, and in tribal warfare, lived in hilltop or hill-brow villages of varying size. Their round huts, built in unsettled centuries, were defended by well-designed systems of banks, ditches and gates. Land access to the lake villages of Somerset was by means of log causeways; they were secure behind their water defences. Iron C villages, best developed in the valleys of south-east England, lay behind extensive earthworks and ramparts. Most of the dwellings within these fortifications were simple huts, but tribal capitals such as Cymbeline's Camulodunum were so extensive that they have been described as towns.

Where a site was well endowed with good cornland or meadows, or was a focus of land or sea routes, or reaped a good yield from the sea, village might succeed village on it. Jarlshof in Shetland shows continuity from its Bronze Age settlement to its medieval farm cluster. Old Sarum has provided evidence of Iron Age, Roman and Saxon occupation, and many Roman forts and towns became medieval towns. At others, like Piercebridge, in Co. Durham, Caerwent, in Monmouthshire, and Castle Acre in Norfolk (Fig. 63), the foundations of the Roman walls to-day encircle villages.

Many of the villages of Lowland Britain were founded by Anglo-Saxon farming groups between 600 and 1,000. Their place-names are largely Saxon and Scandinavian and they predominate in the Domesday Survey. Many of our lowland villages have been in existence for over a thousand years. In Highland and Atlantic Britain, Celtic saints preached to communities in small villages whose names appear on modern maps and are of similar antiquity.

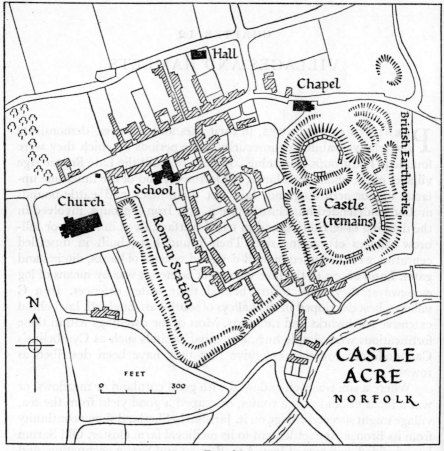

FIG. 63

Castle Acre, Norfolk, a village with a Roman basic plan, a Saxon cemetery and a medieval motte and bailey

The names given to these old-established villages, all basically farm clusters, often describe physical features, vegetation, or potentialities for defence or farming. Among names given by the Early English are *Beorg*, primarily a hill, and *Burh*, a fortified place. Both are responsible for village names that include the words Burgh, Borough, Brough, Borrow, Barrow, Bury, Berry and Bir. *Wick*, or *Vik* in the Northern Isles, for a coastal feature, is a sea rover's name for a creek or haven. Wick, inland, is often an Early English name for a settlement and, especially, one founded as a dairy farm. Villages which worked salt

PLATE XXIII. TEXTILE WORKERS quarter in a nineteenth-century industrial town in the North of England. The one-family house is typical

PLATE XXIV. PART OF THE BOURNVILLE VILLAGE TRUST ESTATE, near Birmingham. The Bournville Estate was founded in 1895 by the late George Cadbury and his work has been carried on by the Bournville Village Trust which he also founded. Mr. Cadbury laid down in the Trust Deed that dwellings should occupy about a fourth part of their own sites, and before being transferred to the tenant or purchaser gardens were laid out and fruit trees planted. This Estate is a separate organisation and residence in it is not confined to the employees of Messrs. Cadbury Brothers Ltd.

deposits have the suffix -*wich*, possible because early saltpans were worked along the margins of creeks. Many coastal saltpans are detailed in the Domesday Book.

Cattle played a big part in the farming economy of the Anglo-Saxons, and settlements which were productive of butter, milk and cheese were given names like Butterwick, Butterley, Birley, Cheswick, Chiswick, Keswick and Smercote. The modern Norwegian word for butter is *smør*. In Scotland and northern England *sett* as a place-name was originally given to a *seter* or summer dairy farm. The Northern Isles have many such Norse place-names (see p. 150). Marshes and poor pastures were identified by names like *moss*, *mire*, *saur*, an area of poor, boggy soil (Sowerby) and *stroud*, an overgrown area of marsh. *Heath* is embodied in the names of Hatfield and Hadley, *chart* is an overgrown common, *hese* is land covered with brushwood (Heysham, Heston), *bent* an area noted for its bent grass (Chowbent) and *bushey* derives from the Early English name for a thicket. *Breck* was uncultivated land or land taken in from the waste and periodically tilled. Names for clearings in woodland and marsh include, in south-west England, elements like *bere*, *beer* and *bear*, and elsewhere *leigh*. In northern England Alsop and Bacup had as their last syllable the Old English *hop*, in their case probably meaning valley, but it also meant a clearing in a fen.

The communally tilled arable land of Anglo-Saxon and medieval villages was given the name *feld* (open country), field, and, in the West Country, where f became v, association with the French *ville* sometimes occurs, both as a settlement and field name. The coasts of the Bristol Channel exchanged settlers in many prehistoric and later periods. This is so in Somerset and Glamorgan and a common field which survives at the western end of the Gower peninsula is known as "Rhosili Vile."

Colonising groups often gave their leader's name to settlements which were known as his *tun* (or *ton*), *ham*, *ing*, *thorp* or *by*. Ceorl is sometimes a personal name but, like *charl*, it could also mean a free peasant or, later, a serf or churl. Names such as Charlton, Chorlton, Chorley, Carlton and Carleton embody these elements. Villages which developed as trading centres and had busy markets took the name *Chipping*, which is also a component of Copenhagen.

Celtic and Gaelic place-names are also descriptive of local topography and vegetation. Hill and vale, rocks and rivers, the predominating colour of the landscape and many other features are described in them. In Cornwall, Wales and Scotland, *lan*, *llan* and *kirk* often preface the names of villages where missionary saints preached, presumably to small communities already settled there. The saint's name and elements descriptive of the locality often follow. The name of the Virgin was often added to that of a medieval township served by a St. Mary's church. Llanfairpwllgwyngyll, "Mary's church of the white hazel pool," is an example. The remainder of this celebrated Anglesey village name was added for the bewilderment of nineteenth-century tourists.

In the prehistoric villages of Celtic and Gaelic-speaking Britain, farms were clustered together. Small nucleated villages, the settlements of related groups of farmers, long continued to be characteristic of the leaner lands of Western Britain and of Ireland. The farmsteads huddled together without much order, as if, to quote an Irish observer, they "had fallen in a shower from the sky." Early Anglo-Saxon villages may have housed similar kinship groups, but as they expanded when more lowland was cleared, they usually became more orderly groupings and the farmsteads were set along well-defined streets.

Farmers in Highland and Atlantic Britain tilled limited arable patches and, so long as they depended solely on corn, sheep and cattle, their settlements rarely contained more than a dozen farmsteads. The Irish *clachan*, the farm clusters of the Highlands and Western Isles of Scotland, and many early Welsh and Cornish villages which were based on this economy have their roots in hut-groups like Chysauster in Cornwall and Din Llugwy in Anglesey. These western clusters were the homes of kinsfolk and were each tied to a communally tilled infield which often lay downslope to facilitate the transport of manure. The infield needed dung, and seaweed if it was available, because it was continuously tilled under a system known as *runrig* in Scotland and *rundale* in Ireland. Each household farmed about four or five acres of strips in it. Outfields were periodically ploughed and might be cultivated for up to five years before they reverted to pasture. Hill pasture of varying quality formed the common grazing land of the village and Scottish farmers had their *soumings*, that is their stints of cattle and sheep which might be put on the hill. Common meadows were much less plentiful than they were in the lowlands of England and the infield was naturally much smaller than the common arable fields which developed under the three-course rotation of such areas as the Midland plains. In the Highlands and Western Isles, and in Ireland, farm clusters did not focus on a church and inn as they did in English villages.

The Laws of Hywel Dda suggest that small hamlets of serfs were a feature of a Welsh lord's demesne. The Welsh *maenor* was based on communal cultivation and tenants paid rent in kind, yielding a portion of their grain, stock and honey to sustain the lord's household. Apart from his family this would include his following of freemen who had military duties. The villagers of the main hamlet (the *maerdref* or mayor's settlement), built a hall or *llys* for the lord nearby. All his bondsmen tilled his demesne land and grazed their stock on the lord's waste. They held strips in the common arable fields and lived in small groups of dwellings, most of which would have been long-houses backed by an enclosed croft or paddock. Nucleated hamlets of this type, located near limited patches of good arable land, were often on or near prehistoric sites. The essentials of their economy resembled elements of the medieval English feudal pattern and they co-existed with settlements which grew round the Norman invaders' castles after these had been established on the best land of the coastal fringes and broader valleys of Wales. In such areas there are boroughs with medieval walls, large groups of farmsteads centring on churches and castles, and formerly surrounded by extensive common arable fields, common meadows and pastures, and the smaller clusters of farms which were once Welsh bondsmen's hamlets. There are also old groups of roadside cottages, outside the villages, which were built as encroachments on the road verges which were the lord's waste, and many dispersed farmsteads, which, in the Welsh as in the English lowlands, resulted from the enclosure of the open fields.

In upland Wales dispersed settlement is old-established and G. R. J. Jones has suggested that it was a consequence of the Anglo-Norman occupation and resulted from the dispersal of the freemen. These freemen were grouped in clans (*gwelygordd*) and each occupied a *gwely* or resting place. The *gwely* had its patch of arable and its grazing rights on the hillsides in return for rents and services to the local lord. As the population increased in the relatively stable centuries after the Norman Conquest both arable patches and homesteads multiplied. Inheritance by gavelkind, the equal succession to land of all heirs, which was widespread in western Britain, made for fragmentation of the original *gwely* land and produced holdings which were too small to sustain households. More land was laid out in arable strips and new homesteads were afterwards scattered along their margins, often at the break of slope between the arable and the grazing land. These are not so much hamlets as strings of widely-spaced "beads." Continuing multiplication of farmsteads, bound up with land quality and population increase, completed the largely dispersed pattern of Welsh rural settlement.

English villages which were based on communal farming, first by

Anglo-Saxon colonisers and later under the medieval feudal system, often became large and compact nucleations of farmsteads. Their arable fields, meadowlands and common pastures were often well-delineated before the Norman Conquest and the limits of the land of the villages, which became parish boundaries, were often already fixed. Full cultivation and occupation of grazing land within the parish limits was usually completed by the thirteenth century. Between the mid-thirteenth and mid-fourteenth centuries, villages continued to expand. This prosperous medieval period was one when corn was exported in considerable quantities. The Domesday population of Britain, overwhelmingly rural, has been estimated at 1,250,000. By the mid-fourteenth century it may have increased to about 4,000,000. Towns and villages were then swept by the Black Death, which killed about one and a half million people.

In the fourteenth century a reduced population, due largely to plagues, produced a retraction of the outer limits of cultivation; marginal lands, such as those of the dry chalk wolds, the sandy heaths of Breckland and the high hillsides of western Britain, often ceased to be cultivated. Whole villages were abandoned at this time. Deserted villages had previously resulted mainly from clearances by royal or monastic officials. The use of the New Forest for hunting by William II caused tillage and village to be abandoned at Greatnam, near Lyndhurst, and Hartford, near Beaulieu. The Cistercians, seeking solitude for their abbeys, and sites for their granges, which were both arable and sheep farms, dispossessed other villagers. In Lincolnshire, the Cistercians of Revesby Abbey displaced three villages on the margins of the Fenland about 1150. The monks of Margam Abbey in Glamorgan caused a later desertion of Llangewydd village, on the site of one of their granges. About three hundred villages were cleared to make way for hunting forests or abbeys and monastic granges. During the fourteenth and fifteenth centuries about a thousand more villages were deserted, and their arable lands, as well as their pastures, were turned over to sheep. The villagers were evicted and their common lands enclosed.

The sites of these villages are now turf-covered lines of banks and ditches, some covering as much as twenty acres. Villages deserted because the land could be more profitably used for sheep can be found in counties of the Midlands which produce good grass but are less satisfactory cornland. Both large and small villages were depopulated by their manorial lords in counties like Warwickshire, Rutland, North-

PLATE 25   WORCESTER CATHEDRAL, mainly twelfth and thirteenth century, on the River Severn.

PLATE 26 FOUNTAINS ABBEY, Yorkshire. The finest British Cistercian Abbey-ruin, twelfth century with a fifteenth-century tower.

ampton and Leicestershire. In the latter county, which has sixty deserted villages, fifty-two desertions have been attributed to clearances for sheep-farming. The East Riding of Yorkshire also has many deserted villages of this period, and in the sixteenth century, enclosures for sheep-farming deprived many Northumberland villagers of their livelihood. Later, and notably in the eighteenth century, emparking of parts of large estates swept away more villages. Well-known instances are Harewood, near Leeds, and Westonbirt, near Tetbury in Gloucestershire. By this time, displaced villagers were often rehoused in model villages, as they were at Ickwell in Bedfordshire, Wimpole in Cambridgeshire and at Milton Abbas in Dorset, where the neat new village dates from 1787. Partly reorganised villages, like St. Fagans in Glamorgan, where some houses were moved from the valley slopes to create pleasure gardens, can also be found. Shrunken villages, due to a variety of causes and dating from many periods, are widely distributed.

In Highland Britain, a land of hamlets with plentiful grassland, fewer villages were deserted because of enclosure for sheep-farming in the Tudor Period. Deserted hamlets here are more likely to be the results of "clearances" (in Scotland), of the later shift to the coalfields, of migration and emigration, or the ephemeral settlements of the early years of the Industrial Revolution. They may be lines of ruined stone cottages by a stream which once turned a water wheel to power an early cotton or woollen mill. Shrunken or deserted hamlets which once clustered round early paper mills or forges can also be found in the valleys of western Britain.

The immediate setting of the nucleated English village was the group of arable fields in which each farmer held a number of strips initially graded to give all holders shares ranging over fields with varying soil, drainage and aspect (Fig. 64). In the fifteenth and sixteenth centuries there was already a free market in land among the small peasantry. In Lancashire and other northern counties most of the communally worked fields appear to have been infields and periodically cropped outfields similar to those of Scotland. Many of them were enclosed at an early date. Piecemeal enclosure there of a few acres of the plentiful hill grazings, as farms were dispersed, was taken for granted. Many Essex and some Surrey open fields had been enclosed in the Middle Ages and in Essex and Sussex, Devon and Cornwall, these had largely disappeared by 1500. North Devon can nevertheless still show one in Braunton Great Field. Around the Fenland, where cattle

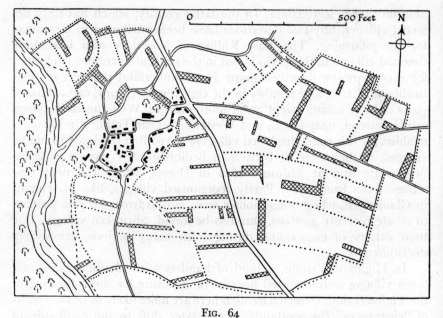

FIG. 64

An irregular West German village (*haufendorf*) and its common fields. The strip
holdings of one household are cross-hatched

were important in the farming economy, there was a great deal of early
enclosure.

But in spite of piecemeal enclosure by tenant farmers, and large-
scale enclosures for sheep-farming, half the arable lands of England
were still unenclosed in 1700. Between 1760 and 1800, parliamentary
enclosure acts accounted for the disappearance of 4,500,000 acres of
common arable, meadow and pasture land. This phase of enclosure
was completed in the mid-nineteenth century and during the following century most villages lay among hedged or walled arable fields,
enclosed meadows and pastures. As reallocated fields were often in
compact groups, many new farmsteads were built in the century following 1760 among their newly grouped fields, leaving some village farmsteads to be occupied by craftsmen or farmworkers.

The open-field system had been wasteful of time and labour and it
succumbed to population growth, rising prices of both the land and its
produce, and to the introduction and spread of root-crops in the seventeenth and eighteenth centuries. The need for these crops to remain in
the ground after the period of corn harvest, when the stubbles were

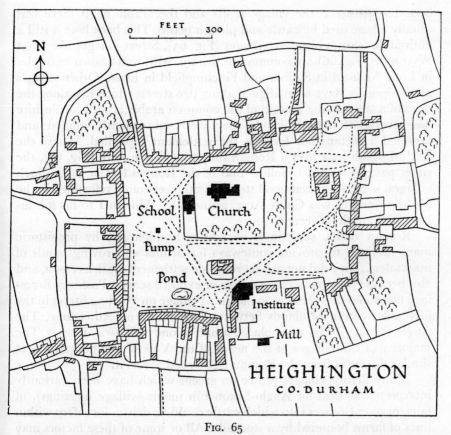

FIG. 65

Heighington, Co. Durham, a village set around a green which was originally rectangular

turned over to the cattle, made enclosure necessary. The few farmers
who still cultivate open fields claim that hedges are wasteful and that
the winds can sweep over their strips and dry the corn. Modern
mechanised farming, with its large fields, is again producing in the
English lowlands and downlands a hedgeless open landscape, though
the varied bands of crops of the old strip fields are better seen to-day
in the Paris basin than in the English Midlands where they were once
so characteristic.

Many English villages are aligned along one or more village streets
with the farmsteads and cottages backed by crofts which were always
enclosed. Beyond their bottom hedges lay the open fields, and along the

boundary between the village crofts and the arable fields there was usually a lane used by cattle and plough teams. This back lane is still a noticeable feature of many villages (Fig. 65). Street villages like West Wycombe (Fig. 66) are common in Britain, with well-known examples in Long Melford in Suffolk and Finchingfield in Essex. Other villages may originally have been aligned along two streets which ran along the sides of a strip on the margin of the common arable land. Lincolnshire has several of these villages; they were subsequently infilled and assumed a rectangular form as the settlement expanded. Where the Early English took over a Roman site, as at Castle Acre (Fig. 63), the street pattern tended to follow that of the Roman fort or town. Such villages, because of their good strategic site, were often refortified in the Middle Ages, as was Castle Acre, granted by William I to his son-in-law, William de Warenne.

Roman roads, sometimes on routes trodden out by prehistoric man, survived to provide routeways for armies and roving bands of marauders. They did not attract roadside settlement for this reason, and also because they often ran over dry or exposed scarps. Professor Beresford has noted that there is no medieval village on Watling Street in the fifty miles of the Midlands between Towcester and Atherstone. The Anglo-Saxon villages were placed a half to one mile away from it. The majority of the villages of the north of the Vale of Glamorgan are at similar distances from the Roman ridge-road across it.

Many British villages centre on greens which have been variously interpreted as sites for Anglo-Saxon tun moots (village meetings), of fairs, or as enclosures into which cattle could be driven for safety within lines of farms bounded by a stockade. All or some of these factors may have been responsible for some of the attractive village greens of Britain. The largest greens were used for horse-racing and many have recently deteriorated, under recreational pressures, into car parks. East Scotland, Northumberland, Durham, the North Riding of Yorkshire, Cheshire and eastern England have many of them. Hilltop villages in Celtic Britain, which formerly had cattle fairs, also have greens. Mathry, in north Pembrokeshire, is one of them. There are a hundred green-villages in County Durham, mostly on the undulating lands south and east of the River Wear. Many of their names have -ton and -ington suffixes and probably date back to the Anglian occupation of the county. Heighington (Fig. 65) was the capital of one of the shire units and, in 1183, was peopled by twenty-seven families. Its green is unusually large and was originally square. Churches were more usually built off the

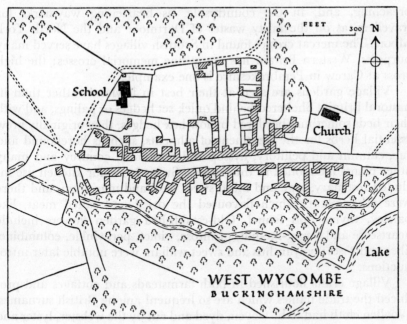

FIG. 66

West Wycombe, a street village in Buckinghamshire

green, which was preserved as a grazing area with rights restricted to the farmsteads facing on to it. There are great variations in the forms of village greens, but clustering of farmhouses and cottages on their margins, and back lanes beyond the paddocks and crofts, were characteristic of all of them.

On the margins of greens and at the junctions of lanes leading into villages, inns are usually found. They frequently adjoin the church and refreshed the worshippers after morning services. It was not unknown for them also to provide diversions such as Sunday cockfights. Village inn-signs largely depict features of farm life and names like Wheatsheaf, Hop-Pole, Waggon and Horses, and Barley Mow are as common as white and black horses or lions on them. An inn on an old pilgrim route may be called the Lamb and Flag. National heroes, or their best-known battles, like Wellington and Waterloo and Nelson or Trafalgar, are also commemorated, as are kings, though not Cromwell. The coats of arms of local landowners are frequently shown on inn-signs.

Crosses often adorn the centres of villages, as, for example, Lambourn and Eastbury in Berkshire. They were used for meeting and preaching, and, in the countryside, as heartening waymarks for travellers, as on the misty wastes of Dartmoor and the North York Moors. The mercat crosses found in Scottish villages have served many purposes. Western Britain has many fine memorial crosses; the high cross at Carew in Pembrokeshire is one example.

Village gardens are seen at their best in lowland rather than in pastoral Britain. Sheltered behind quick-set hedges or palings, and with their beds sometimes bordered by low box hedges, they originally grew essential herbs for the treatment of ailments, such as horehound and rue, catmint and pellitory, hyssop and camomile, comfrey and many other plants mentioned in the herbals. Sweet herbs for kitchen use included rosemary, sage and mint, sweet basil and marjoram, and there were other plants which flavoured the dried and salted meat, like parsley, thyme and fennel. Old-established garden flowers include heartsease and forget-me-not, primrose, violet, periwinkle, columbine, lilies and roses; polyanthus and sweet william were notable later introductions.

Village crafts flourished in both farmsteads and cottages and produced the trade names which are so frequent among British surnames. Woollen cloth had to be woven, dyed and cut by the webster, lyster and shepster, bread was baked by baxters and ale brewed by brewsters. The smith's trade was essential to the village, but, because its thatched roof was often fired, the smithy was usually separated from the main cluster of houses. At Heighington it was the isolated house at the road junction nearest the right-hand margin of Fig. 65. Blacksmiths were allowed to keep a cow on the village waste, and Sir John Clapham stressed their importance by pointing out that, even as late as 1851, they were a more numerous British trade group than the entire labour force of the mines of Northumberland and Durham.

Corn mills were also essential to the village community, and so long as they were the property of the lord of the manor, with a duty on the part of tenants to grind their corn there, they were also a source of dissatisfaction. Both water- and windmills were usually on the outskirts of villages. The Romans had used watermills and the Domesday Survey of 1086 records 7,500 of them. Their wheels later powered not only corn-grinding stones, but were used in trades like fulling of cloth, brewing, paper-making, early textile-weaving and in metal-mining. The large water-wheel of the Laxey lead mines in the Isle of Man still impresses visitors. Villages on estuaries used the sea to power their corn-mills. Kent, Sussex, East Anglia, the Fylde and Pembrokeshire all have examples of tide mills. The Northern Isles of Scotland had mills with horizontal wheels which developed from the rotary quern. They can still be seen in the Norwegian countryside from which their design spread to Orkney and Shetland. Like windmills, watermills declined as steam power took over in the eighteenth century. Windmills, well suited to windswept islands on the fringe of the eastern Atlantic, spread in Britain from the late twelfth century and were common by the seventeenth century in eastern Britain. The Luttrell Psalter has one of the earliest drawings of a windmill. The first type was the post-mill, so called because it revolved round a central post. In tower-mills, a late fourteenth-century introduction, only the cap at the top of the mill rotated according to wind direction.

Western villages, especially those near creeks which are backed by slopes covered with acid soils, often have limekilns near the shore. Both coastal and inland villages in our wetter west have ruins of corn-drying kilns which were used in years when harvests were difficult.

Fishing villages in western Britain, and on some eastern coasts like those of the North Riding of Yorkshire and parts of Northumberland, Fife and Angus, have special characteristics. Houses often huddle for shelter near the harbour in a narrow valley bottom, and are close-set along narrow lanes. High tides used to flood up the seaward ends of the lanes. Polperro (Plate 19, p. 172) and Looe (Plate XVI, p. 177), are typical villages which formerly depended on fishing. Many such villages, picturesque and poised on the seashore which has become a national playground, now benefit from the tourist trade. Their narrow lanes provide the car-borne tourist with the sort of problem which would have confronted him had he been introduced into medieval London. Cottages in fishing villages may now be occupied by retired folk or have only holiday use. Fishermen's wives may be engaged in the tourist rather than the fishing trade. Formerly they handled the catch, cleaning, salting and hawking it. Fishwives also knitted for their menfolk the jerseys and guernseys which took their name from wool sent in Tudor and Stuart times to the Channel Islands to be knitted up by women and old men. The fishwife's work did not attract other women and the men of fishing villages have often married women from fishing, rather than farming, families. There are many traditions of objections to the marriage of farmers' daughters to fishermen, sometimes on the grounds that fishermen were strangers who had come in from the sea, but the objections are more likely to be rooted in the dangers and insecurity of a fisherman's life.

The Industrial Revolution spread new types of villages over the coalfields of Britain. Old textile villages, near swift streams which drain from the Pennines, Rossendale Fells, Cheviots and the Welsh hills, were made up of a few rows of sturdy stone cottages set by small stone mills and by mill-ponds whose embankments were also built of local stone. They lacked the beauty of the medieval East Anglian and Cotswold villages, which had put the profits of their wool trade into fine churches, merchants' houses and guildhalls, but they were well adapted to a difficult terrain and blended well with it. Iron-working and coal-mining villages, and the larger industrial villages which developed in the nineteenth century and until the 1930s, were often placed as near to the pit-head or mill and their waste heaps as possible. Workers' houses were often aligned along busy roads, railways and polluted rivers. The inadequate and worn-out houses which resulted are now being replaced, on the whole at a slower rate than similar houses in large towns. Such villages are often in regions of declining industry. Nonconformist chapels rather than churches dominate them and their concern for education and social welfare is seen in large buildings which originated as mechanics' halls and workmen's institutes. Some industrial undertakings built model villages for their employees. An early example was the New Lanark of Robert Owen (1771-1858). Modern housing standards and well-treed gardens can be seen in the model villages of Port Sunlight and Bournville, respectively engulfed now by suburban Merseyside and Birmingham (Plate XXIV, p. 225).

The Highlands and Western Isles of Scotland have many deserted farm clusters, but the desertion of these clachans came much later than that of the villages of the English lowlands. Until the eighteenth century these small farming settlements were sustained by infields of perhaps twenty acres which produced, year after year, oats for meal and barley for drink. Rye was grown on poorer land in the Outer Isles. Cattle provided milk and the only cash income of these farmers. Their pastures were often extensive and for two months in the summer the cattle grazed shielings at some distance from the clachan and were tended by the women and children who lived in shieling huts. Winter feeding of cattle, because of the general scarcity of meadow hay, was so difficult that in spring, when the cattle were first turned out on the hill, the process was often literally "the lifting." Southern Scotland grew more beans, peas, flax, hemp and clover and winter feeding was less problematic there.

The potato came into western Scotland about 1750 and after an

PLATE 27   Bow Church, Cheapside, London. Though the church was ruined in the war of 1939–45, the spire still stands as one of Wren's masterpieces which had much influence in New England.

PLATE 28   LAVENHAM CHURCH of St. Peter and St. Paul. A fine example of the
churches of the fifteenth and sixteenth centuries built during the prosperity of the wool-weaving industry in East Anglia.

initial slow spread was more widely cultivated, as was clover, by the early nineteenth century. "Ireland's lazy root" became almost the sole crop cultivated in the infields of western Scotland and the population increased as the potato spread over the cornfields. Arable holdings were sub-divided until they could hardly support families. The potato famine of the late 1840s completed the deterioration of the clachans and their holdings. Throughout the period 1750-1850 the population had increasingly been forced to desert the clachans as sheep-farmers took over. The lairds became landlords rather than military leaders after the quelling of the Highlands which followed the '45 rebellion. Their lands were rented to sheep-farmers who had flocks of, typically, 5,000 sheep, and took over the grazing land, including the shielings, cleared the clachans and sometimes destroyed the homesteads. Whole glens were cleared, the most notorious cases being in Sutherland where, between 1810 and 1820, valley clachans were cleared and their people were displaced to the bare moors of Sutherland's north and east coasts where they were expected to become fisher-farmers. As from other cleared areas, many emigrated to America, or moved to the industrial Midlands of Scotland, or gathered as rootless and landless folk in clusters of hovels larger than the clachans which they had been forced to desert. The old way of life had been broken up by warfare, by over-concentration on one crop, and by short-sighted policies which depopulated Highland and Atlantic Scotland and produced problems which have still not been solved. The clachans based on runrig cultivation had largely disappeared by 1850 and have been replaced by scattered modern cottages set in fields laid out in geometrical patterns.

The differing village patterns described above can still be discerned. They vary from the large nucleated villages of the English lowlands to the tiny hamlets of the western uplands. The squire's hall, or rectory, which dominated them may now serve other purposes, the church may be less well attended than in previous centuries, and the village inn may cater not only for the village but for guests from distant towns. Village shops may have lost trade to nearby towns and to mobile shops based on them. Village crafts have markedly declined and working smithies are rare. But the village garage is busy servicing agricultural machinery. The small yeoman farmer is also a rarity; poachers are not now farm labourers who were forced to poach on the squire's demesne and risk hanging to vary a diet of bread and cheese, but gangs from the towns who steal for profit. Television has not replaced other forms of entertainment as it has so often done in suburban settings; villagers can still create their own forms of entertainment and here Women's Institutes have played a leading part.

Many villages, particularly in south-east England and the Midlands, have acquired accretions of new housing on their margins and act as dormitories for city workers. Everywhere, and particularly in villages attractive to tourists, road traffic has produced a deterioration in the village environment. But on the whole, modern systems of welfare and education have given village people better conditions and opportunities than they formerly had.

CHAPTER 13

TOWNS

A VOTE FOR choosing the most charming and interesting small
town in England would bring strong support for Ludlow, King's
Lynn, Winchester, Rye, Chipping Campden, Cirencester and Lavenham. Among larger towns, Bath, Lincoln, Norwich, Shrewsbury,
Chester and York would have strong claims, as would others before
their bombing or redevelopment. Edinburgh stands out among the
great cities of Britain while Liverpool has great buildings, both old and
new, and fine Georgian streets (Plate XXII, p. 209) to balance her
meaner quarters. Bristol, in a dramatic setting, has splendid churches
and public buildings which reflect the wealth of the merchants and
manufacturers of this old-established port. But, broadly speaking, the
dullness of our towns and cities shows how deficient they are as modes
of social expression. London's unique series of fine buildings of the past
nine centuries is in an environment which is already overcrowded at
ground level and could develop increasingly skywards, so that its
historic buildings would be as dwarfed as are the older public buildings
of Boston, Massachusetts. Both London's spacious royal parks and
Boston's Common provide fine settings for fringes of contemporary
dwelling-houses. A few cities of quite special character stand apart.
Oxford (Plate XVII, p. 180) and Cambridge, and Durham, on its
great rock, are among them. The site and cathedral close of the village-
city of St. David's (Plate XVIII, p. 181), a meeting point of routes from
pilgrims' landing places, are also of interest.

A few Iron B fortress-villages, like Maiden Castle and Bagendon,
had considerable populations. Iron C settlements at, for example,
Colchester, Wheathampstead on the Lea in Hertfordshire, and Prae
Wood above the Roman town of Verulamium, were large and sprawl-
ing collections of huts defended by long banks and ditches. The planned
walled towns introduced by the Romans had either administrative
functions, as had London and Verulamium, or were centres for trading
with local tribes, like Caerwent. Others, like Chichester, were cantonal
capitals, or were *coloniae* for retired soldiers, like Lincoln and Gloucester

(see p. 110). Medieval and modern towns grew on many of the good sites selected by the Romans for their forts and towns. Recent excavations have suggested that decaying Roman buildings may have been reoccupied by early English settlers. Roman street plans may be repeated in medieval layouts; Roman town and fort walls were frequently embodied in medieval walls and their towers and gatehouses were refortified. Colchester shows this on a large, and Caerwent on a small, site.

The former English capital, Winchester, is on a site which has been continuously occupied since pre-Roman times. It was a Belgic fortified town and became the Romans' Venta Belgarum. The Saxons squatted in its forum and other public buildings when they arrived in the fifth century, and after their conversion it became Wintanceastre and developed into the capital of Wessex and of England. It was Cnut's capital and the royal city of William the Conqueror. Its Saxon minster was the forerunner of the medieval cathedral and it became a centre of the medieval wool trade and held an important fair (St. Giles) outside its walls. These walls are partly Roman-based, and re-used Roman brick can be seen in several buildings in the city. Like many county towns in the lowlands of England, Winchester and its setting reward the thoughtful visitor.

The Anglo-Saxons lived mainly in villages, but small towns gradually developed. Yeavering in Northumberland, within a wooden wall, was a royal Anglian town. Pre-Norman mints, or fortress mounds like those of Oxford, Cambridge and Thetford, characterised the developing nodal points. While kings and nobles had wooden halls in them, most of their people appear to have lived in squalid huts like those found at Canterbury and Southampton. Many of the Danelaw burgs developed into medieval towns. The great impetus in town-building came with the Norman conquerors and was in some measure an extension of similar developments in France. Medieval walled boroughs focusing on castles, abbeys and guild churches multiplied on both existing and new sites. Canterbury and Chichester (Figs. 67 and 68) are two of many examples of towns where medieval vestiges are visible and where older features are deeply buried by centuries of occupation.

Oxford, lying at crossing points of the branching Thames and Cherwell, and in the frontier zone between Mercia and Wessex, was one of the burgs founded by Alfred the Great in which favourable tenures brought in settlers from the countryside. Many facets of town develop-

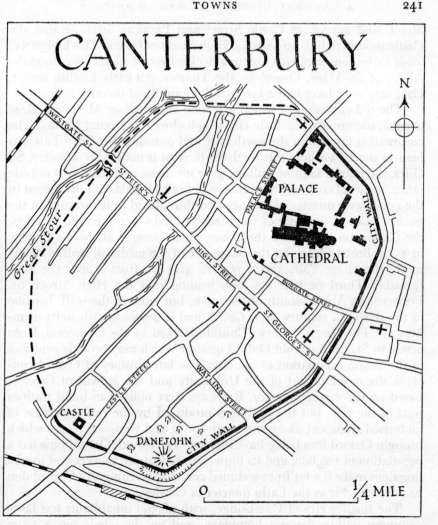

FIG. 67

Canterbury, a medieval walled city with a basic Roman plan. The cathedral lies in its close, apart from the city centre

ment are illustrated in its subsequent growth. The city centres on Carfax (*Quadrifurcus*), the crossing point of north-south and west-east routes. The line of the north-south route is along Banbury Road, St. Giles, Cornmarket and St. Aldates. The west-east road includes the Magdalen Bridge crossing of the Cherwell, High Street and Queen

Street, and curves, as Castle Street and Paradise Street, round the Castle mound to link up with the High Street of Osney. This high street leads to the church of St. Thomas à Becket beyond which once stood the Abbey of St. Mary, Osney, by the Thames. An early English settler, Osa, may once have had a farmstead on an island there.

The old city wall, of which a section still encloses Merton College garden, surrounded the little city which clustered around Carfax. The cornmarket lay within the north gate and outside it St. Giles' Fair was held in the area where the north-south road is noticeably broader. St. Giles, the patron saint of pedlars, gave his name to similar fairs outside other medieval trade centres. Henry II built his palace of Beaumont in the north-west quarter of the city and thus added to its prestige in the twelfth century. Because of wool trading and sheep fairs on St. Giles, the Cistercians built there the abbey which became St. John's College in 1555. Broad Street, on the outer side of the medieval wall, was formerly the Horse Fair, and a postern gate led from it into the Turl (possibly Thurl or hole), a lane leading into the High Street. St. Frideswide's Abbey, south of the town, but close to the wall, became in the sixteenth century *Aedes Christi*, and is thence known to its members as "The House." Christ Church, backed by the Cathedral, looks across to St. Ebbs, an old Oxford quarter which may provide evidence of the Saxon occupation of the city. The later history of Oxford concerns the development of the University and the growth of Cowley, based on the motor industry. Railways were obliged to build stations west of the city, but the problems produced by the rapid increase of motorised transport along the north-south and west-east routes which brought Oxford into being have still not been solved. Oxford now has a population of 108,880, and its important industrial, market and tourist functions make it a far from secluded centre of learning. An Oxford don has described it as the Latin quarter of Cowley.

The smaller city of Cambridge, with 98,390 inhabitants has large commons within the city boundary, and on the whole has a more spacious layout than Oxford, but similar service functions and expanding light engineering industries produce comparable traffic and development problems there.

Lavenham in Suffolk is an example of a medieval and Tudor industrial centre which has survived, as well tended as its surrounding countryside, to delight many visitors. It has only 1,300 inhabitants today. Merchants and craftsmen engaged in the East Anglian woollen industry enriched this town, notably in the prosperous sixteenth

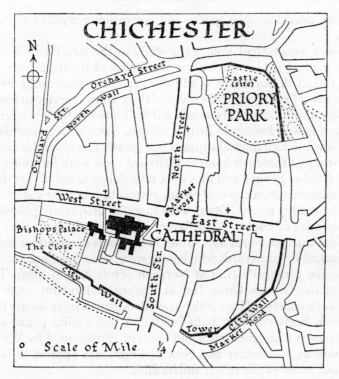

FIG. 68
Chichester. The medieval layout follows, in general, the Roman street plan

century, from which its Hall of the Guild of Corpus Christi (Plate 13, p. 128), the Swan Hotel (once also the meeting place of a guild) and the Church of St. Peter and St. Paul (Plate 28, p. 237) largely date. Lavenham has charming street frontages of contemporary merchants' and craftsmen's houses. Several Cotswolds townlets have fine churches and domestic buildings, but the latter tend to be less homogeneous architecturally than those of Lavenham.

Medieval towns had narrow streets, but the layout of their dwellings was not that of the congested old quarters of modern towns, now so often being redeveloped. A long narrow croft ran back from a narrow street frontage, and each household produced food there. Burgesses also held strips of common arable and meadowland, and shares of common grazing land, outside the town walls, and were able to sustain their families from local produce. Many of the town meadows and commons provided open spaces and recreation grounds for townsfolk to-day.

Houses usually had their gable-ends to the street and a series of steeply pitched gables would line both sides of it. Merchants' houses ·which included workshops gradually expanded backwards from the narrow street frontage. Small groups of these houses survive in towns like Norwich; a fine series of Hanseatic gabled houses in the Norwegian city of Bergen is well known to British visitors. Such an arrangement promoted warmth and mutual support but greatly increased the fire risk in timber-framed thatched houses. Thatched roofs were forbidden in the City of London in 1212 and tiles were introduced to reduce fire dangers. Water drained down copiously from gutters between the gabled houses on to the muddy streets. Doors were therefore frequently placed at the backs or sides of houses, or, in larger houses and inns, in the covered entry into the courtyard. The broad housefronts of wealthier townsfolk were backed by courtyards which gave some seclusion—one such house became the Stranger's Hall at Norwich (Plate XX, p. 189). The exterior of the Golden Cross Inn at Oxford still retains some of the features of a courtyard into which travellers came to seek shelter for man and steed. Early students' halls in Oxford had similar plans, and the idea of courts with gatehouses and covered entries, used by William of Wykeham at Winchester and New Colleges, was applied in both the older and many of the newer universities.

On the main streets of medieval towns some of the ground floors of the narrow houses would be shops. They were workshops working to order, such as the London workshops of the Flemish weavers of Edward III's day, or of the sixteenth-century silk-weavers of Shoreditch and Spitalfields. Exposure of goods for chance sale was a feature of markets and fairs. Corporate towns had the right to hold weekly markets. Some held them on two days, hence the Saturday and Tuesday market-places at King's Lynn, the former dominated by St. Margaret's church, the latter still a fine large square. Fairs were held annually or seasonally and were usually linked with church festivals, largely because these festivals marked many of the crucial dates of the climatic and agricultural calendar. The fairs attracted pedlars and countryfolk, and still do so in many towns which strive to maintain them against the opposition of some resident shopkeepers and motorists.

Many British cathedrals stand in closes entered by a fine gateway, and in this respect they contrast with typical French cathedrals which stand on what is, or was, the central market-place. The dwellings in

PLATE XXV.   INTER-WAR FACTORIES along the Great West Road, an early stage in the industrialisation of the approaches to London

PLATE XXVI. EDINBURGH, aerial view showing in the centre the Castle and the old High Street. To the left is the drained loch, now gardens, and the planned extension set out at the end of the eighteenth century on either side of George Street. Princes Street faces the gardens. Calton Hill is seen beyond Princes Street

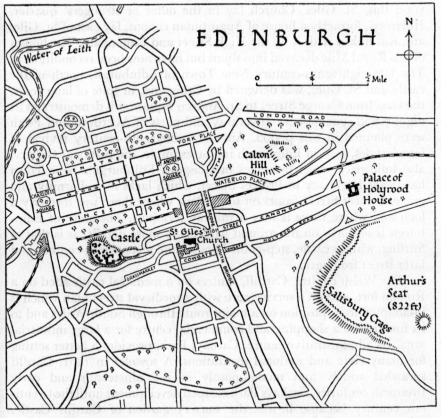

FIG. 69

Edinburgh. The medieval city lay around the castle and High Street. The late eight-teenth century New Town lies around George Street and St Andrew Square. Between them is Princes Street, now the main shopping street

cathedral closes, which are rich in late seventeenth- and eighteenth-century houses, are among the most comely domestic buildings in England. Old grammar schools, mainly Tudor foundations, often adjoin cathedral closes and the chief churches of market towns.

Edinburgh and London, with their collections of monuments and buildings connected with national administration and royal ceremony, are our two truly metropolitan cities. Edinburgh is strikingly charac-terised by its distinct, yet contiguous, elements derived from different periods (Plate XXVI, p. 245 and Fig. 69). Its finely poised castle, begun in the early Middle Ages, protected a small flanking town. Beyond this, St. Giles' Church lay in the outer or strangers' quarter. Holyrood, formerly a house of Augustinian canons, lay east of St. Giles and was linked with it by the High Street and Canongate. The houses of this Royal Mile decayed into slums but have now been reconditioned. The late eighteenth-century New Town of Edinburgh, north of the castle and St. Giles, was designed by Craig and, in spite of later scars, the view from George Street to St. Andrew Square still demonstrates its dignity and spaciousness. Inveraray and parts of Aberdeen and Perth were planned in this period. An early nineteenth-century revival of Greek styles, seen in Edinburgh in, for example, the National Gallery, also influenced street frontages in Glasgow. Edinburgh's New Town has yielded primacy to Princes Street, which lacks its uniformity and grace. Princes Street fronts on to gardens where there was formerly a loch and where there is now a railway terminus. The story of Edinburgh is set forth on the ground with many more details, as is that of Stirling, with its castle, step-gabled houses and seventeenth-century and later street frontages.

The Welsh capital, Cardiff, centres on a medieval castle sited on a Roman fort, and on a service core with a medieval street plan which is ill-adapted to its position on a major route through South Wales and to its function as a shopping and commercial centre for a large industrial area. Its administrative centre, Cathays Park, provides a better setting for many civic and national institutions. A townlet in 1801, Cardiff sprawled widely and monotonously in the nineteenth and early twentieth centuries. Cathays Park escaped development until the twentieth century because it was the nursery garden of Cardiff Castle. Narrow flood plains along the Taff provide a long green belt which stretches for three miles from the castle to and beyond the little cathedral city of Llandaff on the north-western outskirts of the city.

Camden described Cardiff as "a propper fine towne (as townes goe in this country) and a very commodious haven." Welsh native society may have supported a few small market centres like Pwllheli, but Wales had no equivalent of the Anglo-Saxon burgs built to repel Danish invaders. Its first towns were built by Norman and later English invaders for security against the native Welsh. Many of them, well-sited and in relatively fertile coast plains and valleys, function as market and tourist centres to-day. In some, such as New Radnor, grass-grown medieval walls surround fields and a tiny village, in others, like Harlech, tourism and retirement has only recently led to the expansion of settlement on and below a lean hillside. The best-known series of planned

Welsh castle towns, Edward I's bastides, which were provisioned by
sea and aimed at containment of the turbulent Welsh, were Flint,
Rhuddlan, Conway, Beaumaris, Aberystwyth and Caernarvon (Plate
XXIX, p. 272). Many south and east Welsh market towns were
founded before this series and have charters giving them rights to hold
markets and fairs which are based on that of the Norman town of
Breteuil. They are still dominated by ruined castles and some, like
Tenby, preserve massive town walls and the gracious town houses of
later centuries. Urban planning, as practised in the prosperous cities of
Britain in the late eighteenth century, ran as a spent wave across Wales
and on its western limits left a feeble, though interesting, small imprint
on the early nineteenth-century core of Milford Haven, the townlet of
Tremadoc and the small port of Aberaeron. Among these, only Milford
Haven has shown any marked expansion since the early nineteenth
century.

During a drive into a town many features which are indicators of
our social evolution may be noted. While still a few miles from the
town centre we come upon what would like to consider itself a village
but is now largely a dormitory for the more prosperous families of the
town. Its modern houses will show a contrast between those built before
and after the servant problem became too acute to retain its place as a
subject of conversation. Larger houses built in the expectation of
domestic help will have trees or walls round their gardens as a screen of
privacy; smaller houses built for family housework will be compact and
in their small gardens flowering shrubs, small lawns and garages will be
prominent. Cottagers may still grow vegetables but frequently the
larger gardens have no labour and the smaller ones inadequate space
for both vegetables and flowers.

The dormitory ex-village is usually inhabited by those whose experience is wide enough to give some of them a historical sense. Beneath all this there is the half-conscious feeling that the industrial and
technological revolutions have cut our old roots of social life. When we
realise how much our historical background means in our national life,
with our unwritten constitution and our centuries of continuity of ceremonial, we should not wonder that the families now living in the ex-
village hanker after historic roots, especially as they are apt to have
social aspirations. These attitudes have often expressed themselves in
the building of sham timber-framed houses or sometimes in dignified
copies of eighteenth-century town houses. The old squire's house may
have become a residential hotel or a social centre for a large manu-

facturing firm in the town, and is likely to look as *depaysée* as the medieval village church. If this were personified, it would have a puzzled look at its present congregation, so different from the "rude forefathers of the hamlet" for whom it was built in the days when a village three miles from the town was "right in the country."

The ex-village has often been disappointed in its hopes of keeping a green belt between itself and the town. Ribbon development of the inter-war period, and post-war housing estates, may now fill the former houseless zone. Bus services, the profit motive and the availability of public utilities explain roadside ribbon development. The ribbon may include Victorian dwellings (Plate 23, p. 220) and an infilling of modern detached houses, but as we drive towards the town semi-detached houses become more common and shops, garages and bank branches surround road junctions. Houses in continuous rows with tiny gardens and names on their gates such as St. Helier, Clovelly, or some other honeymoon spot, then appear. They are succeeded by gardenless terraces and gaunt schools of the Bleak Age, as the Hammonds called the period 1810-50. Towards the inner end of the zone of small terraced houses the eye catches here and there a house surviving from the Georgian Period which even in its decadence suggests a dignity that the Industrial Revolution destroyed and replaced by a heightened desire for display. Some of the terraced houses which once had small gardens have often had the ground floors converted into shops built out over the gardens to provide a shop front on the street. These curious streets with shops projecting from houses are a characteristic feature of nineteenth-century Britain.

In the zone of small gardenless houses one finds mission-halls and chapels, and here and there a rather forlorn church. It usually dates from the Gothic Revival but occasionally is an eighteenth-century building with more meaning. Near the town centre there may be Georgian chapels, perhaps including one built by a Presbyterian group who gathered around a minister ejected after the Act of Uniformity in 1661. Several groups of this character became Unitarian in doctrine in the late eighteenth century. Another denomination which may have an old and modest building, with a small burial ground, is the Society of Friends (Plate 16b, p. 145). These religious groups were able to build meeting places in towns after the Puritan Revolution of 1688, though it was long afterwards that their ministers had the right to conduct marriage or burial services in them.

The deracinated farmworkers who flocked into the rapidly growing towns were a crowd rather than a community. Social tendencies began to work in and through the Nonconformist, largely Methodist, chapels. Their early nineteenth-century ministers tended to condemn play as taking time off from work that might lead to success in this world and the next. John Wesley's sympathy for the poor too often took this unattractive form. Chapels and churches were also associated with Victorian dress displays on Sundays and with the influence of repressive employers who were often leading men in church and chapel. An alternative outlet for social tendencies, apart from the public house, was the Friendly Society, especially the Oddfellows. These Friendly Societies, and soon the trade unions, helped to train the wage-labourers for their citizenship responsibilities. They are characteristic of our British system of proceeding by voluntary association, at least until the experimental phase of a movement is well advanced.

Many an Oddfellows Hall or mechanics' institute is now used for other purposes, and chapels near town centres, built when business folk lived above and behind their shops, may now lie among worn-out buildings and have small congregations. In England, chapel folk who moved to the suburbs often became members of the State Church. New suburban churches now being built may adjoin new community centres, or may themselves have rooms used as such. The most advanced architecture is usually seen in new Roman Catholic and Mormon churches.

Town centres may retain Elizabethan timber-framed houses whose ground floors have become shops. Such buildings have even been jacked up and removed to new sites. On both sides of the Welsh border, market houses in narrow squares are characteristic, typically raised on arches to provide shelter for market folk (Plate 20, p. 173). There may be Assembly Rooms, sometimes attached to an eighteenth-century town hall, sometimes independent; large inns often had their own ballrooms with galleries for the orchestra (Plate XXI, p. 208). These rooms testify to the social life of the more leisured folk before the Industrial Revolution. After the 1688 revolution, towns expanded and country landowners acquired or built town houses and spent part of the winter in them rather than travel in over roads which were deep in mud and infested with highway robbers. Many of these eighteenth- and early nineteenth-century town houses may now be offices or flats but they retain their dignity. In shopping streets chain stores, multiple shops and supermarkets have fascias and window displays which usually compete with each other in vulgarity. The Civic Trust's street improvement schemes, initiated some years ago in Magdalen Street in Norwich, have given a lead in the introduction of seemly street frontages and street furniture.

The town centre will often have a few modern public buildings built as copies of older styles. County and town halls often show a series of extensions, ranging from Neo-Gothic to modern functional, to accommodate their expanding staffs. Many towns with more than 50,000 and most of those with over 100,000 people have a centre which is almost uninhabited at night. Even the centres of new towns, or those with re-developed town centres, have this night-dead heart. It is associated with the high values of central sites and the expansion of offices in either purpose-built blocks or above shops. Town centres typically have offices of the leading banks occupying positions as conspicuous as those of the hotels, while insurance companies, though less fully represented than banks, are also quite conspicuous. Towns in the Lowland Zone often have a Cornmarket Hall which is now more often than not used by a seed merchant. The Carnegie United Kingdom Trust has financed lending and reference libraries in many towns and local authorities with vision have added a lecture hall, museum and art gallery. Attendances at lectures have fallen markedly since the advent of television and many lecture halls could well be used as extensions of reference libraries, for displays relating to the town, or as discussion and social centres. Devoted curators are now attempting to modernise their museums and galleries which often contain much that could be discarded.

Towns which expanded rapidly during the Industrial Revolution, when the ideal of "toil, thrift and triumph" was held up so often for popular admiration, still have too many crowded obsolete houses (Plate XXIII, p. 224). Back-to-back houses became illegal only in 1909, and in spite of a great deal of slum clearance much remains to be done to improve the crowded quarters of our towns. Open spaces and playgrounds have increased since the mid-nineteenth century when Puritan administrators left to wage-labourers only alcohol, sex and betting by way of relaxation. Since 1855 it has been legal to convert town churchyards into gardens or playgrounds, and school playgrounds have also been improved. But more play spaces are needed, as are more footpaths or bridle ways leading out into the open country.

Our towns and cities lag behind several continental ones, especially those whose wealth was not based on coal, like Copenhagen and

Zürich. Local authorities and bodies like the Civic Trust face a long battle in the face of public apathy, or resentment of planning schemes, and local resources are often inadequate for the comprehensive redevelopment of towns. The authorities who have developed new towns have been able to dispose of more liberal funds and to plan shopping centres with separate pedestrian and vehicle access, well-designed street plans, well-placed schools, and public buildings with adequate open spaces around them. They have built a variety of houses and flats to attract the young families who form a big part of their populations. Regional studies which are now proceeding will lead to the establishment of more new towns and of large additions to existing conurbations, for example those of Severnside and Humberside. The apt, if unbeautiful, term *conurbation* was invented by Patrick Geddes, who added that the name was all the more apt because conurbations were in themselves unbeautiful. Manchester, Salford and Stretford have long ceased to be distinguishable from one another on the ground, and this conurbation pushes out tentacles in all directions to engulf towns and villages in Lancashire and Cheshire.

Satellite towns built to house the overspill of conurbations have multiplied since 1945, but they originated in the nineteenth century and are a product of the revulsion against industrial slums. One of the first new towns was Saltaire, three miles north-west of Bradford, built as a model town in the Aire valley by Titus Salt between 1851 and 1871. Later in the century Ebenezer Howard fostered the idea of the garden city and published his ideas in *Tomorrow: A Peaceful Path to Real Reform* in 1898. His followers formed the Garden City Association in 1899, and Letchworth Garden City (1903) was the first fruit of this movement. Bournville and Port Sunlight garden villages had already been built, and the hybrid form, Hampstead Garden Suburb, planned by Raymond Unwin, followed in 1907. Some of these early ideas in town planning were adopted by local councils and housing associations in the inter-war period, but, generally speaking, it was the speculative builder who then left the greatest imprint on our towns and on their outskirts. Authorities responsible for overspill towns, which may house thousands of uprooted families from the obsolete sections of nearby towns, strive to build community facilities so that symptoms ranging from loneliness to lawlessness, rife among nineteenth-century urban populations, do not manifest themselves. This can be a heavy burden on small local authorities. Good new schools, which are often equipped for evening classes, characterise overspill towns and estates, and their welfare services are well developed, but other public buildings such as libraries do not always have the priority which they deserve.

Problems of rehabilitation are nowhere more acute than in our sub-metropolitan cities and they are being vigorously tackled there. These cities may have originally depended on one major activity, but they now have large areas given over to specialised industry, particularly engineering industries, which may supply automobile, shipbuilding, textile, chemical or building industries. Their warehouses and old office blocks, often centrally placed, usually need replacement or dispersal. These cities have cultural independence in some measure, and have theatres as well as cinemas (which have not become bingo halls as have many cinemas in smaller towns) and concert halls where there are performances by a professional orchestra. They often have a university, a college of advanced technology, a hospital system with a wide range of consultants, libraries, art collections of aesthetic value and a cathedral, which in some cases is an adapted parish or collegiate church. Birmingham and Manchester are typical. Leeds city hall is more pleasing than that of Manchester, but its church is not a cathedral. Ripon, over twenty miles away, is the bishop's seat, but vicars of Leeds are men of high standing in the Church. Sub-metropolitan cities often maintain learned societies which have old-established headquarters with libraries and meeting rooms and publish annual journals. Manchester has more than one, though the fine Georgian house of its oldest learned society, which had survived among cotton warehouses, was destroyed in 1941. Recruitment of a younger generation of members has recently proved difficult for provincial learned societies.

London is unique in Britain in its sprawl, wealth, power and in the opportunities provided by its riversides for setting off fine buildings. The banks of the Thames, John Burns's "liquid history," are still disfigured by decayed commercial properties, power stations and incongruous development, and many years will pass before they are replaced by public buildings and recreational facilities which will provide daily and evening entertainment for London's citizens and visitors. Both these riversides, and the imaginative Lee Valley Scheme, could be of immense benefit to a population with increased leisure time. But the dynamic city already offers continuous interest in its existing buildings, parks, squares, markets, quarters which have a very marked individuality, and many institutions which have a long history. London was recognised as a centre of communications by the Romans and our road and rail network, though less markedly than that of France, still hinges

PLATE XXVII.   JOHN WESLEY'S CHAPEL, City Road, London. A typical
      eighteenth century design

PLATE XXVIII. PART OF THE BAYEUX TAPESTRY representing a Motte and Bailey Castle at Dinan

on the capital city. London's railway stations are themselves a remarkable series of buildings, but as in many other cities, duplication by competing companies has left a legacy of surplus stations and other railway property. Closures of London's rail termini have already started and plans exist to develop some of their extensive land-holdings for housing and other purposes.

In Bede's day London was already "a mart town of many nations which repaired thither by land and sea." It was the Lundunaborg of the Icelandic sagas, a burg defended by Roman walls which had been restored by King Alfred. Southwark, the southern fort of the Domesday Book, was a distinct settlement on the Surrey bank which was not finally incorporated until 1554. It came to be a place where London's citizens sought amusement via London Bridge, the only bridge until 1729. The walled City of London, packed with the houses of merchants and craftsmen, preceded the royal City of Westminster, and its leading citizens, guilds and livery companies have wielded great power. The dichotomy between the two cities is perpetuated in many ways, for example in the halts in royal ceremonial progress past the former Temple Bar. Medieval and later kings gave the city rights in exchange for funds; Dick Whittington helped to finance the wars of Henry IV and V. Religious houses, such as those of the Knights Templars, were usually outside the city walls. The medieval City of London preserved an identity almost independent of king and Church. A king from another trading nation, William III, founded the Bank of England in the City.

Until the Tudor voyages of discovery London was something of an outpost on the edge of Europe. But in the sixteenth century it became a terminus of Atlantic and other ocean highways, a growing, bustling entrepôt which was already spilling over the fields beyond the walls and had coalesced with the City of Westminster. The Strand, with aristocratic houses fronting on to the river, linked the two cities. The fire which raged during the first week of September, 1666, destroyed many of the City of London's half-timbered houses and numerous churches, which included the Gothic St. Paul's. The replanned city, and the City of Westminster, expanded in the eighteenth century and produced Georgian London. Its dignified terraces and splendid squares still partly survive to delight the eye, as do the proud Regency frontages of Nash's buildings around and beyond Regent's Park. Regent Street, the southern end of this audacious layout, was unfortunately rebuilt in a particularly uninspired period. London's explosive nineteenth- and twentieth-century growth was northwards to and beyond the London clays north of the "New Road" (Euston Road-Marylebone Road), on to former marshes behind the docks which lay east of the Tower, and along the gravel terraces of the Thames. London's tentacles ramified with each extension of the public transport systems and its green belt is now rather tattered.

Londoners have an appreciation of the many ceremonial occasions offered by their city and a great capacity for enjoyment. London archers were breaking down hurdles set up to enclose fields around the city as early as 1516. Moorfields, in the City of London, where refuse was tipped, was used for recreation in the fifteenth century and was laid out as a pleasure-ground after 1625. The neighbouring Finsbury Fields were used as a military training ground. Outside the city wall, Lincoln's Inn Fields were preserved in the seventeenth century for the relaxation of the only students London then had. They were so preserved until 1894. Far beyond the City of London, races were held in Hyde Park in the seventeenth century, and St. James's Park, the hunting-ground of Henry V, was landscaped in the reign of Charles II and was well known as a pleasance where the court took exercise and played "pall mall" along the north-west boundary. More popular pleasure-grounds were at Vauxhall, west of London, which functioned from the mid-seventeenth century until 1859, Ranelagh Garden across the river in Chelsea, and the once notorious Battersea Fields, which became a respectable royal park in 1858 and got back some of its gaiety during the Festival of Britain. London's large open spaces include well-landscaped parks like Regent's Park, dating from 1800, Kew Gardens, set by a village which dates from the fourteenth century, and Hampstead Heath on the hills of north London. All now cater for both organised and informal recreation. What is now called audience participation probably goes back to Roman times in London. Pepys watched wrestling in Moorfields in 1661. Individual games like golf and tennis have been played for centuries in London, and lawn tennis, team games and organised sport as we now know them, date from the second half of Queen Victoria's reign and are well catered for by clubs and by local authorities.

London's millions and other large urban populations to-day need more sites for informal recreation and for unorganised sport, both within and on the borders of cities. The need to escape from dull streets takes many town dwellers to neighbouring countrysides and seashores whose inns, cafés, funfairs and amusement arcades could be provided in open settings in or near to towns. Only a minority of town dwellers prefer the empty countryside and there is an urgent need near towns for amenities which will attract crowds and smaller family groups. But the greatest need, so far imperfectly communicated to most townsfolk, and to some of their elected representatives, is that urban environments in which 80 per cent of the British people live, should become better places in which to live, work and relax.

CHAPTER 14

CHURCH AND CASTLE

CHRISTIANITY, INTRODUCED into Britain in a late phase of the Roman occupation, temporarily bifurcated into the Church of Lowland Britain, closely linked with Rome, and the more isolated Celtic Church, monastic in organisation, which was centred on Atlantic and Highland Britain (see Chapter 6). By the end of the seventh century both churches conformed to the Roman tradition and in the course of this century many prehistoric and pagan shrines were destroyed and were replaced by small rectangular churches. These were probably as simple as the Romano-British church at Silchester, the earliest church known in Britain. In eastern England Roman building materials were re-used in the churches built by St. Augustine's converts in the late sixth century. St. Peter-on-the-Wall, at Bradwell in Essex, of which the nave survives, and some Kentish churches, date from the time of St. Augustine. Massive boulders were often used to build primitive Celtic churches in Highland and Atlantic Britain; only their foundations survive. Round towers of refuge, similar to the more numerous Irish round towers, are found in Scotland at Abernethy by the lower Tay, and at Brechin at the east end of Strathmore.

In the seventh century fifteen dioceses were formed in the main Anglo-Saxon territorial units. The villages which became bishops' seats sometimes proved unsuitable for peoples with true urban centres and in 1075 William the Conqueror abolished the Anglo-Saxon dioceses and founded sees based on towns. Thus, in East Anglia, Dunwich (631) and Elmham (673) were amalgamated and sited at Elmham in 870, moved to Thetford in 1078 and to Norwich in 1094. In Northumbria the devastation of Lindisfarne was followed by a transfer to Chester-le-Street in 883 and to the defensible site at Durham in 995. The bishopric at Winchester, the capital of Wessex, was founded in 663, and as this more densely peopled and long-settled area needed more sees, the diocese of Selsey was added in 709 (and centred on Chichester from 1075), and Sherborne was created in 705 west of Winchester. In 1075 Sherborne was moved to Old Sarum which, in its turn, was deserted for Salisbury in 1228. In the north-west of Mercia the diocese of Lichfield, founded in 669, extended north to the Ribble and west to the Dee. Worcester (679) and Hereford (678), more centrally placed in Mercia, were also early bishoprics.

St. David's, Bangor, St. Asaph and Llandaff are Early Christian centres, as is St. German's at Peel in the Isle of Man. Here it is claimed that the diocese of Sodor and Man was founded in 447. The Southern Isles (Sodor), i.e. the Hebrides, were detached from the see of Man in the fifteenth century. The sixth-century Celtic "sees" are territories over which missionary saints ranged widely, rather than bishoprics in the modern sense. In 1966, celebrations in the diocese of Llandaff dated back to the refoundation in 1266. The ancient Scottish bishoprics began about 1107 at St. Andrews after Queen Margaret and her son, David I, encouraged the Roman to absorb the Celtic Church in Scotland. St. Magnus' cathedral at Kirkwall followed St. Andrews in 1137 and when David I died in 1153 nine cathedrals had been founded. The archiepiscopal sees came to be at St. Andrews for the east, and Glasgow for the west coast. Good sea communications brought many pilgrims to the shrine of St. Mungo in the crypt of Glasgow Cathedral. Farther south, similar journeys to harbours narrower than the Clyde carried pilgrims to St. David's—the main bishoprics of both mountainous lands were most readily approached by sea.

New British dioceses were created during the Reformation when, for example, the Benedictine abbeys at Peterborough, Chester and Gloucester became the cathedrals of new bishoprics. Population increase and industrialisation have transformed parish, abbey, or collegiate churches into cathedrals at such centres as Newcastle, Bristol, St. Albans, Manchester, Brecon, or Newport in Monmouthshire. New cathedrals have been built at Coventry, Guildford, Truro and Liverpool, where the Neo-Gothic Anglican cathedral, still incomplete, now contrasts with a striking Roman Catholic cathedral completed in 1967.

Most early Anglo-Saxon churches are likely to have been built of wood and their stone churches may carry ornament which imitates timber work. The finest Anglo-Saxon masonry is seen in the church of St. Lawrence at Bradford-on-Avon (Fig. 70). One of the seventh-century bishop's seats, the Minister of the Holy Cross at Elmham, appears to have had a small choir, nave and presbytery. In the ninth century, Brixworth, near Northampton, was a square church with an apse. During the tenth and early eleventh centuries, splendid churches, of which fragments survive, were built by Benedictine communities

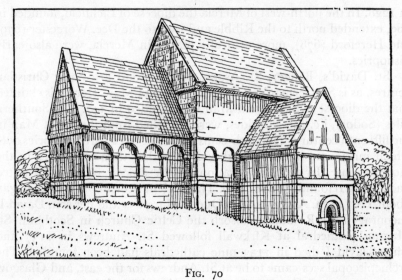

FIG. 70
The Saxon church of St Lawrence, Bradford-on-Avon, Wiltshire

inspired by St. Dunstan. They are found in areas where Jurassic building-stone was near at hand, or could be transported by river, and include the first abbeys at Peterborough and Ramsey, on the fringe of the
Fenland, Winchcombe in the Cotswolds and Dorchester-on-Thames,
where the diocese once extended far along the Jurassic Way. Deerhurst
Church, on the Severn near Tewkesbury, is an interesting Benedictine
church, with Anglo-Saxon details, which was completed in 1056. The
Romanesque Westminster Abbey, built by Edward the Confessor in
1045-50, appears on the Bayeux Tapestry; the semicircular arch which
is basic to it is shown on Fig. 71.

Building traditions from the lower Rhineland, where Charlemagne
had built an eighth-century church at Aix-la-Chapelle, and beyond it
from Lombardy, Ravenna and Constantinople, influenced pre-Con-
quest architecture in Britain. These traditions were largely superseded
by French styles and by buildings designed more specifically for the
ceremonies of the Roman Church after 1066. Orientation towards the
east, elongation of naves and the erection of aisles and ambulatories
became usual. The chapel in the White Tower of London, built a
decade after the Conquest, has an apsidal east end separated from its
surrounding ambulatory by closely spaced pillars. Semicircular east
ends, flanked by chapels which counteracted the thrust of the walls of

the apse, became as normal in the greater churches of Britain as they were in those of northern France. They were built in the new cathedrals of London and Winchester and in churches like St. Bartholomew, Smithfield, which belonged to the Hospital founded by Rahere, the minstrel of Henry I. Some eastern influences came in again after Jerusalem was captured by the Crusaders in 1099 and the Templars built their twelfth-century round churches with a centrally placed altar like that of the Church of the Holy Sepulchre in Jerusalem. The Temple Church in London, the Churches of the Holy Sepulchre at Cambridge and Northampton, and the chapel at Ludlow Castle are examples.

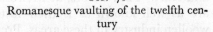

After 1066, the Norman conquerors gave a strong impetus to the building of both churches and castles. Native masons, already capable of good work in the Romanesque style, carried out most of the building. Existing monasteries were extended and many others were erected in previously remote western and northern areas conquered by the Normans. Secular churches as magnificent as those of the Benedictines arose after

FIG. 71
Romanesque vaulting of the twelfth century

1075 when the cathedrals were founded in the expanding Anglo-Norman towns. The semi-circular Romanesque arch was beautifully adorned with chevrons (and, by some masons, with animal heads) in the twelfth century. Doorways and windows were recessed and their several orders provided larger surfaces which could be ornamented to break the plain surfaces of the massive Norman walls. Examples of ornate Romanesque work can be seen on the great doorway of Durham Castle and in the Galilee and nave of its cathedral. More imposing than the adjoining castle, in its present form, Durham Cathedral has been described as "half house of God, half castle against the Scots." Parish churches like those of Tickencote, in Rutland, and the richly adorned Kilpeck and neighbouring churches in the Welsh

Marches, are others where such work has survived. When Norman doorways and windows increased in size, fine churches like that of Tewkesbury Abbey, with a single great recessed arch occupying most of its west front, became possible. In the twelfth century the cult of the Virgin became particularly important in Britain. Facilities for devotion to Our Lady took the form of Lady chapels. Norman builders placed them either at east, or, in the case of the Durham Galilee, west ends of churches. Later Lady chapels usually adjoined the choir.

The powerful Benedictine Order, whose work in Britain dates from 597-8, greatly expanded its influence after 1066. The Benedictines of Durham influenced the Scottish court, and by 1153, fourteen abbeys had been founded in Scotland. Monks of the Order of Tiron, a branch of the Benedictines, came from France to Selkirk in 1113 and began to build their finest British abbeys in Scotland, at, for example, Kelso in 1128 and Arbroath in 1178. Members of the reformed branch of the Benedictine Order, the Cluniacs, came into Britain a decade after the Conquest and built their main house at Lewes in Sussex. The Cluniac reform was not in the direction of austerity. It was Cistercian monks who rejected the wealth and magnificence of the Benedictines and sought the lonely valleys of northern England, the Southern Uplands and Wales. They accommodated large numbers of lay brothers and needed a complex of monastic buildings. Their monasteries, more severe in style than those of the Benedictines, were begun in the early twelfth century and partly survived the Reformation to enhance many secluded valleys in Highland Britain. Cistercian houses in the Yorkshire Dales and North York Moors, at Melrose in Scotland and a dozen in Wales are as well known as is their fostering of sheep-rearing and of the woollen industry in these areas. Premonstratensian Regular Canons, or White Canons, complemented their work. About thirty Premonstratensian churches survive; one example is at Talley in Mid-Wales. Orders of Regular Canons like the Augustinians, or Black Canons, worked from the early twelfth century in the same field as the Benedictines. In territory under Anglo-Norman military control, such as Wales, Benedictine priories were usually built near the castle from which lordships were administered, and if isolated in the countryside they were fortified, as is Ewenny Priory in Glamorgan. In the austere Carthusian monasteries the monks lived in separate cells, while the orders of preaching friars travelled in the countryside, were not allowed to hold endowments and seldom built large churches. The best known of these mendicant orders were the Dominicans (the Order of Preachers), the

PLATE 29 PILGRIM'S WAY, an ancient trackway along the southern flank of the North Downs, used in the Middle Ages by pilgrims to the shrine of St. Thomas à Becket at Canterbury.

PLATE 30   *a.* COWSIC CLAPPER-BRIDGE, Dartmoor.

b. PACKHORSE BRIDGE, Arennig, North Wales.
Before the eighteenth century, mules and horses carried packed goods
and bridges were characteristically narrow. Local stone is used in
both cases; long slabs of Dartmoor granite make an arch unnecessary
at Cowsic.

Franciscans, the Carmel-
ites and the Austin Friars,
who all established British
houses in the first half of
the thirteenth century.
Several Benedictine nun-
neries antedated the Con-
quest and, like those of other
orders, increased after it.
Sisters of St. John of Jerusalem had their general
house at Buckland in Somerset. This military order took
over the houses of the
Knights Templars when
that order was suppressed in
1311-12. Colleges of secular
priests were communities
of priests and deacons who
served dioceses and parishes
and helped to improve standards in outlying churches.
Manchester Cathedral was
a collegiate church which
had its college in what is
now the charity school,
Chetham's Hospital. Pre-
Reformation foundations in
Oxford and Cambridge
were similar in organisation
and groups of scholars were attached to them.

FIG. 72
Early Gothic vaulting of the late twelfth and
early thirteenth century

In the great churches of monasteries, choirs for the monastic community were separated from the nave by choir and rood screens; the
rood screen served as a reredos for the altar of the laity. Crowland and
St. Albans Abbey, and Ewenny Priory too, show this well. It was
usually the nave used by the common people which survived the destruction of the monasteries. Rood screens in the churches of Devon
and Mid-Wales, which sometimes escaped later destruction, are often
their best features. The monks also built parish churches for the laity,

FIG. 73
Middle Gothic vaulting of the early fourteenth century

as at Bury St. Edmunds, but this abbey did not thereby escape spolia-
tion; it is now being restored to some of its former glory. Fountains
Abbey, west of Ripon, still indicates the massing of monastic buildings
around a fine church, and is one of the few cases where the Cistercians
broke their rule and, in the fifteenth century, added a tower (Plate 26,
p. 229). Near the west end of a monastic church lay the outer parlour
where contact with the outside world was maintained through a *curia*
or court. This was surrounded by domestic offices and was often entered
through a great gate. In monasteries like Canterbury, Norwich and
Peterborough, the walled court also contained guest and private houses.
These courts subsequently became cathedral closes, and abbey-
cathedrals, now flanked by lawns enclosed by walls and beautiful

medieval gatehouses, are more characteristic of Britain than cathedrals set on medieval market-places. Post-war attempts to link cathedrals with town life by erecting modern buildings as neighbours for them have had varying success. Those at Worcester, itself heavily restored (Plate 25, p. 228), have rightly attracted adverse comment.

In the second half of the twelfth century, Romanesque features were replaced by pointed arches in the style which Renaissance architects called Gothic, or "barbarous." The purity of Early Gothic (1150 to 1250), lent itself to high-gabled, narrow-windowed, slender buildings in which the Cistercians excelled (Fig. 72). The more ornate Mid-Gothic or Decorated style (1250-1330) produced broader buildings with a wealth of decoration (Fig. 73). Exeter Cathedral shows this well. After about

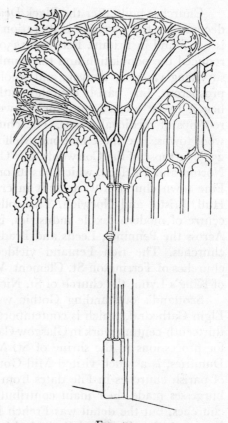

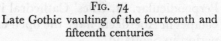

FIG. 74
Late Gothic vaulting of the fourteenth and fifteenth centuries

1350 the Late Gothic (Perpendicular) style introduced large windows and fan vaulting, and church walls were fragmented until they became stone screens and frames for glowing glass (Fig. 74). Light shone on to altars through rose windows; in the ruins of Cistercian abbeys like Tintern they may now act as a frame for a fine outward view. The Perpendicular towers added to great churches in the fourteenth century, like that which adorns the thirteenth-century cathedral at Salisbury, are among the finest achievements of medieval engineers and masons. St. Mary Redcliffe at Bristol, St. George's Chapel at Windsor, Henry VII's Chapel at Westminster and King's College Chapel at Cambridge are some of our beautiful Late Gothic churches.

Churches built after the Black Death tend to be more restrained in decoration; the excessive elaboration of the French Flamboyant style is not found in Britain. Between 1350 and 1550, after the Plague had reduced the population and the numbers of urban craftsmen, and the surviving yeomen, weavers and wool merchants became increasingly prosperous, fine parish churches rather than abbeys and cathedrals began to be erected and their towers pointed skywards above the rooftops of medieval towns. The churches built in the East Anglian wool towns, like those of Long Melford and Lavenham (Plate 28, p. 237), or those of the Cotswolds, like Cirencester, Northleach, Chipping Norton and Fairford, which has its original glass, are the best known. Fine town churches were built in craft centres and ports like York, Hull, Bristol and Norwich. The collegiate church at Manchester, a centre of modern textile industries, is a fine Perpendicular building. Across the Pennines, Leeds and Bradford have good fifteenth-century churches. The rich Fenland yielded wealth which produced the churches of Terrington St. Clement, Walpole St. Peter and, in its port of King's Lynn, the church of St. Nicholas.

Scotland's outstanding Gothic work includes that of the ruined Elgin Cathedral, which is contemporary with Salisbury, and the mid-thirteenth-century work in Glasgow Cathedral whose crypt was designed for processions to the shrine of St. Mungo. Sweetheart Abbey, near Dumfries, is a much visited Mid-Gothic building, and a good group of parish churches in Fife dates from this period. As in England, the burgesses made their main contribution in the form of Late Gothic churches, but the detail was French Late Gothic rather than English Perpendicular. St. Giles' Cathedral in Edinburgh, and King's College Chapel in Aberdeen, have the open crown steeples characteristic of this period in Scotland.

Britain has a very wide range of building-stones. Some of our oldest rock was quarried to build St. David's Cathedral, a plum-coloured shrine in a green western hollow which is flanked by a bishop's palace made gay by chequered purple, cream and white stonework. The Jurassic escarpment not only sustained sheep; its numerous quarries provided valuable building-stone and flags for roofing. Many Romanesque abbeys and Gothic churches are built of Jurassic rock. Abbeys found quarry ownership profitable; Barnack quarry, for example, owned by Peterborough Abbey, provided stone for five other abbeys, including Ely. Transport was easier and cheaper by water and the Normans encouraged the use of Caen stone from Calvados. It is similar to our cream-coloured Bath stone and came into southern Britain both unworked, and, partly because it is most readily carved soon after it is hewn, in worked form. Caen stone was widely used until Normandy was lost in the mid-fifteenth century. Bath stone comes from the Upper Oolite series of the Jurassic, while the Lower Oolite was worked at such quarries as those around Dundry, near the Avon at Bristol; Ham Hill in Somerset, whose orange stone is well seen in Sherborne Abbey; Clipsham near the Fenland or those round Chipping Campden. Stonesfield quarries, near Oxford, provided oolitic roofing-slabs.

Portland stone comes from more recent Jurassic deposits, and although it was used near the Isle of Portland and in London in the fourteenth century, it became popular only when London and its churches were rebuilt after the Great Fire. The limestone known as Purbeck marble has been used for columns, effigies and the paving stones of churches since the Middle Ages, as has clunch, a chalk formation from which the arcade of Ely Lady Chapel was carved. Carboniferous Limestone was widely used in churches on or near the flanks of the Pennines and Peak District. Magnesian Limestone from Yorkshire's lower hillsides and broad vales was used locally and farther afield; Eton College leased a quarry at York in the fourteenth century. A pale cream limestone, which was formed during the erosion of Carboniferous Limestone by Liassic seas, was used by masons in South Wales for decorative work. This stone takes its name from Sutton, where, on the Vale of Glamorgan coast, a line of small quarries follows the outcrop just above the shore; it was used for the fine Romanesque chancel arch of Llandaff Cathedral. Red sandstones of differing ages give glowing warmth to the churches of Cheshire and Devon.

The skilled masons of East Anglia had patrons who could import limestones, but they also overcame the problems of working in the local stone. This was usually flint. Because of the lack of good building-stone, this was used for walls, and stone was reserved for their angles and for door- and window-frames. As conventional towers needed much stone at their angles, round flint towers sometimes replaced them. Eventually flints were halved and set in panels of stone tracery, giving the flush-work characteristic of East Anglia. The magnificent timbering of roofs, screens and stalls of our churches owes much to the oak forests of the Midlands and of the major valleys which flow towards them. Many lead roofs originated in the mines of the Mendips and of the Peak District and Pennines.

The people of the vibrant and questing Tudor Period rejected

Gothic styles. Their overseas contacts brought in ideas from France, Flanders and Italy, and though many fine secular buildings date from the Tudor Period no uniform style is characteristic of Elizabethan or Jacobean ecclesiastical work. In the first half of the seventeenth century, Inigo Jones built in the manner of the Italian, Palladio, for Stuart kings and others. Palladian buildings, based on a revival of classical traditions, had multiplied and been modified since the sixteenth century in France and Wren, Vanbrugh and Hawksmore, influenced by French Palladianism, introduced a late flowering of Renaissance architecture into Britain which had great originality and gave us some of our most handsome buildings.

Many London churches were rebuilt after 1666, but the fifty new churches provided for in an early seventeenth-century act did not materialise. The fifty-three churches built by Wren after the Great Fire include St. Paul's, St. Clement Danes' and Bow Church, Cheapside (Plate 27, p. 236). Thirty-three of Wren's churches existed in 1939 and seventeen of them were destroyed or gutted in the war of 1939-45. Hawksmore, who produced some of the late designs for St. Paul's, built six London churches; among them at St. Mary Woolnoth and St. George, Bloomsbury, with its Roman portico. As other towns began their modern growth in the eighteenth century, some rather staid churches on classical lines were built in them and earlier styles were rejected. At Llandaff Cathedral an odd classical temple, since swept away by restorers, was built within the ruined Norman and Gothic walls. Profits from root-crops and newly enclosed land, and from overseas trade, were used to adorn eighteenth-century churches with chancel screens, pews for the squire's family, and well-lettered memorials to local magnates.

From 1689, dissenting chapels began to be built. When persecuted, rural dissenters had met in barns, and their early chapels were equally simple and modest (Plate 24b, p. 221). In the towns simplicity and dignity are seen in such early chapels as Cross Street, Manchester (originally Presbyterian but later Unitarian). John Wesley's chapel in City Road, London, is a famous eighteenth-century example (Plate XXVII, p. 252). In the late eighteenth century a revival of Anglican preaching led to the building of churches such as St. Chad's, Shrewsbury, which were primarily auditoria.

The Gothic Revival of the nineteenth century produced trite copies of a style which had been inspired by visionaries and had achieved much in Britain as it slowly matured in monastic solitudes. The influence of Sir Walter Scott, the growth of sober faiths preoccupied with morality and material prosperity, rich patrons with a love of display, and growing industrial populations, brought forth numerous churches and chapels in the Gothic style. In the new Truro Cathedral an attempt was made to imitate the succession of styles which would have occurred during the building of a medieval cathedral. Lifeless copies of Gothic originals were erected in a period when mechanical production by contract had replaced handicraft. Copies of the beautiful Sainte Chapelle in Paris were among the least successful churches. Sir Patrick Geddes used of one of them the words of Genesis, Chapter 28, verse 17: "How dreadful is this place. This is none other but the house of God." Restorations and stained glass of the Gothic Revival, which impoverished and disfigured so many churches, are perhaps most regrettable in the countryside, where they replaced small buildings well set in the landscape which could have been readily adapted to the needs of small modern congregations. The Gothic Revival style is at its most absurd when applied to secular buildings like the Law Courts in London, the Town Hall of Manchester and its first purpose-built University building. Sir Gilbert Scott's design for Whitehall buildings, which became St. Pancras station hotel, could hardly be bettered as a monument to Victorian pomp and will probably be preserved as such.

Twentieth-century church-building shows no uniformity and has often lacked confidence. Since 1950, some good buildings have been erected by the Anglican, Roman Catholic and Mormon Churches, often with special attention to social and, especially, youth services. Intellectual perplexity has reduced congregations and the number of functioning churches. After rebuilding, several bombed churches have acquired modern treasures which have made them centres of a new form of pilgrimage. Coventry Cathedral, and Llandaff with Epstein's *Majestas*, are outstanding. Moreover, an increasingly mobile mass of visitors has flocked in the post-war period to the ruins of monasteries and castles maintained by the Ministry of Public Building and Works, as they have to fine secular buildings which are publicly or privately maintained.

The earliest British castles are the Scottish brochs, the well-fortified homesteads of the islands and Highlands of Scotland. About five hundred are known and they reached their widest distribution in the first century A.D. Brochs had immensely thick walls, access was through a narrow well-guarded entrance-passage, and they were often sur-

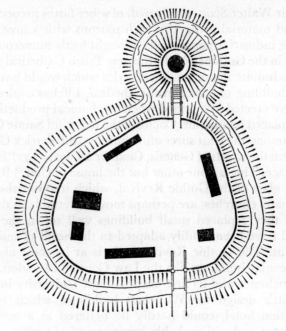

FIG. 75

Diagrammatic ground plan of a motte and bailey castle. The blocks on the bailey
indicate that domestic or farm buildings could have been built there

rounded by banks and ditches (see p. 101). Brochs keep their mystery;
they may have been built for defence against Roman slave-raiders or
their mercenaries.

In Alfred's day fortifications were again erected against raiding
armies, in this case Scandinavian. Burhs, the prototypes of medieval
walled cities, occasionally centring on defensive mounds, were built in
the English Midlands (see p. 156). Castle mounds or mottes began to be
constructed during the reign of Edward the Confessor, but mottes and
baileys were most widely built during and after the Norman Conquest
(Fig. 75). They are found throughout England, and in the late eleventh,
and in the twelfth, century many were built along the lowland and
coastal lines of Norman penetration in Wales, and in similar good land
in Scotland, notably in the south-western coastlands and river valleys,
in Aberdeenshire and in the adjoining coastal lowlands. In both Wales
and Scotland settlement by Norman families, and patterns of feudal
tenure, accompanied the building of mottes and castles. Many mottes

PLATE 31 CLIFTON SUSPENSION BRIDGE over the Avon, below Bristol. Designed by
Sir Isambard K. Brunel and built 1832–64.

PLATE 32   *a*. WATERLOO BRIDGE, London. Designed by Sir Giles Gilbert Scott and built 1937–42 to replace Rennie's fine old bridge.

b. FORTH BRIDGE, near Edinburgh, over one mile long. Designed by Sir Benjamin Baker and built 1882–89.

never had stone castles but were expendable features of Norman campaigns. Others became strongpoints which dominated Anglo-Norman boroughs, and still more were the strongholds of local lords.

Though the Normans built stone castles in Britain from the outset of their occupation, many mottes were at first surmounted by wooden towers. Hope-Taylor argued, as a result of his excavation of the Abinger motte, that the massive wooden stilts which supported the tower reached down through the motte and that the mound was thrown up against them. This has been questioned, though stone towers embedded in mounds have been found. The wooden tower could have been faced with square wooden panels bristling with lances which could have been pushed through them. The Romans used stilted signal towers and the Bayeux Tapestry shows a stilted and palisaded tower on the motte at Dinan (Plate XXVIII, p. 253). Such towers were very vulnerable to fire.

Spurs on chalklands similar to those of Normandy, or within natural moats provided by rivers, were among sites favoured by Norman builders. Windsor and Oxford Castles use the Thames as part of their defences, while on flat sites moats and ramparts encircled both motte and bailey. The first large motte and bailey was built at Berkhampstead in 1066 and here the surrender of London was received. Plate XVa (see p. 176) shows the motte and embanked horseshoe-shaped bailey. Windsor Castle (Plate XXXI, p. 288) has a great thirteenth-century shell keep on the Conqueror's motte, and beyond it the bailey embankments terminate at the cliff-edge above the Thames. A second bailey was added at Windsor in the twelfth century, and this outer ward gave this and other fortresses an hour-glass ground plan.

Stone towers, less vulnerable to fire, were early additions to entrances through the ramparts. Shell keeps replaced the wooden stockades around the tops of mottes. The first castle at Rothesay, with a wall nine feet thick, was such a shell keep. Round towers were added to it in the thirteenth century. In the twelfth century stone keeps replaced timber towers. Rochester's keep is an early example which was soon followed by other hall keeps in southern England, such as the Tower of London, Colchester and Norwich keeps, and farther afield Scarborough and Richmond in Yorkshire or Tretower in Breconshire, where the Norman knight Picard built one. The stump of the latter castle now encloses a round keep of the type which replaced square keeps late in the twelfth century, after many square keeps had been mined by sappers. Orford in Suffolk has an early round keep, and Pembroke Castle a particularly massive one. The spectacular donjon of Bothwell Castle, on the Clyde, is a thirteenth-century example of a great round tower which could serve as a citadel if the curtain-walls were breached. The weight of a massive stone keep could not be supported by most mottes and if the risk was taken their masonry was liable to collapse, as it did at Duffus Castle near Elgin.

In the late twelfth century the trebuchet, a gigantic catapult which advanced behind a shield of wet hides, began to hurl projectiles over the low ring-walls of castles and to damage many keeps. High curtain-walls with wall-towers, and perimeter defences, henceforth replaced keeps. The walls and projecting bastions of Roman forts were sometimes re-used, as they were at Cardiff and Caerwent. Framlingham, in Suffolk, built about 1190, has early towers which are merely projections from the wall. Returning Crusaders brought home many new ideas of fortification and later towers, including those of the gatehouse, are semicircular or octagonal (Plates XXXI and XXIX, pp. 288 and 272). The octagonal towers of Caernarvon originally rose from water defences, a protection against mining. Many moated castles were built in the thirteenth century and around one of the largest of them, Caerphilly in Glamorgan, the water defences included lakes whose dams were fortified. To allow the garrison to see wall-bases, crenellated parapets, and later, projections, were built along the tops of high curtain-walls. Projecting machicolation, seen in an early form at Cooling Castle in Kent, survived for ornamental purposes. This false machicolation can be seen in Britain's northernmost castle, that built on Muness on the Shetland isle of Unst in 1598.

The basic castle plan which had evolved by the thirteenth century is shown on Fig. 76. It combined the functions of military stronghold, garrisoned by a permanent force of perhaps two dozen men, with that of a residence for the lord and his household. This was the plan, adapted to the local terrain, which Edward I used in the castles of the North Wales seaboard, and it evolved into the concentric castle so beautifully displayed at Beaumaris. Fine gatehouses, which were the homes of their constables, characterise the splendid fronts of the North Welsh castles; behind them lay walled bastides like Flint and Caernarvon, which they dominated. The castles of Edward I are the climax of medieval military architecture. Similar castles, with square courtyards and massive corner towers, were built in the west of Scotland at, for example, Inverlochy at the Fort William end of the Great Glen, and Dunstaffnage on Loch Etive, near Oban. The concentric castle is repre-

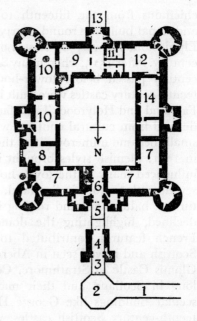

FIG. 76

Plan of a late medieval castle. 1. Timbered causeway across the moat. 2. Fortified bridgehead. 3. Drawbridge. 4. Barbican. 5. Drawbridge. 6. Gatehouse. 7. Barracks for the garrison. 8. Chapel and priest's room. 9. Hall. 10. Lord's private rooms. 11. Butteries and pantries. 12. Kitchen. 13. Causeway and entrance for the Lord's use. 14. Possibly kitchen and dining hall for garrison

sented in Scotland by Caerlaverock on the Solway shore in Dumfries-shire, whose gatehouse is virtually a keep.

Smaller castles and fortified manor houses continued to be built in the fourteenth century. Tretower Court, walled and with a massive gatehouse, is a more spacious dwelling than the adjoining Picard's Tower, but it is still heavily fortified. The Wars of the Roses encouraged much refortification and peel towers were being built even later as dwellings which would withstand marauders on both sides of the Scottish border. In England and Wales the Tudor peace and the end of feudalism brought an end to the building of castellated houses and initiated their replacement by brick or stone mansions which might have high gatehouses but were of more decorative than military value. The few castles built by Tudor monarchs, such as those which guarded the Cornish harbours, had to have immensely thick walls which could withstand gunpowder. In the Civil Wars of the seventeenth century the obsolete castles were sometimes dismantled by local people to prevent their use by either side, or they were besieged, taken, and partly destroyed. Towers which were mined then can be seen at Corfe and Caerphilly.

In Scotland tower-houses continued to be built by turbulent

chieftains from the fifteenth to the seventeenth centuries, though additional buildings round courtyards usually supplemented the tower. Elphinstone Tower, in East Lothian, dates from the mid-fifteenth century. After 1513, when many Scottish leaders died at Flodden, a half-century passed before tower-houses proliferated again. Palatial six-teenth-century castles were built in the interval at Linlithgow, Stirling, Falkland and Holyrood. Their façades have early Renaissance features derived from cultural contacts with France. Tower-houses, large and small, became numerous after the accession of Mary, Queen of Scots, in 1561. Flemish styles brought in by Scottish nobles and merchants influenced many of the tower-houses which were built until the mid-seventeenth century in Scotland. In the larger tower-houses exuberant turrets, balustrades and roofing blossomed forth as defensive features declined, highlighting the domestic quarters in the upper stories. French features contributed to a style which became peculiarly Scottish and is well seen in Aberdeenshire and in the central block at Glamis Castle in Strathmore. Courtyards and castle towers lingered long in Scotland and their mark is strong on seventeenth-century secular buildings like George Heriot's School in Edinburgh. Nine-teenth-century Scottish castles, with their trite multiplication of the good features of earlier tower-houses, are the so-called "Scots Baronial" buildings which were responsible for many inept turrets on Victorian mansions built south of the border.

After the risings of 1715 and 1745, forts were built at strategic points in Scotland. They contained governors' residences and barracks and were defended by stone-faced banks and gateways. The well-planned Fort George, near Inverness, built after the '45, is still the head-quarters of the Seaforth Highlanders. Such fortification was inter-national in style and was resorted to later during the Napoleonic Wars. Milford Haven has a fine series of forts, built of massive blocks of local limestone, which were initiated in the mid-eighteenth century but were mainly planned as defences against Napoleon I and Napoleon III. The fortifications of Pembroke Dock include martello towers which take their name from a tower on Cape Mortella, in Corsica, which was captured in 1794. Martello towers, superficially akin to Norman round keeps, are most numerous along the shores of south-east England which the Normans, but not Napoleon I, successfully invaded.

PLATE XXIX. CAERNARVON CASTLE and its dependent "Bastide" Town
planned by Edward I. Note the parallel streets within the wall

PLATE XXX. STOKESAY CASTLE, Shropshire. A moated manor, partly thirteenth-century

CHAPTER 15

COMMUNICATIONS AND TRANSPORT

FOR MOST prehistoric periods lines of communication by land and sea can be determined only by the patterns of artefacts and other human traces left on the landscape of Britain. In Palæolithic and Mesolithic times, small hunting bands, ranging widely, can have made few pathways except in the vicinity of their temporary shelters. Neolithic peoples came to these islands by sea and they and the Bronze Age peoples established lines of communication in and between areas favourable to settlement. Ridgeways above forested lowlands, isthmian routes across necks of peninsulas which were fringed by tide-races, rivers and their gravel terraces, and relatively low passes through mountain barriers are all known to have been in use.

We know little about the boats in which prehistoric men reached Britain. Several dugout canoes have been found, either on river beds or beneath the waters of lakes. Coracles, still used on the rivers of south-west Wales (Plate 4, p. 49), are of great antiquity; Caesar describes native boats made of interwoven withies and covered with hides. Much larger skin-covered, or wooden, craft are a possibility from the Bronze Age or earlier. The skills which the peoples of Wessex applied to metal, stone (and by inference from Stonehenge, wood) in the Early Bronze Age could also have been applied to boat-building. Pacific peoples with a Neolithic material culture made voyages in the open ocean which were longer than the coastwise journeys which Neolithic folk are likely to have made in their colonisation of the Mediterranean and West European shores. The large well-designed canoes of Pacific peoples such as the Maori are well attested and Thor Heyerdahl's east-west crossing by raft proved that more unwieldy craft could also have been used.

Settlement and communication patterns in the Neolithic and Bronze Ages can be discerned from a few dwellings, many more tombs, and from artefacts lost or buried by their owners. In the Secondary Neolithic, stone axes, polished or half-finished, were traded from the factories shown on Fig. 12. The necessity to bring together tin and copper supplies, and the lure of gold, amber and faience, fostered Bronze Age trading and communication by land and water. The main settlement areas of the megalith builders and Secondary Neolithic peoples (Figs. 11 and 12) were broadly those favoured by Bronze Age man, and, with slight changes of emphasis, by Iron Age peoples. The best-known lines of communication between them are the ridgeways which radiated from Salisbury Plain along the chalk scarps of which it is the node, and the Jurassic Way which ran from Dorset and the Cotswolds to the Humber estuary.

In the earlier stages these ridgeways are likely to have been belts of transit rather than well-marked paths, and even when they had become established as tracks some sections of them were duplicated. Scarp-top and scarp-base trackways were made for use according to wind, rain, and the need for water and shelter. The routes along the chalk hills include the Ridgeway which runs from the Marlborough Downs along the Berkshire Downs, past Wayland's Smithy and a number of Iron Age forts, to the Thames at Goring. Its lower counterpart, along the Greensand, also crosses the Thames at the Goring Gap and both tracks continue as the frequently duplicated Icknield Way along the Chilterns. The Icknield Way continues more or less along the line of the Peddar's Way through the north-west Norfolk chalk belt to the sea. The best-known prehistoric track east of Salisbury Plain is again on lightly forested chalkland above former forests and swamps. For most of its length on the North Downs it is known as the Pilgrims' Way because it was later used by pilgrims to St. Thomas à Becket's tomb at Canterbury; the main route runs to the Dover Strait. This old track has also been called the Harroway and it has both hilltop and hillside sections (Plate 29, p. 260). Shorter routes for prehistoric ridge walkers probably included the scarp-tops of the Yorkshire Wolds and Moors, the ridgeways between what became the South Wales mining valleys, and those on the limestone flanks of the Aire and Stainmore gaps which communicated with East Yorkshire by such features as the York moraine and with the Lake District fringes by means of high shelves of limestone. The prehistoric peoples of Lowland Britain settled round harbours such as the Essex, Suffolk, Medway, Hampshire and Dorset estuaries. They also travelled on rivers and on their gravel terraces.

In Atlantic and Highland Britain prehistoric man depended largely on sea and river transport, though some land routes can be postulated in western Britain. Coastal finds are common, and islands, or peninsulas which protrude into the seaways, were relatively densely peopled, especially if they were intervisible in good weather with distant coasts. The Northern Isles, Kintyre, Arran, Bute, the Galloway peninsula, the Isle of Man, Anglesey, the Llŷn and Pembrokeshire peninsulas, Gower, the Vale of Glamorgan, which protrudes into the Bristol Channel, the South-West peninsula and the Scilly Isles were all inhabited by a succession of prehistoric peoples who were linked by sea. To avoid tide-races off their headlands, isthmian land routes developed across many peninsulas. Among them are that followed by the Crinan Canal across Kintyre, the Llanllyfni-Cricieth route which avoids the tide-races between Llŷn and Bardsey, several hill and river routes behind the Pembrokeshire headlands, St. Ives Bay to Mount's Bay, Padstow-Fowey (largely a river route) and, probably, intermediate routes in Cornwall. Craft such as coracles (Plate 4, p. 49), or skin-covered canoes or curraghs, could have been carried over the relatively short land journeys involved in many of these routeways.

Flint, stone and bronze axes, ore or scrap, or metal goods, were carried on all these prehistoric routeways. The products of the Graig Lwyd axe factory, for example, appear to have been traded both coast-wise and overland. Those which reached Wessex could have been taken round the Welsh coast or may have been carried up the Conway, down the upper Dee and down the Severn, always one of our major arteries of trade. They may then have gone down its estuary and up the Bristol Avon and along the route postulated for the conveyance of the Presely bluestones to Stonehenge. Professor Atkinson's experiments have shown how the transport of these large masses of stone, both by raft and for short land journeys, and that of the sarsen stones, could have been accomplished by a large and well-directed labour force.

Although prehistoric men must have used landmarks as sighting points their tracks were not straight; they curved considerably according to the lie of the land. The Roman road network, designed for military and civil control rather than for peaceful trade, was made possible by skilled engineers backed by slave labour. The major elements in this network are shown on Fig. 24. Roman roads centred on London: Salisbury Plain, the focus of prehistoric routes, lost its supremacy. Planned to facilitate troop movements, roads aimed straight for legionary and civil headquarters. From landing places in Kent, roads were built to the lowest firm crossing place of the Thames, where Londinium was established. Roads then spread fanwise throughout the area south-east of the Jurassic Way. Much of this track became the

Fosse Way. Beyond the Jurassic scarp, after some years, road-building continued to York and to the Welsh borderland through conquered country which was added to the Roman civil zone. Northern England, southern Scotland and Wales became military zones and their roads connected forts, rather than the cantonal capitals of the civil zone. Troublesome tribes which retreated to the mountains were contained within networks of forts and roads, like those on either side of the Pennines, or the major rectangle round Wales, or those in the valleys of the Southern Uplands. Minor transverse roads were made as links between the major containing roads; their routes are gradually being discerned on the ground.

Roman roadways were built on excavated beds and on a foundation of large stones topped by smaller stones and gravel. Kerbstones supported this road bed which was flanked by ditches and cambered. Major Roman roads were sometimes wider than their successors, as they are in Caerwent in Monmouthshire. On peat-bogs Roman roads were paved, like that over Blackstone Edge in the territory of the Brigantes. Causeways of logs were built over lowland bogs, as had occurred on many Iron Age tracks. The Roman roads which led to Corinium (Cirencester), Lindum (Lincoln) and many other places are now buried under modern roads, but the lines of ditches and the low banks which were once cambered roads, now grassed over, can often be followed across countrysides where they rapidly became disused after the Romans left Britain.

Roman engineers built the first British canals, the Foss Dyke which runs from Torksey, on the Trent, to Lincoln, and the Car Dyke from Lincoln to the Fenland. The former is still navigable and the latter still drains a part of the Fenland. The next British canal was not built until the sixteenth century; this Exeter Canal was built well before the main period of canal-building. New roads as good as those of the Roman network began to be built only in the eighteenth century, and our main contribution to the development of communications in the intervening centuries was made on our estuaries and on the seas beyond them.

Roads suitable for medieval and Tudor farming economies, for slow ox teams and the leisurely life of largely self-supporting communities, ran their winding ways around and between settlements. Rural roads which followed the margins of common arable fields, and were hedged during piecemeal enclosures, to-day present the motorist with a succession of right-angled bends. Straighter roads were usually made during the parliamentary enclosures of the eighteenth and early nineteenth centuries.

But no medieval community was completely self-contained. Salt was a necessity for curing meat after the autumn killings, and Salt Ways developed from mines like those of Droitwich or Cheshire, or from coastal saltpans to the interior. Human porters and packhorses carried salt and most of the other loads carried by land. Neither needed broad roads or bridges, and packhorse (or mule) tracks are narrow. Packhorse trains could be seen in Highland Britain until well on into the nineteenth century. One famous track which they used is the paved "Roman Steps" on the route from the Merioneth coast (Dyffryn Ardudwy), eastwards over Bwlch Drws Ardudwy towards the Arennig massif (Plates XVb and 30b, pp. 176 and 261). It may follow a Bronze Age route. Sharply arched packhorse bridges can be found near towns which had well-known fairs. They may now lie on field paths like that north of Hawes, in the North Riding, which is linked with Hawes by flagged paths through the brilliant meadows typical of the Yorkshire Dales. Packhorse bridges in Dartmoor, built of long granite slabs, could have originated in the Late Bronze Age when Dartmoor farmers became accustomed to handling such massive boulders and built house and field walls from them. A late Devonshire pack-mule path is shown on Plate XXXII (see p. 289).

On the inadequate medieval and later roads, merchants transported their goods by ponderous long wagons, or *chars*, drawn by oxen or horses. Hadfield estimates that a horse can draw about two tons on a level road and from 50 to a 100 tons on a good waterway. It is hardly remarkable that coastwise shipping and river transport were used where possible and that improvement of water transport generally received more attention than the improvement of roads until increased trade in the early stages of the Industrial Revolution made both necessary. Where slopes were too steep for wheeled traffic, sledges were used. Sometimes small solid wooden wheels were fitted to them. Hay and peat were the chief products carried on sledges, and large hay sledges with steel-shod runners are still being used and made in areas such as the Yorkshire Dales.

Until railways were built, cattle, sheep, and even pigs and geese walked from Highland to Lowland Britain for fattening and marketing. The drove roads, the drovers' inns and pounds, and occasionally the smithies where the cattle were shod, can still be seen on many hillsides in southern Scotland and northern England, notably in the Cheviots,

and in Wales. Continuations of Welsh drove roads east of the lower
Severn are called Welsh Ways. On the borders of Leicestershire and
Lincolnshire, both counties with fattening pastures, the Drift was a
drove road. About ten major drove roads crossed Wales and cattle
walked them from western collecting centres over the hillsides to the
border and on into the Midland Plain. Many drove roads are now green
walking-tracks with fine views. They sometimes incorporated prehistoric trackways and they rarely became major roads. When turnpike roads were made, the drovers kept to their ridge tracks. Drovers
acted as bankers and newsmen for the upland communities and
Carmarthenshire had a Bank of the Black Ox which was founded by a
drover. Local branches of Lloyds bank, into which it was merged, had
black oxen on their cheques.

Until the late nineteenth century, parishes were responsible for the
upkeep of roads, but this system was never effective, particularly in
thinly peopled hill parishes. Urban roads gradually improved as
coaches became more common. Elizabeth I complained of the dis-
comfort of travel in a coach presented to her by a Dutchman in 1565.
In Charles II's day a Company of Coach and Harness Makers improved the springs of coaches and used glass more widely for their
windows. Queen Anne used a heavy glass coach drawn by six horses.
Stage-coaches for public use, with practically no suspension, had been
introduced before the Civil War. By 1739, the three-quarters of a million
inhabitants of London used 22,639 horses, 2,484 private carriages, and
1,100 carriages which plied for hire. Sedan-chairs, first licensed in
1634, were also available; they were useful in narrow or congested
streets and provided work for many pairs of chair-men.

In 1663, the first toll-gates were erected at Wadesmill, near Ware,
in Hertfordshire and private companies began to be formed to improve
roads. These turnpike companies were given powers to erect gates at
which tolls would be levied on users to pay for the maintenance of the
roads. During the eighteenth-century turnpike trusts, roads and toll-
gates multiplied, as did regular coach services on them. Turnpikes were
fairly direct routes and gradients were often steeper than those of
modern main roads. Oxen were even used for supplementary traction
on their steepest sections, and these stretches have become, like drovers'
roads, green ways or country lanes. Until the railways took over long-
distance passenger transport, the turnpike system fostered the growth
of fashionable watering-places like Bath, and coach tours, by the same
social class, of the valleys from which the "horrid" mountains of the

Lake District could be observed; fell walking was then an odd practice of the hardy natives. Turnpike roads also attracted the skills of engineers of the calibre of Thomas Telford (1757-1834) and John Loudon Macadam (1756-1836), but the system did not provide a national network.

Parishes were responsible for the upkeep of roads other than the 23,000 miles of turnpike roads until 1894, though after 1835 statute labour was replaced by rates. The dreadful conditions on many roads were often described by agricultural improvers like Arthur Young (1741-1820) and deplored by manufacturers like Josiah Wedgwood (1730-95) whose fragile goods had to be carried on them. The development of canals, and particularly railways, delayed reform of road administration and railways also ruined the stage-coach companies and most of the turnpike trusts. In south-west Wales agrarian discontent and grievances against tolls crystallised into the Rebecca Riots of 1839 and 1842-3 when Genesis, Chapter 24, verse 60: "And they blessed Rebecca and said . . . let thy seed possess the gate of those which hate them" was invoked and "Rebecca and her daughters" broke down the toll-gates. The first statutory abolition of a turnpike system followed in South Wales in 1860. The last British turnpike trust was abolished in North Wales in 1895.

In the nineteenth century, more varied horse-drawn passenger vehicles became common on urban roads. After 1830, these included hackney carriages, hansom cabs, the four-wheeler and horse-omnibuses. The wagons of firms of carriers, many of them with a long history, added to the traffic, as did horse-drawn tramways from 1868 in Liverpool and 1869 in London. From 1863, London's first underground trains, those of the Metropolitan Railway, took some passenger traffic off her roads. The first experimental vehicles with internal combustion engines driven by petrol appeared on British roads in the 1880s and early 1890s, and in 1903, "motor-cars," with a speed limit of 20 miles per hour, were licensed for general use. Roads began to be improved and Macadam's name was perpetuated in tarmacadam; untarred macadam had produced much dust as traffic speeds increased. The hard smooth surfaces of Macadam's turnpikes, made of pounded stone, had allowed coaches to reach 10 miles per hour in the knowledge that changes of horse-power were available at coaching inns.

The advent of the motor-car meant that railways would soon cease to dominate our inland transport system. The number of motor vehicles of all types rose from 17,810 in 1904 to 265,182 in 1914. By

1939, over three million vehicles used 180,000 miles of motorable roads in Britain. The rapid post-war increase in car ownership, and its damaging effects on the urban environment, produced the report on *Traffic in Towns* in 1963. In it Professor Buchanan estimated that, by 1970, 18 million, and, in 2010, 40 million vehicles might be attempting to use the roads of Britain, and that the most rapid increase would come before 1980. Even now, 80 per cent of our goods traffic goes by road. In the eighteenth century the country gentry built town houses for winter use because the roads then became impassable. The dignified quarters which resulted have proved vulnerable to modern road improvements which could prove to be only short-term solutions to one of our most urgent problems. Outside towns the construction of new roads and motorways hardly keeps pace with the increase in motor traffic, particularly of freight traffic formerly carried by rail.

Fords, and then bridges, were once fought over and defended by local armies. Some bridges, like those at Warkworth or Monmouth, were fortified. Medieval bridges often had chapels where alms were given for maintaining the bridge. Bridges began to be designed and built by architects when, in the early eighteenth century, wide Palladian arches were used for them. On the Thames, London Bridge was the only bridge until Westminster Bridge was built in 1738 and London's watermen flourished until the Thames bridges multiplied in the nineteenth century. Engineers joined architects as bridge designers after iron bridges proved durable and the first, built in 1779 at Iron Bridge, Coalbrookdale, still stands, as does Telford's Menai Bridge, completed in 1826. The old London Bridge was replaced by Rennie's bridge in 1831; in 1967 this bridge was sold because it was too narrow. Rennie's Waterloo Bridge was replaced by that shown on Plate 32a (see p. 269). Our fine suspension bridges include that at Clifton (Plate 31, p. 268), the Forth Bridge (1964) which partners the iron railway bridge dating from 1890 (Plate 32b, p. 269) and that across the Severn estuary which was opened in 1966.

Modern industry finds the slowness of inland water transport intolerable. There are exceptions; coal is transported to some power stations in the Midlands by barges. The transport of "sea coal" from Tyneside to London has continued from medieval times and, like the trade in wool, and fishing, provided training for seamen. Small sailing ships of 10-60 tons, many of them based on the creeks of Atlantic Britain, accomplished remarkable journeys in Tudor times, trading not only to the Mediterranean but to Newfoundland for salted cod.

They also brought in goods to coastal harbours and traded up rivers to ports like York, Norwich, Oxford and Cambridge where merchants and fairs depended greatly on waterborne goods. The great Stourbridge Fair at Cambridge is a case in point. Overseas trade led to an increase in the size and number of ships, many of them being chartered by companies like the Merchant Adventurers, the East India and Hudson's Bay Companies. By the nineteenth century, schooners from many British harbours were carrying emigrants to the colonies which had followed the Tudor voyages of discovery and expansion of trade. As steam replaced sail the small harbours languished. Oil imports have replaced coal exports as a major part of our trade, and docks which were built in the nineteenth century are now becoming obsolete. Tankers of 300,000 tons discharge cargoes at a tank farm on Whiddy Island in Bantry Bay, followed by shipment in tankers of 100,000 tons to a refinery on Milford Haven, where ships of 250,000 tons now trade. Tankers may eventually become so large that they may have to berth far out beyond our coasts and discharge their cargoes through undersea pipe-lines; they already berth well offshore near some sources of crude oil.

Transport of freight on inland waters has been carried on since prehistoric craft first plied on our lakes and rivers. As river trade developed, little inland ports, such as Bewdley on the Severn, became the focus of packhorse routes for further distribution of goods. Bewdley still has a Packhorse Inn. The Severn and Thames were the main navigable waterways, followed by the Trent, Tyne, Tees and Fenland rivers, and the Clyde in Scotland. In the reign of Elizabeth I, improvement of navigation on these and many other rivers was initiated, and this later resulted in groups of trustees or companies undertaking to make rivers navigable and levying tolls on users. In the mid-seventeenth century, acts were passed to make navigable the Medway, Stour, Lugg, Wiltshire Avon and Itchen. The Aire and Calder Navigations allowed ships in the wool trade to reach Leeds and Wakefield after 1700 and at this time the Trent was improved to Gainsborough. In the early eighteenth century the south Lancashire rivers and the Weaver, in Cheshire, were made navigable for the benefit of the coal, textile, salt and pottery trades. These river navigations involved dredging, cuts through the necks of meanders, and, as early as Elizabeth I's reign, the use of pound-locks with sluice-gates to replace flash-locks which were wasteful of water. River navigations were opposed by millers, riparian farmers and landowners, and towns which had previously been at the head of navigation, but by 1724 there were 1,160 miles of river navigation in Britain and in the Lowland Zone most traders were within fifteen miles of navigable water.

But trade and industry continued to expand in the eighteenth century and, as supplies of wood decreased, poor folk demanded cheaper coal. In France the Canal du Midi was completed from the Mediterranean to the Gironde in 1681. Only the Exeter Canal, built between 1564 and 1566, then existed in Britain and it had not yet been enlarged. The St. Helen's Canal was largely completed to the Mersey in 1757, and two years later the Duke of Bridgewater obtained his act for a canal from his pits at Worsley to Manchester. It was opened in 1761 and its most remarkable feature was the Barton aqueduct over the Irwell. Francis, third Duke of Bridgewater, had studied the Canal du Midi and he and his engineer James Brindley, a former millwright from Derbyshire whose spelling was unconventional, produced several of the links in our canal network which made possible the rapid growth of industry. Linked with river navigations, the canals made feasible water transport between Thameside, Severnside, Merseyside and Humberside by 1790 and allowed the Industrial Revolution to take its hold on the Midlands and northern England. In South Wales a number of short canals had been built after 1770 to connect pits with the sea. The iron industry, sited farther inland on the north crop of the South Wales coalfield, needed from its inception in the mid-eighteenth century better transport than the packhorse and mule trains which went down to the ports along ridgeways first trodden out in the Bronze Age. The Glamorganshire Canal from Merthyr Tydfil to Cardiff was opened in 1794 and was soon followed by canals which led from other ironworks down the Neath and Swansea valleys, and by the Brecon and Monmouthshire Canal. Long tramroads ran over hills and through valleys down to these waterways. On the Penydarren Tramroad, which ran from Merthyr Tydfil to the Glamorganshire Canal at Navigation (Abercynon), Trevithick's locomotive ran in 1804, making possible by 1840 the end of canal dominance in industrial transport and the later supremacy of Merthyr's ironworks as producers of iron and steel rails for many railway systems.

In North Wales the Ellesmere Canal, with its graceful aqueducts over the Dee and Ceiriog valleys, was completed in 1805. The canals of Scotland were those which linked the Forth with the Clyde estuary, opened in 1790 by a sea-going sloop, the Crinan Canal across the neck of the Kintyre peninsula, engineered by Rennie and opened in 1801, and the Caledonian Canal, completed in 1822, which runs between and through the lakes of the Great Glen but never took the large ships which Telford, its builder, had hoped to see on it. Canals across the Pennines, such as the Rochdale Canal, from 1804, and the Leeds and Liverpool Canal, from 1816, carried local and long-distance traffic through the textile areas. The Gloucester and Berkeley Canal, completed in 1827, was for many years the deepest in Britain. A few other canals were built after the Napoleonic Wars, but the opening of the Stockton and Darlington Railway in 1825, and early railway speculation, discouraged further new canal projects. Many existing canals were improved before the real rivalry with the railways started.

The last canal built in Britain was also the greatest. The Manchester Ship Canal, opened in 1894, quickly made Manchester the fourth British port. Ships of up to 12,500 tons tower above the Lancashire plain as they come up to Manchester Docks. This canal is not administered by the British Waterways Board; it is classified as a dock undertaking and its control extends over the Duke of Bridgewater's first canal. Nearly all British canals (2,064 miles), and river navigations other than the Thames and Broads, came under the control of the British Transport Commission in 1948. There were then 6,000 working boats on British canals.

The towpaths of our canals can still be walked for many miles and about 1,400 miles of canals maintained by the British Waterways Board are still navigable. They lead to or past some of the most important sites for industrial archæologists and their courses run through pleasant countryside or through industrial dereliction. Canals were responsible for much interesting urban growth; Stourport, for example, was created after the Staffordshire and Worcestershire Canal was completed to the Severn, and Kendal expanded after the Lancaster Canal was completed to it. After 1794, Merthyr Tydfil, with its four ironworks, sprawled quickly, as did Cardiff, its port. The walker can find fascination in canals and their tramroads. Many improvements, either for commercial or recreational use, have recently been carried out by the British Waterways Board. Many more are needed, on canals and rivers, both in the towns, where they could be linked with imaginative redevelopment schemes, and on their fringes. We need large schemes like that proposed for the Lee valley, and a variety of smaller recreational schemes based on water; it is the biggest magnet for those in search of recreation.

The advent of railways slowed down the development of both roads and canals, while coaching inns, and to a lesser degree canal-side inns, lost their trade. Railways had their origins in the tramroads which carried coal from pits to ports or hauled iron ore and limestone to ironworks and took their products to canal wharfs. By 1840, when railways began to dominate canals in inland transport, the Industrial Revolution had taken place. Industrialisation had already brought ugliness and dereliction in the form of slag-heaps, deforestation and crowded dwellings, but most towns retained some seemliness and workers' cottages were usually stone-built and trim. Railways proliferated in almost the bleakest age of individualist politics and paid little regard to the amenities of the towns they served. They gave a wide circulation to bricks and other standardised building materials and made possible rapid urban growth in the form of grim blocks of mean streets. Most of our major cities are disfigured by railways and, now that many of the lines, goods yards and stations built by former competing companies are redundant, opportunities arise to restore some of the amenities which they destroyed. In London surplus railway land may have to be largely built over, but elsewhere disfiguring derelict tracks could give way to landscaped pleasure-grounds. One of the earliest railways, the Mumbles Tramroad completed in 1804, and a later line, follow the lovely curve of Swansea Bay and restrict access to the beach. Their removal, to make way for Miss Sylvia Crowe's redevelopment scheme, is long overdue. Many rural railways will revert to scrub and their cuttings will provide increasing interest for naturalists. On other redundant lines, problems of bridge maintenance, drainage and fencing need to be tackled so that more of them can be used by walkers and pony-trekkers. Old tramroad tracks have often survived as fine walking and bridle paths, and sections of abandoned railways, such as the Scarborough-Whitby line, the Merthyr to Talybont-on-Usk line over the Brecon Beacons, that running south from Coniston, the Wye valley lines and many more could be so used.

Air transport in Britain uses Heathrow, Gatwick and Prestwick, which are internationally important, and thirty other airports, spaced between the Isles of Scilly and the Scottish Midlands, which are used for local or international flights. Our civil airways network was not planned as such; many airports were built as services airfields. A number of large and smaller airports are owned by municipalities and there are several helicopter stations. The Scottish Highlands and Islands are served by eight airfields and their situation is almost similar to that of Iceland where, in one generation, transport by pony has been replaced by journeys by plane. Since 1945, the piston engine has been largely superseded by the jet engine and supersonic speeds are adding supersonic booms to the noise already created by air traffic. A suggestion has been made that palls of smoke will be replaced by blankets of noise unless major airports are better sited in relation to built-up areas. In the nineteenth century the railways cut swathes through towns with subsequent deterioration of adjoining residential property. This feature could be repeated on a much greater scale on land which lies under the approaches to runways or under flight paths between airports. The railways brought direct or indirect benefit to a large proportion of the community; it is doubtful whether the benefits of supersonic flight will be enjoyed by a similar number of people.

The Agricultural and Industrial Revolutions showed up the weaknesses in our transport system, but networks of canals, roads and railways were gradually laid down for the benefit of both town and country. The Technological Revolution finds Britain with largely derelict canals, some efficient ports and others which need to be modernised, an increasing number of redundant railways and a dense road network which is nevertheless inadequate for the demands which are being made upon it. Air traffic, for civil or defence purposes, engenders demands on lowlying land which is often high-quality farmland and adjoins densely peopled areas which are already subjected to noise from other forms of traffic. Arthur Young said of the Preston-Wigan road: "I know not, in the whole range of language, terms sufficiently expressive to describe this infernal road." The improvements in width and surfaces which he advocated have come, but his views on our numerous overloaded main roads would have been of great interest.

CHAPTER 16

POPULATION

ESTIMATES OF THE population of Britain prior to the decennial census reports, first issued in 1801, involve a great deal of guesswork. We may hazard a guess that the pre-Roman population, living in defended villages or isolated farms, perhaps numbered a quarter of a million. In the most stable phase of the Roman occupation, the Romano-British population may have been three-quarters of a million. The walls of Roman London enclosed an area of 325 acres. London was larger than most Roman cities north of the Alps and may have housed 20,000 inhabitants. Half a dozen larger *coloniae* or legionary forts may have averaged 3,500 each and about fifty other towns around 1,000 each. This gives an urban population of about 120,000, and if a proportion of 80 per cent is added for the rural population, England and Wales could have had a total of about 600,000 inhabitants (see p. 105).

Estimates based on the Domesday Book suggest that in 1086 England may have had a population of one-and-a-half or even two millions and that the population had risen after the Conquest. The Domesday Survey shows that the fertile lands of East Anglia and Kent were then the most densely settled parts of England. There appear to have been further considerable population increases in 1150-1200 as more land was brought into cultivation, and in the thirteenth century, when the rise in the number of villeins brought about land hunger. The population of Scotland in about 1250, during the reign of Alexander III, is thought to have been about 600,000. In the mid-fourteenth century recurrent outbreaks of the Black Death reduced the population total by 30-40 per cent, and by 1500, when recovery was still slow, it may have been two-and-a-half to three millions in England and Wales. Ninety per cent of this total are likely to have lived in the countryside which was still, for the most part, thinly peopled. Between 1500 and the mid-seventeenth century the population increased by 75 per cent, from less than three to more than four-and-a-half millions. About a million and a half of this increase was in rural areas where 80 per cent of the population lived. Here, by the mid-seventeenth century, land hunger and relative poverty were again apparent. London shared in this increase; in 1534 her population may have been 60,000; in 1582, possibly 120,000 and in 1605 about 250,000. By 1700 London's population was about 674,000 and in 1821 it was 1,274,000. Estimates for other trading cities, during the reign of Henry VIII, include 12,000 for Norwich, 10,000 for Bristol and 8,000 each for York, Salisbury and Exeter. It has been suggested that the population of Wales numbered 251,800 in the mid-sixteenth century and 275,000 in the early seventeenth century. In the second quarter of the seventeenth century, plague and famine slowed down the rate of growth in both towns and countryside, but until then, population increase, fostered by Tudor prosperity, had alarmed both Elizabeth I and James I, especially because of its effects on overcrowded London. In the seventeenth century the plague of 1665, the Fire of London in 1666, and the New River Scheme, reduced overcrowding and improved the water supply. Other towns, such as Norwich, Ipswich and Exeter were overcrowded. The wool manufacturing areas in East Anglia, the West Country and the North, and areas with craft industries in the Midlands, also increased their populations. In the countryside, increases of as much as 50 per cent in Hertfordshire and Leicestershire, during the reign of Elizabeth I, made necessary enclosure of common fields and improvements in cropping.

Gregory King's tables of 1688 estimate the population of England as 5,500,520; they are largely based on hearth-tax data. Sir John Clapham's suggestion for England and Wales in 1700 was 5,800,000. In 1707, the date of the Union with England and Wales, the people of Scotland may have numbered about a million, with about 12,500 in Glasgow. By 1801 the Scottish population numbered 1,610,000. A mid-eighteenth century estimate by Dr. Alexander Webster, minister of the Tolbooth Church in Edinburgh, gave a figure of 1,265, 380 in 1755. A fifth of them were described as fighting men aged 18 to 65 years, younger men being too weak and older men too infirm to bear arms. In 1755, Scotland was still largely a farming country and the most densely peopled counties were Banff, Fife, Clackmannan, Midlothian, West Lothian and Berwick, in the rain shadow of the wet hills. Between 1801 and 1841, another million was added to the Scottish population and in the following century the figure doubled again.

The more rapid eighteenth-century growth of population in Britain came in the second half of the century. In 1750, England and Wales probably had about seven million people. Industrialisation and improvements in medicine, to which Scots doctors contributed considerably, produced the figure of 8,890,000 for England and Wales by 1801. There had probably been an overall increase of 50 per cent in the British population in the eighteenth century. In areas which were affected by the first phases of the Industrial Revolution it grew more rapidly. Lancashire probably had about 160,000 people in 1701. In 1801, 695,000 were recorded there. The largest Welsh town in 1801 was Carmarthen, an old-established market town supported by a good agricultural hinterland. In 1801, Merthyr Tydfil had grown from a tiny hamlet to an "iron town" of 7,705 and by 1831, 22,000 people lived in the nightly glare of its ironworks. Carmarthen had grown only slowly, to 9,955 in 1831. Cardiff, the modern capital of Wales (259,700 in 1966), and a commercial rather than an industrial centre for much of the nineteenth century, had only 1,870 in 1801 and 6,187 in 1831.

Nineteenth-century population movements within Britain often extended over only relatively short distances between rural and new industrial areas. Northerners went into Lancashire and Yorkshire industries, and to Tyneside and the Northumberland-Durham coalfield. From neighbouring Welsh counties rural folk flocked to the iron towns, mining valleys and ports of Glamorgan and Monmouthshire. Between 1801 and 1861 Birmingham's population grew from 70,000 to 300,000, partly by natural increase but also by migration from the Midlands and the Welsh Marches. In 1801, Birkenhead was a village of 700 people; in 1861 it had 50,000. In the same period the little textile town of Bradford, with 13,000 people, grew until it had 100,000 inhabitants. Glasgow was a magnet for much of Scotland and parts of northern England. In 1707 it was a port and market town of 12,500 inhabitants. It grew to a town of 77,000 in 1801 and of 283,000 in 1841 and at this time rivalled Manchester as leader of the cotton industry; Clydeside's engineering industries were prodigious both in growth and fame. Glasgow laid claim to the title of second city of the Empire as early as 1830; its population was estimated at 979,798 in 1966. Throughout Britain old-established provincial cities also expanded in the eighteenth century. The elegant town of Bath, with a population of 30,000 in 1801, was then the ninth largest British city.

The figures since 1801, and the annual rates of increase, are shown opposite.

In 1801-1901, the population of Britain multiplied from 10.5 to 37 millions. It doubled in 1801-51 and again in 1851-1911. English decennial increases were never less than 10 per cent in the nineteenth century but in the next decade a reduction in the size of families was

PLATE XXXI. WINDSOR CASTLE. An eighth-century mound and a thirteenth-century round tower altered in the fourteenth century and again by George IV. The Upper Ward has buildings remade under Charles II. The Lower Ward has St. George's Chapel (1473–1507)

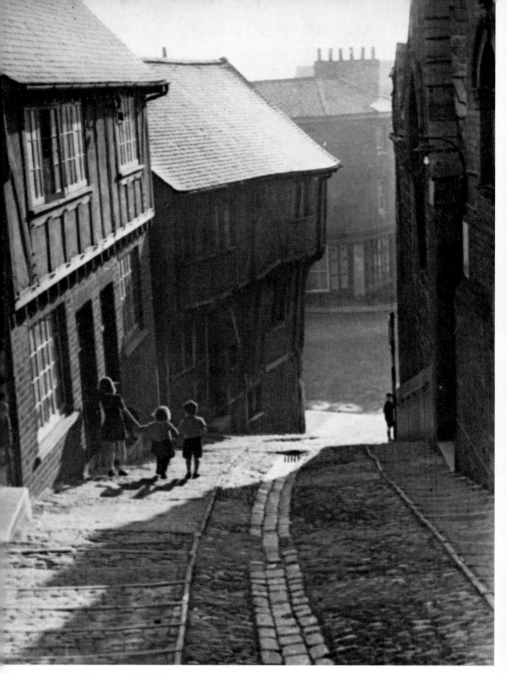

PLATE XXXII. MULES' STEPWAY, Exeter. Steps are broad for pack-
mules taking loads from the old port up to the city

Year	England and Wales—Population in millions	Percentage annual increase	Scotland—Population in millions	Percentage annual increase
(first 1801 census)	8.89	—	1.61	—
1811	10.16	1.43	1.81	1.23
1821	12.00	1.81	2.09	1.58
1831	13.90	1.58	2.34	1.30
1841	15.91	1.43	2.60	1.08
1851	17.93	1.27	2.89	1.02
1861	20.07	1.19	3.06	0.60
1871	22.71	1.32	3.36	0.97
1881	25.97	1.44	3.74	1.12
1891	29.00	1.17	4.03	0.78
1901	32.53	1.22	4.47	1.11
1911	36.07	1.09	4.76	0.65
1921	37.89	0.49	4.88	0.25
1931	39.95	0.55	4.84	-.08
1951	43.74	0.47	5.10	0.26
1961	46.07	0.51	5.22	0.24

becoming apparent. The birth-rate per thousand had been about 37 in 1800, 32 in 1850 and 30 in 1900. The growth-rate throughout the nineteenth century was slower in Scotland than in England and Wales, and noticeably slower in the first half of the twentieth century. Emigration was largely responsible, though Irish immigrants partly replaced the loss. In 1881-91, 217,418 Scots emigrated, and between 1900 and 1930 nearly 900,000 Scots are thought to have left Scotland. In 1921-31, for example, there was a net migration from Scotland of 391,903 and a 0.08 per cent decrease in her total population. Wales lost many migrants in this decade; only England increased her population by 6 per cent. In 1931-51 Scotland lost a further 220,000 by migration while England and Wales gained 745,000 by immigration. Irish migrants made up a large part of this total.

The decay of the older industrial areas such as Lancashire, Tyneside, the Scottish Midlands and South Wales, which had too great a dependence on too few declining industries, resulted in migration from them to areas of newer and more diversified industries. South-east

England, the Midlands and the Bristol area took many of these migrants between about 1922 and 1939.

After two centuries of rapid growth the population of Britain grew much less rapidly until the Second World War. This decline was a feature of many European countries. In 1930 the birth-rate per thousand was 16; its continuing fall was reduced in 1933 and after 1941 it began to rise and was 20 per thousand in 1946-7. After a fall in the mid-1950s the birth-rate again rose by the end of the decade. The mid-1966 population figures were 48,098,700 for England and Wales and 5,190,000 for Scotland. In each year since 1960, births have exceeded deaths by more than a quarter of a million, but there has been a slow decline in the birth-rate since 1964. The provisional figure for the birth-rate in England and Wales in 1966 was 17.7 and for Scotland 18.6. The 1968 rate (16.9) for England and Wales was the lowest since 1959. The crude death-rate for 1966 was 11.7 and for Scotland 12.3.

Improvements in sanitation, medical care and diagnosis have greatly decreased the death-rate since the mid-nineteenth century, and the reduction in infant mortality is among the most striking changes. In England and Wales in 1966, this figure was 18.9 per thousand, the lowest ever recorded, and 23 in Scotland. In 1956 the figures had been 23.7 in England and Wales and 29 in Scotland. In 1939, in England and Wales, 50 deaths per thousand had been recorded but at the end of the nineteenth century, 150. Our infant mortality-rates for 1966 are comparable with those of Australia and Denmark; Sweden and the Netherlands have lower rates of 13 and 14 per thousand. In the mid-nineteenth century, infectious diseases accounted for one death in three; they now account for one in fifteen. Scarlet fever, typhus and tuberculosis (except lung tuberculosis) have markedly declined as environmental conditions and food supplies have improved. Diseases of the circulatory system, and especially heart diseases, now account for more than a third of deaths, and cancer for 15 per cent of them. Improved diagnosis and increased longevity (cancer mainly affects older age-groups) help to explain this high proportion. In 1966 deaths from heart diseases and cancer reached their highest recorded totals. The proportion of people aged over sixty-five in the total population is about five times that for the end of the nineteenth century. Deaths from respiratory diseases, like bronchitis and pneumonia, though proportionately less common than they were in the mid-nineteenth century, still account for 9 per cent of all deaths.

In 1951-61 a total of 1,962,000 was added to the population by natural increase and 352,000 by immigration. The decennial rates of increase were 5.4 in England, 1.6 in Wales and 2.4 in Scotland. Regional rates of increase varied. In the East and West Riding and in north-west England the rates were well below the national average and there was a continuation, much reduced in numbers, of the drift from these areas, and from Wales, to south-east England and the Midlands. In 1962-6, the drift to the south-east appeared to have stopped. Greater London's growth-rate declined in 1951-61, but many of the English counties which showed the greatest increase were within commuting distance of London. Other conurbations and their rural neighbourhoods showed the same pattern.

It has been obvious for some years that the people of Britain will be far more numerous in 1970 than was predicted in pre-war and early post-war surveys. It has been suggested that by 1981 the population could be 61.5 millions and 65 millions by the year 2,001, but economic and other factors could restrict this predicted large growth. What is certain is that more intensive land use, both in urban and food-producing areas, will be necessary to house and feed this increasing population. In 1961 the population density in Britain was 306 per sq. km. and our annual rate of increase in 1958-61 was 0.7 per cent. In Europe only the Netherlands, with 346 per sq. km., and a 1.3 per cent increase, exceeded these figures. The corresponding figures for Belgium were 301 and 0.5 per cent, for the Federal Republic of Germany 217 and 1.2, for Italy 164 and 0.7 and for France 83 and 1.0.

Since 1801 there have been marked changes both in the proportions of rural and urban populations and in the regional growth of the population. In 1801 three-quarters of our ten-and-a-half million people still lived in the countryside and a third still farmed the land. Country villages as well as towns had grown in the eighteenth century, but migration from rural areas had already started. By 1851 half the population of rather more than 20 millions lived in urban surroundings and in the rapidly growing industrial towns many were so overcrowded that the reduction in death-rates was temporarily slowed down. Migration to these towns had been mainly from the rural uplands of Britain, many of which have suffered a continuous decline of population since 1821. Craftsmen from lowland villages were also attracted into industrial centres in the first half of the nineteenth century, but it was not until its second half that the population of the rural lowlands declined. Between 1871 and 1881 about 100,000 farm labourers left the land and arable fields were increasingly laid down to grass. Agricultural depression, amalgamation of farms and the decline of craft industries all contributed to a peak in migration and emigration from rural areas from about 1870 to 1890, which continued well into the twentieth century, slowing down with the reduction in the birth-rate. By 1961 the British population was only 19.2 per cent rural and this figure includes as rural many commuters who work in the towns. Only 4 per cent of the population is now employed in agriculture, a proportion which is the lowest in Europe though here, too, desertion of rural areas is a common twentieth-century phenomenon. This 4 per cent of our population is responsible for 5 per cent of our gross national product. In France, 26 per cent of the working population are employed in agriculture and produce 13 per cent of the national product; in U.S.A. the figures are 10 and 7 per cent respectively.

Areas of difficulty in Highland Britain now have very sparse populations. They include the Scottish Highlands and mountainous islands, the Southern Uplands, the north Pennines, the heart of the North York Moors, the mountain spine of Wales from Snowdonia to the Brecon Beacons, Exmoor and north-west Devon. These areas have large empty tracts of country, thinly scattered ageing populations, and are bordered by many smaller areas with declining populations. Only well-planned multiple use of land, providing employment in farming, forestry, water storage and tourism, will maintain a population in our remote and beautiful uplands in future years. The rapidly growing urban population will be increasingly mobile. As many families will have two cars by the end of the century, and a smaller proportion will have both town and country dwellings, and all may have more leisure time, the need for a high standard of land use in rural areas, and for improvement of neglected services in depopulated areas, becomes urgent. We have taken for granted that rural depopulation is a feature of most mature industrial societies but only a small part of the urban population has returned, as yet, to the deserted hills in its leisure time. The greater part of the population still prefers to take its holidays in urban settings along our coast.

Population estimates for 1966 include figures of 7,913,600 for Greater London, 2,573,551 for Rome and 485,313 for Oslo. In 1961, 38.7 per cent of the population of England and Wales lived in six conurbations and 42.1 per cent in other urban centres. Eighty per cent of the people of Scotland live in the seventh conurbation, in the narrow industrial belt between and around the Forth and Clyde estuaries. Five of these conurbations are centred on coalfields and two on great estuaries. In all of them growth is most rapid on their outer fringes. The regional details for 1966 are as follows:

Population Estimates: England and Wales: 30th June, 1966, in thousands:

	Male	Female
North	1,630.9	1,685.9
Tyneside Conurbation	411.2	436.9
Remainder: North	1,219.7	1,249.0
Yorkshire and Humberside	2,300.3	2,431.8
West Yorkshire Conurbation	826.8	901.0
Remainder: Yorks and Humberside	1,473.5	1,530.8
North-West	3,232.6	3,499.3
South-East Lancs Conurbation	1,177.8	1,275.6
Merseyside Conurbation	656.0	717.2
Remainder: North-West	1,398.8	1,506.5
East Midlands	1,633.0	1,665.5
West Midlands	2,492.8	2,528.6
West Midlands Conurbation	1,205.0	1,232.1
Remainder: West Midlands	1,287.8	1,296.5
East Anglia	789.8	792.7
South-East	8,226.1	8,845.8
G.L.C. Area	3,778.9	4,134.7
Outer Metropolitan Area	2,452.8	2,556.5
Remainder: South-East	1,994.4	2,154.6
South-West	1,763.9	1,855.1
Wales	1,323.0	1,378.2
Wales I (South-East)	952.8	982.5
Wales II (Remainder)	370.2	395.7
England and Wales	23,392.4	24,682.9

This table indicates the concentration of the urban population in Greater London and the South-East, the Midlands, on both sides of the southern Pennines and on Merseyside. Beyond this axial belt Tyneside and Tees-side and south-east Wales are densely peopled. In all these areas population density averages over 1,200 to the square mile: the overall average for England and Wales is 790. The Edinburgh and Glasgow areas also have over 1,200 to the square mile. Coastal areas with discontinuous patches with the same high density, which could soon coalesce, include Humberside, the Lancashire coast, the coast of north-east Wales, much of the coasts of Kent and Sussex and the Hampshire coast. Industrial growth based on oil, electricity and gas, movement of retired folk to the coast, and increased provision of holiday facilities have all contributed to this growth of densely peopled coastal belts and will continue to do so. In south-east England as a whole in 1951-61, the population increased at five times the rate of northern Britain. South-east Wales is also likely to experience more rapid increases of population than the remainder of Wales. Rapidly developing industrial areas will increase their populations and their expansion is being carefully planned. One of them is the East Midlands Industrial area, between Derby, Nottingham, Mansfield and Chesterfield, where a 24 per cent increase of population is predicted in 1964-81. Surveys have shown that, in 1966, the East Midlands had the same area and population as had the Black Country in 1900. By 2,000 it could have a population total comparable to that of the Black Country in 1966.

The 1966 estimates show a marked preponderance of females. In 1951-61 the decennial increase of males was 5.5 and of females 4.2. In 1966 in Britain there were 106 male to 100 female births and male births predominated throughout the decade 1951-61 (foetal mortality had previously operated selectively against males) but women live longer, on the average, than men and their preponderance is very marked in the older age groups. London, with an excess of women workers, and the south coast with large numbers of retired widows, are among the areas with a large total of females. In many rural areas men predominate because the women have left to work in the towns. This is particularly true of thinly peopled uplands.

Overcrowding in the conurbations, often in obsolete dwellings, led to the New Towns Act of 1946 and to the Town Development Act of 1952. Some inter-war housing estates had acted as overspill areas, though they were less carefully planned than the post-war new towns.

In 1921-31, Dagenham, thirteen miles from the centre of London, completed the greater part of its growth, from 9,000 to 90,000. Under the 1946 Act, new towns were planned to provide well-designed dwellings, roads, work and leisure facilities. They were to be self-contained units spaced far enough from the larger cities so as not to become dormitories for them. In practice their populations do largely work locally and on the whole their industries have been sufficiently diversified to have survived trade fluctuations. The new towns, like post-war university buildings, have attracted the skills of some of our best post-war architects, and some fine layouts and housing schemes can be found in them.

London's overspill population has gone to the ring of new towns which includes Hatfield, Harlow, Hemel Hempstead, Welwyn, Stevenage, Bracknell, Crawley, Basildon and Luton. It is now intended to build an outer ring beyond these: one of its new towns will be in and around Milton Keynes in Buckinghamshire. New towns built or planned in the Midlands include Corby, on the Northamptonshire ironfield, and Telford in Shropshire; between the two Lancashire conurbations, Skelmersdale is partly built and Runcorn is planned. In north-east England, Newton Aycliffe, Peterlee and Washington will be completed, and in Scotland, Cumbernauld, East Kilbride, Livingston and Glenrothes. The Welsh new town is Cwmbran which has been largely filled by people who have moved eastwards from the mining valleys of Monmouthshire. By 1961, the first twelve new towns of England and Wales had absorbed a year's growth of its population, viz. about 300,000. The new towns are intended to take totals varying from 25,000 to 80,000. In 1961, Basildon, Crawley, Harlow and Hemel Hempstead exceeded 50,000 and Corby, Cwmbran, Stevenage and Welwyn had over 30,000 inhabitants. Around London and other conurbations, under the Town Development Act, large additions to existing towns have been or will be built to receive overspill populations. King's Lynn, Ipswich and Swindon are among southern examples. Many schemes exist for the enlargement of small towns in the most densely peopled belt of England which extends from the south-east, through the Midlands to Lancashire.

The migrations of the twenties and thirties, from Scotland, northern England and South Wales, to the Midlands and southern industrial areas, are now much reduced. Added to First World War casualties, these losses of young families removed a valuable section from the older industrial communities. A quarter of a million people moved from

Breconshire, Glamorgan and Monmouthshire in 1921-31 and in the same decade the net migration from Scotland was 391,903. Rural Scotland had by then known a century of migration and emigration, but many Scots in 1921-31 left declining industrial areas.

A decreasing flow of emigrants to Commonwealth countries, and to the U.S.A., continued both before and after the Second World War. In 1966, 165,700 Britons emigrated to Canada, Australia and New Zealand. Immigration, however, has been a more outstanding feature since 1931 and between this year and 1961 over a million immigrants entered Britain and the flow has continued since 1962, though at a reduced rate. In 1931-9, large numbers of Irish immigrants and a smaller total of refugees came into Britain. The total entering in 1939-51 was about three-quarters of a million. There are now estimated to be about two million non-native inhabitants of Britain, including over 700,000 born in Eire, 500,000 West Indians, 300,000-350,000 Australians, New Zealanders, Canadians and South Africans (many of whom will return home), 250,000 Asiatics, and 400,000 Polish-born, Italian-born and German-born, many of whom are now British subjects.

The rapid increase in immigration from the Commonwealth in the late 1950s placed heavy burdens on the housing, social and education services of the conurbations in which the immigrants mainly settled and made necessary the Commonwealth Immigrants Act of 1962. This so reduced the net gain from immigration, which had been 225,000 between mid-1961 and mid-1962, that the net inward movement in 1962-5 averaged only 48,000 a year. In 1966 the figure was 35,000. Women and children can still enter to join their menfolk, and thus escape the restrictions on the immigrant inflow, but the 1962-5 rate is expected to be halved in the 1970s. The 1962 Act resulted from the rapid inflow of non-white Commonwealth immigrants. They became concentrated in densely peopled urban areas and in them manned understaffed transport, catering and health services. They also took over heavy work in factories, building, or extractive industries which had often previously been undertaken by Irish labourers.

Britons have been critical of immigrants, from whose services they have often benefited, in past centuries. In 1601, Elizabeth I arranged for the deportation of a group which was consuming her people's food. She was "discontented at the great number of Negroes and blackamoors who had crept in since the troubles between Her Majesty and the King of Spain." During her reign, in 1572, the first group of Huguenots came in from northern France after the St. Bartholomew's Day massacre. They were joined by many more in the seventeenth century and established valuable craft industries in south-east England, of which the Spitalfields silk industry is best known. The Huguenot name of Courtauld is one which is still in the forefront of the textile industry.

In 1656 Cromwell allowed the Jews to immigrate into England again; many had been expelled by Edward I. Their first synagogue was opened in Bevis Marks in 1701 and, in the eighteenth and nineteenth centuries, the descendants of these Jews, mainly Sephardim families from the Iberian peninsula, played an important part in financial and political life, as they still do. The flow of Ashkenazim Jews from Eastern Europe started in the eighteenth century and was augmented after the pogroms which followed the assassination of Czar Alexander II in 1881. By 1914 there were 300,000 Jews in Britain. In 1964, owing to natural increase and Nazi persecution, the total was 450,000. This is less than 1 per cent of our population and it is indicative of Jewish learning and respect for learning that 5 per cent of the Fellows of the Royal Society are Jewish.

When the potato famine started in Ireland in 1846, about 400,000 Irish already lived in Britain. These Irishmen worked on the land and as navvies, the canal "navigators" having by 1846 moved into a variety of building work. Many lived in Scotland: exchanges of population between western Scotland and northern Ireland had gone on for centuries. Over half a million Irish landed at ports on the east side of the Irish Sea in the famine years. Many settled in Britain; in 1881 one in eight of the population of Liverpool was Irish-born. Many more joined the thousands who went from Ireland to U.S.A. until the First World War. From 1900 until 1929, when the United States lowered its quota further, to an annual total of 18,000 Irish, the Irish emigrated increasingly to Commonwealth countries. Since 1930 over 80 per cent of the Irish emigrants have come to Britain and they form our largest minority group. Between 1946 and 1962, 422,000 came into Britain. Many of our large post-war building projects could not have been completed without their labour and Irish girls have helped to man the health services.

About 15,000 Negro slaves were employed in Britain in the eighteenth century. They have been absorbed into our population. In the nineteenth century, West African sailors made their homes in British docklands and married British women. Cardiff's dockland, which also had and has a Muslim minority of seamen, became the notorious "Tiger Bay." Clearance schemes have radically altered it and have partly dispersed its population throughout suburban Cardiff where many quadroon and octoroon citizens stem from this former dockland population. Cardiff's dockland is no longer notorious: troubles resulting mainly from competition for housing, with resulting overcrowding, were at the root of Tiger Bay's disturbances. There is no colour problem in the city to-day.

It is to be hoped that similar improvements in housing and social services, in spite of a difficult economic situation, will reduce friction between other British and Negro and Asiatic groups. The rapidity and size of the influx of West Indian families in 1951-62, and of Indians and Pakistanis in 1955-65, makes the problem a serious one, and though many Pakistanis, in particular, intend to return home, the children of all groups may well remain here. Since the war we have also gained students of many nationalities, and 33,000 Cypriots, 130,000 Poles and 24,000 Maltese. The million immigrants of the period 1946-62 have tackled some of our hardest jobs. Italians work in the Bedfordshire brickfields, Poles have reclaimed marginal land in Mid-Wales and have reared trilingual children there, West Indians man London's underground services, Indians and Pakistanis provide much of the labour in the factories of Southall and many immigrant girls and young doctors make it possible to run our hospitals. Integration is a very complex process, but it will not be integration with pure Anglo-Saxons. For many centuries Britain has absorbed waves of incomers. The Anglo-Saxons arrived rather late in our story and the other peoples who had occupied Britain for the four thousand previous years have left strong imprints on our population. Rising unemployment could bring friction during integration, but it should not be forgotten that when labour was lacking for difficult jobs it was the immigrant population which accepted the unskilled work. We should all remember too, the work of the teachers who have educated large groups of immigrant children, and the social workers who have worked among their parents, in both cases often under very trying conditions.

EPILOGUE

HAVING NOW come to the thin and ever-moving curtain, always impenetrable, that separates the past from the future and is called the present, it behoves us to have a care about suggestions of prognostication. In 1850 no one would have foreseen the changes in social life and equipment that were to follow the advent of transmissible electric power and the invention of the internal combustion engine, the crises of thought that would follow the penetration of the idea of evolution into the problems of society, the new methods of spreading information that radio and television would bring, the claims of the workers to well-being that were to follow the spread of education for all. The quickening of the pace of change, over all the world, is perhaps the most salient fact of our time; we "plan" and want to see results ourselves. Rarely do we realise that this haste, however inevitable we may have made it, is a new and dangerous portent in the realm of the natural history of man.

Some of the difficulty is due to the old-time acceptance of the idea of creation of the universe by *Fiat* in six days about 6,000 years ago. That idea of creation is dead, but a subconscious residue remains and leads men, unwittingly, to think of change on a great scale in short periods. If the universe were 6,000 years old, the last 2,000 years would represent one third of its duration. The geologists have estimated the age of the earth, as a body with a solid crust, at far more than 1,000,000,000 years. Human time has become some 600,000 years. This makes the period since men emerged from mere collecting and hunting into the more organised life of food production little more than the last one per cent of the human age. During the previous 99 per cent of men's life on earth they lived in small in-bred groups often much isolated from other groups. And life of small groups went on, for a great part of our British population, until barely two centuries ago, when agglomeration metamorphosed so many members of small social groups into isolated units in a crowd.

It has become clear that men drifted into Britain from the south in the long intervals between the ice-phases of the Pleistocene Period, and, so far as stone implements allow us to judge, made only quite moderate advances over a period of 250,000 years. Later on, hunters with means of action at a distance show an appreciable amount of evolution of their tools in, perhaps, 25,000 years. After the ice finally retreated a gradual amelioration of climate and of Mesolithic material culture occurred over a period of about 5,000 years.

Then comes the great change, introduced into Britain by immigrants from the Mediterranean and continental Europe, from precarious subsistence by hunting and collecting to organised food-production by herding and cultivation. Ritual, trade and crafts developed, partly under the leadership of successive groups of immigrant families and partly through intermarriage with the Mesolithic population. A strong indigenous element is represented in Neolithic B cultures, and in the pottery made by its womenfolk. Intermingling of populations in Neolithic and Early Bronze Age times was probably analogous with that described in the beginning of the sixth chapter of the book of Genesis. The surviving megalithic and henge monuments suggest that there must have been a considerable labour force. They imply, as do later Iron Age forts, increases and agglomerations of population made possible by more plentiful food supplies resulting from an extension of cultivation and a multiplication of herds.

Through coastal landing places, new waves of immigrants came in from time to time, bringing in new ideas which spread inland through trade. From the south and east coasts of Britain, cultures spread to and sometimes beyond the Jurassic scarp. Seaborne diffusion was characteristic of Atlantic Britain; its rugged coasts had limited pockets of lowland which often became relatively well peopled. New ideas infiltrated slowly into Highland Britain, and down to our own century its moorlands and mountains have preserved in their isolation, cultures based on small inter-related groups in which kinship is of great significance.

Towards medieval times the fact of relationship-grouping seems to have given place on the lowlands to proximity-grouping. A little mobility of population had become possible and agglomeration had certainly increased, so that relationships between individuals became hard to trace. The humbler folk still mainly chose wives from within a radius of a few miles; the wealthier people often married farther afield.

Tradition in a hierarchical society obtained until the eve of modern times. Then diversities of belief and ritual engendered new ways of thought, commerce brought wider contacts and refugees from religious persecution gave Britain an intellectual and spiritual élite and a fount of initiative.

So we find a growing population seeking to maintain its sociality of small groups by gathering around chapels, small collections of like-minded people on a voluntary basis and full of initiative in various directions. They prepared the way not only for the Industrial Revolution but also for increasing freedom of conscience.

Conversion of arable land to pasture, and the spread of root-crops, led to the enclosure of the common fields. These enclosures were often amicably arranged and resulted in greater productivity. But enclosing and engrossing were sometimes carried through with heartless disregard of the welfare of humbler folk. Goldsmith's *Deserted Village* remains a classic on this subject. The agrarian and industrial revolutions meta-morphosed humble families into a sort of social flotsam and jetsam, and changed man from his former status as a member of a small group into an often lonely unit in a crowd. A great deal in his mental make-up that had been accumulating and consolidating during hundreds of thousands of years of small-group-membership was left to atrophy, and an attempt was made to start what was almost a new mentality. We cannot wonder, therefore, that there have been conspicuous maladjustments and that the old deep-rooted tendencies have shown their vigour once more in the efforts to create the Welfare State.

Our thinkers are face to face with a triple problem. Production and distribution of many goods and services have to be thought out on a world basis. Social life has to be reshaped on the basis of groups that are not too large. Personality and initiative have to be cherished as the fountain of originality and the only means of keeping social life and thought from mechanised direction by authoritarian doctrine.

BIBLIOGRAPHY

ABRAHAMS, H. M. (Ed.) (1959), *Britain's National Parks*
ALCOCK, L. (1968), Excavations at South Cadbury, *Ant. J.*, 48, 6-17
ALLEN, D. (1967), Iron Currency Bars in England, *Proc. Prehist. Soc.*, 33, 307-35
ARBMAN, H. (1961), *The Vikings*
ARMSTRONG, A. L. (1939), Palæolithic Man in the North Midlands, *Mem. Manchr. Lit. Phil. Soc.*, 83, 87-116
ARMSTRONG, A. L. (1940), Note on Mother goddess, *Antiq. J.*, 20, 541
ARTHUR, D. R. (1969), *Survival, man and his environment*
ARVILL, R. (1969), *Man and Environment*
ASHBEE, P. (1960), *The Bronze Age Barrow in Britain*
ASHBEE, P. (1966), Fussell's Lodge Long Barrow, *Archæologia*, 2nd series, 50
ATKINSON, R. J. C. (1951), *Excavations at Dorchester, Oxon*
ATKINSON, R. J. C. (1959), *Stonehenge and Avebury*
ATKINSON, T. D. (1947), *Local Styles in English Architecture*

BARLEY, M. W. (1961), *The English Farmhouse and Cottage*
BARLEY, M. W. (1963), *The House and Home*
BARR, J. (1969), *Derelict Britain*
BATSFORD, H. and FRY, C. (1938), *The English Cottage*
BATSFORD, H. and FRY, C. (1944), *The Greater English Church*
BEAUJEU-GARNIER, J. (1966), *Geography of Population*
BEDDOE, J. (1885), *The Races of Britain*
BEDDOE, J. and ROWE, J. H. (1907), Ethnology of West Yorkshire, *Yorks Arch., J.*, 19, 31-60
BELLOC, H. (1935), *The Old Road*
BENNETT, H. S. (1937), *Life on the English Manor, 1150-1400*
BERESFORD, M. W. (1954), *The Lost Villages of England*
BEST, R. H. and COPPOCK, J. T. (1962), *The Changing Use of Land in Britain*
BETJEMAN, J. (Ed.) (1968), *Collins Guide to English Parish Churches*
BLOCH, M. (1931), *Les Caractères originaux de l'Histoire rurale française*, Vol. I
BLOCH, M. (1956) (Ed.), Dauvergne, R., Vol. II
BOAS, F. (1940), *Race, Language and Culture*
BOLTON, J. (1922), *Architecture of Robert and James Adam*
BORROW, G. (1901), *Wild Wales, its people, language and scenery*

BOSWELL, J. (1785), *The Journal of a Tour to the Hebrides with Samuel Johnson, LL.D.*

BOWEN, E. G. (1954), *The Settlements of the Celtic Saints in Wales*

BOWEN, E. G. (Ed.) (1957), *Wales*

BRACEY, H. E. (Ed.) (1963), *Industry and the Countryside*

BRADBROOKE, W. and PARSONS, F. G. (1922), Anthropology, Chilterns, *J. Roy. Anthrop. Inst.*, 52, 113-26

BRAUN, H. (1951), *An Introduction to English Medieval Architecture*

BREUIL, H. (1939), Pleistocene succession, Somme valley, *Proc. Prehis. Soc.*, 5, 33-38

British Museum Handbooks, Man the Tool Maker, The Neolithic Revolution, and on the Bronze and Iron Ages, Roman Period and Anlgo-Saxon antiquities

BRØGGER, A. E. (1929), *Ancient Immigrants*

BRØNDSTED, J. (1960), *The Vikings*

BRUCE-MITFORD, R. L. S. (1926), *Recent Excavations in Britain* (Mawgan Porth, Jarlshof, Abinger motte and London)

BUCHANAN, C. D. (1964), *Traffic in Towns*

BULLEID, A. and GRAY, H. ST. GEORGE (1911-1917) *Glastonbury*, 2 vols.

BULLEID, A. and GRAY, H. ST. GEORGE (1953-1954), *The Meare Lake Village*, 2 vols.

CARR-SAUNDERS, SIR A. M. (1936), *World Population*

CARR-SAUNDERS, SIR A. M. (1949) (as chairman), *Royal Commission on Population*

CARTER, H. (1965), *The Towns of Wales*

CARUS-WILSON, E. M. (1967), *Medieval Merchant Venturers*

CERAM, C. W. (1966), *The World of Archæology*

CHADWICK, H. M. (1907), *Origin of the English Nation*

CHADWICK, N. K. (1963), *Celtic Britain*

CHAMBERS, J. D. and MINGAY, G. E. (1966), *The Agricultural Revolution, 1750-1880*

CHARLES, B. G. (1934), *Old Norse Relations with Wales*

CHARLESWORTH, M. P. (1949), *The Lost Province or the Worth of Britain*

CHILDE, V. G. (1931), *Skara Brae*

CHILDE, V. G. (1935), *The Prehistory of Scotland*

CHILDE, V. G. (1947), *Prehistoric Communities of the British Isles*

CHILDE, V. G. (1958), *The Prehistory of European Society*

CHRISTIAN, G. (1966), *Tomorrow's Countryside*

CLAPHAM, SIR J. H. (1949), *A Concise Economic History of Britain from the Earliest Times to 1750*

CLARK, J. G. D. (1936), *The Mesolithic Settlement of Northern Europe*

CLARK, J. G. D. (1940), *Prehistoric England*

CLARK, J. G. D. (1952), *Prehistoric Europe. The Economic Basis*

CLARK, J. G. D. (1954), *Excavations at Star Carr*

CLARK, J. G. D. (1957), *Archæology and Society*
CLARK, SIR KENNETH (1969), *Civilisation*
CLARKE, R. R. (1960), *East Anglia*
COLLIE, G. F. (1948), *Highland Dress*
COLLINGWOOD, R. G. (1930), *Archæology of Roman Britain*
COLLINGWOOD, R. G. and MYRES, J. N. L. (1936), *Roman Britain and the English Settlements*
CONDRY, W. M. (1966), *The Snowdonia National Park*
CONWAY, M. (later Lord Conway) (1901), *The Domain of Art*
CONZEN, M. R. G. (1949), Scientific Survey of North-East England, *Brit. Assoc. Adv. Sci.*, 75-83
COOK, O. (1968), *The English House through Seven Centuries*
COON, C. S. (1939), *The Races of Europe*
COPLEY, G. G. (1958), *The Archæology of South-East England*
COULTON, G. G. (1925), *The Medieval Village*
CRAWFORD, O. G. S. (1928), Air Survey and Archæology, *Ordnance Survey Professional Papers, No. 7*
CRAWFORD, O. G. S. (1940), Report on Sutton Hoo, *Antiquity*, 14, 64-68
CRAWFORD, O. G. S. and KEILLER, A. (1928), *Wessex from the Air*
CROSSLEY, F. H. (1945), *English Church Design, 1040-1540*
CROWE, S. (1926), *Tomorrow's Landscape*
CRUDEN, S. (1960), *The Scottish Castle*
CULLINGWORTH, J. B. (1967), *Town and Country Planning in England and Wales*
CUNNINGTON, M. E. (1923), *The Early Iron Age Inhabited Site at All Cannings Cross*
CURLE, A. O. (1932-35), Jarlshof, Shetland, *Proc. Soc. Antiq. Scotland*, 67, 82-136; 68, 224-319; 69, 85-107; 70, 237-70
CURWEN, E. C. (1946), *Plough and Pasture*

DANIEL, G. E. (1963), *The Megalith Builders of Western Europe*
DARBY, H. C. (Ed.) (1936), *Historical Geography of England and Wales before 1800*
DARBY, H. C. (1940), *The Draining of the Fens*
DARBY, H. C. (Ed.) (1952-67), *The Domesday Geography of England*
DARLING, F. F. (1945), *Crofting Agriculture*
DARLING, F. F. (1947), *Natural History in the Highlands and Islands*
DARLING, F. F. (1955), *West Highland Survey*
DARLING, F. F. and BOYD, J. M. (1969), *The Highlands and Islands*
DARLINGTON, C. D. (1947), The Genetic Component of Language, *Heredity*, I, 269-86
DAVIES, E. and REES, A. D. (Ed.) (1960), *Welsh Rural Communities*
DAVIES, E. and FLEURE, H. J. (1936), Anthropometric Survey, Isle of Man, *J. Roy. Anthrop. Inst.*, 66, 129-88

DAVIES, M. (1945-46), Megalithic Monuments, Irish Sea Coastlands, *Antiq. J.*, 25, 125-44; 26, 38-60

DAVISON, B. K. (1967), Origins of English castles, *Arch. J.*, 124, 202-11

DEFOE, D. (1959), *A Tour through England and Wales* (Everyman edition)

DENMAN, D. R., ROBERTS, R. A., and SMITH, H. (1967), *Commons and Village Greens*

DICKINSON, R. E. (1947), *City, Region and Regionalism*

DIMBLEBY, G. (1967), *Plants and Archæology*

DUCKETT, E. S. (1967), *Anglo-Saxon Saints and Scholars*

DUTTON, R. (1945), *The English Garden*

EDWARDS, K. C., SWINNERTON, H. H. and Hall, R. H. (1962), *The Peak District*

EKWALL, E. (1947), *Concise Oxford Dictionary of English Place-names* English Place Names Society. Series of County Volumes

ELLIS, E. A. (1965), *The Broads*

ELLIS, H. (1904), *A Study of British Genius*

EMERY, F. V. (1969), *The World's Landscapes, 2, Wales*

EVANS, E. E. (1942), *Irish Heritage*

EVANS, E. E. (1957), *Irish Folk Ways*

EVANS, E. E. (1966), *Prehistoric and Early Christian Ireland*

FEACHAM, R. (1963), *A Guide to Prehistoric Scotland*

FEACHAM, R. (1965), *The North Britons. The Prehistory of a Border People*

FLEURE, H. J. (1920), Early Neanthropic Types, *J. Roy. Anthrop. Inst.*, 50, 12-40

FLEURE, H. J. (1947), *Aspects of British Civilisation*, Sir James Frazer Memorial Lecture

FLEURE, H. J. and NEELY, G. H. J. (1936), Cashtal yn Ard, Isle of Man, *Antiq J.*, 16, 373-95

FLEURE, H. J. and DUNLOP, M. (1942), Glendarragh house site, Isle of Man, *Antiq. J.*, 22, 39-53

FLEURE, H. J. and DAVIES, E. (1958), Physical Character among Welshmen, *J. Roy. Anthrop. Inst.*, 88, 45-95

FLEURE, H. J. and DAVIES, E. (1937), The Manx People and their Origins, *J. Manx Museum*, 3, 172-7 and 187-9

FLEURE, H. J. and JAMES, T. C. (1916), Geographical Distribution of Anthropological Types in Wales, *J. Roy. Anthrop. Inst.*, 46, 35-153

FLEURE, H. J. and ROBERTS, E. S. (1915), Archæological Problems of the west coast of Britain, *Arch. Camb.*, 70, 405-20

FLEURE, H. J. and WHITEHOUSE, W. E. (1916), Early Distribution and valleyward movement of population, *Arch. Camb.*, 71, 101-40

FOSTER, I. Ll. and DANIEL, G. D. (Ed.) (1965), *Prehistoric and Early Wales*

FOSTER, I.LL. and ALCOCK, L. (Ed.) (1963), *Culture and Environment*
FOWLER, P. J. (1967), *Wessex*
FOX, A. (1964), *South West England*
FOX, SIR CYRIL (1923), *Archæology of the Cambridge Region*
FOX, SIR CYRIL (1940), The Boundary Line of Cymru, *Proc. Brit. Acad.*, 26, 3-28
FOX, SIR CYRIL (1946), *A Find of the Early Iron Age from Llyn Cerrig Bach, Anglesey*
FOX, SIR CYRIL (1947), *The Personality of Britain*
FOX, SIR CYRIL and LORD RAGLAN (1951-4), *Monmouthshire House*
FOX, SIR CYRIL (1958), *Pattern and Purpose. A Survey of Early Celtic Art in Britain*
FRERE, S. (1967), *Britannia*
FULLARD, H. (1938), Anthropometric Survey, Rochdale District, *Trans. Rochdale Lit. Sci. Soc.*, 20, 29-55
FUSSELL, G. E. (1949), *The English Rural Labourer*

GARDNER, W. (1926), Native Forts in North Wales, *Arch. Camb.* 7, 221-82
GARROD, D. A. E. (1938), The Upper Palæolithic in the light of recent discovery, *Proc. Prehist. Soc.*, 4, 1-26
GEDDES, SIR PATRICK (1915), *Cities in Evolution*
DE GEER, G. (1940), Geochronologica Suedica, *K. Svenska Vetensk Akad. Handl.*, 18, 1-360
GEIKIE, A. (1887), *The Scenery of Scotland*
Geological Survey, Regional Monographs
GERALD OF WALES (1908), *The Itinerary through Wales and the Description of Wales*, (Everyman edition)
GLASS, D. V. (1940), *Population Policies and Movements*
GODWIN, H. (1956), *The History of the British Flora*
GOMME, SIR G. L. (1914), *London*
GRAHAM, H. G. (1950), *Social Life in Scotland in the Eighteenth Century*
GRANT, I. F. (1934), *The Economic History of Scotland*
GRAY, H. L. (1915), *English Field Systems*
GRAY, M. (1957), *The Highland Economy, 1750-1850*
GRIMES, W. F. (1968), *The Excavation of Roman and Medieval London*
GRIMES, W. F. and SAVORY, H. N. (1951), *The Prehistory of Wales*
GRINSELL, L. V. (1953), *The Ancient Burial Mounds of England*
GRUNDY, G. B. (1934-8), Papers on old roads in *Archæol. J.*, 91, 92, 94-5

HADFIELD, C. (1959), *British Canals*
HALDANE, A. R. B. (1953), *The Drove Roads of Scotland*
HAMILTON, H. (1932), *The Industrial Revolution in Scotland*
HAMMOND, J. L. and B. (1919), *The Skilled Labourer*
HAMMOND, J. L. and B. (1925), *The Town Labourer*

HAMMOND, J. L. and B. (1930), *The Age of the Chartists*
HAMMOND, J. L. and B. (1934), *The Bleak Age* (Penguin Book, 1947)
HAMMOND, J. L. and B. (1937), *The Rise of Modern Industry*
HAMMOND, J. L. and B. (1948), *The Village Labourer*
HARDEN, D. B. (Ed.) (1956), *Studies in Dark Age Britain*
HARTLEY, M. and INGILBY, J. (1968), *Life and Tradition in the Yorkshire Dales*
HARVEY, J. (1947), *Gothic England*
HARVEY, L. A. and ST. LEGER GORDON, D. (1953), *Dartmoor*
HAVERFIELD, F. J. (1923), *The Romanisation of Roman Britain*
HAVERFIELD, F. J. (1924), *The Roman Occupation of Britain*
HAWKES, C. F. C. (1940), *The Prehistoric Foundations of Europe to the Mycenean Age*
HAWKES, C. F. C. and J. (1958), *Prehistoric Britain*
HENCKEN, H. O'N. (1932), County Archæologies, *Cornwall and Scilly*
HENDERSON, I. (1967), *The Picts*
HIGGS, J. W. Y. (1965), *English Rural Life in the Middle Ages*
HIGGS, J. W. Y. (Ed.) (1966), *People in the Countryside*
HILTON, K. J. (Ed.) (1967), *The Lower Swansea Valley Project*
HOBSBAWM, E. J. (1968), *Industry and Empire. An Economic History of Britain since 1750*
HORNELL, J. (1938), *British Coracles and Irish Curraghs*
HOSKINS, W. G. (1955), *The Making of the English Lansdcape*
HOSKINS, W. G. (1959), *Devon*
HOULDER, C. (1968) Henge Monuments at Llandegai, *Antiquity*, 42, 216-21
HOULDER, C. and MANNING, W. H. (1966), *South Wales*
HRDLIČKA, A. (1928), Catalogue of Human Crania, U.S. National Museum Collections, *Proc. U.S. Nat. Mus.*, 71, No. 24
HUDSON, K. (1966), *Industrial Archæology*
HUGHES, H. (1907), Excavations at Tre'r Ceiri, *Arch. Camb.*, 7, 38-62
HUSSEY, C. (1955-6), *English Country Houses*, 2 vols.
HUTTON, J. H. (1933), Report, *Census of India*, 1931, Vol. I, 357-69
HUXLEY, E. (1964), *Back Street, New Worlds*
HUXLEY, J. S. and HADDON, A. C. (1935), *We Europeans*

JACKMAN, W. T. (1916), *The Development of Transportation in Modern England*
JACKSON, K. (1953), *Language and History in Early Britain*
JELLIS, R. (Ed.) (1966), *Land and People*
JONES, E. (1945), Settlement Patterns, Teifi valley, *Geography*, 30, 103-11
JONES, F. (1954), *The Holy Wells of Wales*
JONES, G. R. J. (1961), Pattern of settlement in Northern England, *Advancement of Science*
JORDAN, R. F. (1966), *Victorian Architecture*

KEITH, SIR ARTHUR (1948), *A New Theory of Human Evolution*
KELLY, F. M. and SCHWABE, R. (1925), *Historic Costume*
KELLY, F. M. and SCHWABE, R. (1931), *A Short History of Costume and Armour, 1066-1800*, 2 vols.
KENDRICK, T. D. (1930), *A History of the Vikings*
KENDRICK, T. D. (1938), *Anglo-Saxon Art*
KENDRICK, T. D. (1949), *Late Saxon and Viking Art*
KERRIDGE, E. (1967), *The Agricultural Revolution*
KINVIG, R. H. (1944), *History of the Isle of Man*
KIRK, D. (1946), *Europe's Population in the Inter-war Years*, League of Nations Publications, II, A 8
KISSLING, W. (1943), The Hebridean Black House, *J. Roy. Anthrop. Inst.*, 73, 75-100
Kleidung (1926), *Reallexikon der Vorgeschichte*, 6, 380-94
KNOWLES, D. (1949), *The Monastic Order in England*
KNOWLES, D. and HADCOCK, R. N. (1953), *Medieval Religious Houses. England and Wales*
KUCZYNSKI, R. (1942), *The New Population Statistics*

LEEDS, E. T. (1913), *Archæology of the Anglo-Saxon Settlements*
LETHBRIDGE, T. C. (1948), *Merlin's Island*
LEWIS, W. J. (1967), *Lead Mining in Wales*
LOCKYER, SIR N. (1901-05), Notes on Stonehenge, *Nature*, 65, 66, 71, 72, 73

MACKINDER, SIR H. J. (1906), *Britain and the British Seas*
MACLAGEN, E. (1945), *The Bayeux Tapestry*
MANLEY, G. (1952), *Climate and the British Scene*
MARGARY, I. D. (1967), *Roman Roads in Britain*
MARSTON, A. T. (1937), The Swanscombe skull, *J. Roy. Anthrop. Inst.*, 67, 339-406
MATHESON, C. (1932), *Changes in the Fauna of Wales within Historic Times*
MAWER, SIR ALLEN (1924), *Chief Elements in English Place Names*
MEATES, G. W. (1955), *Lullingstone Roman Villa*
MEIKLE, H. W. (Ed.) (1947), *Scotland*
MEITZEN, A. (1895), *Siedelung und Agrarwesen*, 4 vols.
MERRYFIELD, R. (1965), *The Roman City of London*
MILES, R. (1967), *Forestry in the English Landscape*
MITCHELL, J. B. (1962), *Great Britain: Geographical Essays*
MOGEY, J. M. (1947), *The Rural Community in Northern Ireland*
MOORE, I. (1966), *Grass and Grasslands*
MORANT, G. M. (1926), Craniology, England and Wales, *Biometrika*, 18, 56-98
MORANT, G. M. (1930-1), Upper Palæolithic skulls of Europe, *Ann. Eugen*, 4, 109-214

MORANT, G. M. and HOADLEY, F. M. (1931), Crania, Spitalfields, *Biometrika*, 23, 191-248
MUMFORD, L. (1938), *The Culture of Cities*

NASH-WILLIAMS, V. E. (1950), *The Early Christian Monuments of Wales*
NØRLUND, P. (1948), *Trelleborg*
NORTH, F. J., CAMPBELL, B. and SCOTT, R. (1949), *Snowdonia*
NORTH, F. J. (1957), *Sunken Cities*

OAKLEY, K. P. and ASHLEY-MONTAGU, M. F. (1949), A Reconsideration of the Gally Hill skeleton, *Bull. Brit. Mus. Nat. Hist. Geol.* I, No. 2
OLIVER, B. (1929), *The Cottages of England*
O'NEIL, H. (1945), Roman Villa near St. Albans, *Archæol. J.*, 102, 21-110
Ordnance Survey, *Maps of*, Roman Britain, Neolithic Wessex, Trent Basin, South Wales, Britain in the Dark Ages, Monastic Britain.
O'RIORDAIN, S. P. and DANIEL, G. D. (1964), *New Grange*
ORWIN, C. S. and ORWIN, C. S. (1954), *The Open Fields*
OSBORN, F. J. (1969), *Green Belt Cities*
OSBORN, F. J. and WHITTICK, A. (1969), *The New Towns*
OXENHAM, J. R. (1966), *Reclaiming Derelict Land*
OXENSTIERNA, E. G. (1967), *The World of the Norsemen*

PAINTER, K. S. (1964), Regional Archæologies: *The Severn Basin*
PAYNE, F. G. (1947), The Plough in Ancient Britain, *Archæol. J.*, 104, 82-111
PAYNE, F. G. (1964), Welsh Peasant Costume, *Folk Life*, 2, 1-16
PEAKE, H. J. E. (1922), *The English Village*
PEAKE, H. J. E. (1940), The Study of Prehistoric Times, *J. Roy. Anthrop. Inst.*, 70, 103-46
PEAKE, H. J. E. and FLEURE, H. J. (1927-56), *Corridors of Time*, 10 vols.
PEARSALL, W. H. (1950), *Mountains and Moorlands*
PEATE, I. C. (1940), *The Welsh House*
PELHAM, R. A. (1964), The Concept of Wessex, *A Survey of Southampton and its Region*, ed. F. J. Monkhouse, 169-76
PENNANT, T. (1883), *Tours in Wales* (ed. J. Rhys)
PERCIVAL, J. (1921), *The Wheat Plant*
PEVSNER, N. *The Buildings of England*, the Penguin survey by counties
PIGGOTT, H. S. (1939), Timber Circles, *Archæol. J.*, 96, 193-222
PIGGOTT, H. S. (1954), *The Neolithic Cultures of the British Isles*
PIGGOTT, H. S. (1958), *Scotland before History*
PIMLOTT, J. A. R. (1947), *The Englishman's Holiday*
PIRENNE, H. (1925), *Medieval Cities*
POSTAN, M. M. (Ed.) (1966), *The Agrarian Life of the Middle Ages*, Cambridge Economic History of Europe, I

310   BIBLIOGRAPHY

POWELL, T. G. E. (1958), *The Celts*
POWELL, T. G. E. and DANIEL, G. E. (1956), *Barclodiad y Gawres*
POWER, E. (1924), *Medieval People*
PRAEGER, R. LL. (1947), *The Way that I Went*
PRAEGER, R. LL. (1950), *Natural History of Ireland*
PULBROOK, E. C. (1923), *English Country Life and Work*
PULBROOK, E. C. (1925), *The English Countryside*

QUENNELL, M. & C. H. B. (1918-), *A History of Everyday Things in England*

RAISTRICK, A. (1950), *Quakers in Science and Industry*
RASMUSSEN, S. E. (1960), *London, the Unique City*
REES, A. D. (1961), *Life in a Welsh Countryside*
REES, A. D. and REES, B. (1961), *Celtic Heritage*
REID, R. W. and MORANT, G. (1928), A Study of Scottish Short Cist
   Crania, *Biometrika*, 20, 379-88
REPTON, H. (1803), *Observations on the Theory and Practice of Landscape
   Gardening*
RHYS, J. and BRYNMOR-JONES, D. (1900), *The Welsh People*
RICHARDS, M. (1954), *The Laws of Hywel Dda*
RICHARDS, M. (1969), *Welsh Administrative and Territorial Units*
RICHMOND, I. A. (1955), Pelican History of England, I, *Roman Britain*
RIPLEY, W. Z. (1900), *The Races of Europe*
RIVET, A. L. F. (1958), *Town and Country in Roman Britain*
RORIG, F. (1967), *The Medieval Town*
ROSE, E. J. B. (Ed.) (1969), *Colour and Citizenship*
ROSS, A. (1966), *Pagan Celtic Britain*
ROWSE, A. L. (1941), *Tudor Cornwall*
ROWSE, A. L. (1950), *The England of Elizabeth*
Royal Commission on Ancient and Historical Monuments for England, Scotland,
   Wales. County Reports.
Royal Society of Arts and the Nature Conservancy (1966), *The Countryside
   in 1970*
RUSSELL, SIR E. J. (1966), *A History of Agricultural Science in Great Britain*

SALAMAN, R. N. (1949), *History and Social Influence of the Potato*
SANDERS, N. K. (1968), *Prehistoric Art in Europe*
SAVAGE, C. I. (1959), *An Economic History of Transport*
SAVILLE, J. (1957), *Rural Depopulation in England and Wales, 1851-1951*
SCHUBERT, H. R. (1957), *History of the British Iron and Steel Industry, 400
   B.C. to A.D. 1775*
SCOTT, J. G. (1966), Regional Archæologies: *South-West Scotland*
SEEBOHM, M. E. (1952), *The Evolution of the English Farm*
SHARP, T. (1945), *Town Planning*

SHARP, T. (1946), *The Anatomy of the Village*

SHARP, T. (1968), *Town and Townscape*

SIMPSON, W. D. (1939-44), Papers on Castles, *Archæol. J.*, 96, 98, 99 and 101

SKENE, W. F. (1886-90), *Celtic Scotland*, 3 vols.

SMALL, A. (1968), Norse Viking Colonisation of the Scottish Highlands, *Norsk. geog. tidsskr.*, 22, 1-6

SMITH, A. H. (1956), *English Place Names*, 2 vols.

SMITH, I. (1965), *Windmill Hill and Avebury*

SMOUT, T. C. (1969), *A History of the Scottish People*

SOLLAS, W. J. (1913), Paviland Cave, *J. Roy. Anthrop. Inst.*, 43, 325-74

STAMP, SIR L. D. (1962), *The Land of Britain*

STAMP, SIR L. D. (1967), *Britain's Structure and Scenery*

STAMP, SIR L. D. (1969), *Man and the Land*

STAMP, SIR L. D. (1970), *Nature Conservation in Britain*

STAMP, SIR L. D. and BEAVERS, S. H. (1941), *The British Isles*

STAMP, SIR L. D. and HOSKINS, W. G. (1963), *The Common Lands of England and Wales*

STEERS, J. A. (1969), *The Sea Coast*

STEERS, J. A. (Ed.) (1964), *Field Studies in the British Isles*

STENTON, D. M. (1951), *English Society in the Early Middle Ages*

STENTON, SIR F. M. (1927), *The Danes in England*

STENTON, SIR F. M. (1947), *Anglo-Saxon England*

STOESSIGER, B. and MORANT, G. M. (1932), Crania, Hythe, *Biometrika*, 24, 135-202

STOLL, R. (1967), *Architecture and Sculpture in Early Britain*

STONE, J. F. S. (1958), *Wessex before the Celts*

SUMMERSON, J. (1945), *Georgian London*

SUMMERSON, J. (1953), *Architecture in Britain*

SYLVESTER, D. (1948), Hill villages of England and Wales, *Geog. J.*, 110, 76-93

TAIT, J. (1936), *The Medieval English Borough*

TANSLEY, A. G. (1968), *Britain's Green Mantle*

TATE, W. E. (1967), *The English Village Community and the Enclosure Movements*

TAYLOR, A. J. P. (1966), *English History, 1914-1945*

TAYLOR, H. M. (1965), *Anglo-Saxon Architecture*

THIRSK, J. (1957), *English Peasant Farming*

THIRSK, J. (1959), *Tudor Enclosures*

THIRSK, J. (Ed.) (1967), *The Agrarian History of England and Wales, Vol. IV, 1500-1640*

THOMAS, N. (1960), *A Guide to Prehistoric England*

THOMPSON, F. (1957), *Lark Rise to Candleford*

TOCHER, J. F. (1924), *Anthropometric Characteristics, North-east Scotland*

TOUT, T. F. (1934), *Medieval Town Planning*
TOY, S. (1953), *The Castles of Great Britain*
TREHARNE, R. F. (1967), *The Glastonbury Legends*
TREVELYAN, G. M. (1946), *English Social History*
TRUEMAN, A. E. (1949), *Geology and Scenery in England and Wales*
TURNER, SIR W. (1915), Craniology of the People of Scotland, *Trans. Roy. Soc. Edin.*, 51, 171-255
TURNER, W. J. (Ed.) (1945), *The Englishman's Country*
TWISTON-DAVIES, SIR L. and LLOYD JOHNES, H. J. (1950), *Welsh Furniture*

VARLEY, W. J. and JACKSON, J. W. (1940), *Prehistoric Cheshire*
VAVILOV, N. I. (1926), *Studies on the Origin of Cultivated Plants*
V. and A. Museum (1924), *Guide to the Collection of Old English Costumes*
Victoria History of the Counties of England (1912-)

WADE-EVANS, A. W. (1909), *Welsh Medieval Law*
WAINRIGHT, W. J. (Ed.) (1955), *The Problem of the Picts*
WAINRIGHT, W. J. (1962), *The Northern Isles*
WATSON, J. W. and SISSONS, J. B. (Ed.) (1964), *The British Isles*
WEBB, S. and B. (1913), *English Local Government, The Story of the Highway*
WEBSTER, G. (1968), *The Roman Imperial Army*
WHEELER, SIR R. E. M. (1925), *Prehistoric and Roman Wales*
WHEELER, SIR R. E. M. (1927-35), London Museum Catalogues: *London and the Vikings; London in Roman Times; London and the Saxons*
WHEELER, SIR R. E. M. (1943), *Maiden Castle, Dorset*
WHEELER, SIR R. E. M. (1954), *The Stanwick Fortifications*
WHEELER, SIR R. E. M. and WHEELER, T. V. (1936), *Verulamium*
WHITELOCK, D. (1952), *The Beginnings of English Society*
WICKHAM, A. K. (1933), *The Villages of England*
WILLAN, T. S. (1938), *The English Coasting Trade, 1600-1750*
WILLIAMS, D. (1955), *The Rebecca Riots*
WILSON, D. M. (1960), *The Anglo-Saxons*
WOOD, E. S. (1968), *Collins Field Guide to Archæology*
WRIGHT, W. B. (1939), *Tools and the Man*

YARWOOD, D. (1952), *English Costume*

ZEUNER, F. E. (1957), *Dating the Past*
ZEUNER, F. E. (1963), *A History of Domesticated Animals*

INDEX

Figures in bold refer to pages opposite which illustrations appear.